Interdisciplinary Perspectives on Fairness, Equity, and Justice

Meng Li • David P. Tracer
Editors

Interdisciplinary Perspectives on Fairness, Equity, and Justice

Springer

Editors
Meng Li
Department of Health and Behavioral Sciences
University of Colorado Denver
Denver, CO, USA

David P. Tracer
Departments of Health and Behavioral Sciences and Anthropology
University of Colorado Denver
Denver, CO, USA

ISBN 978-3-319-58992-3 ISBN 978-3-319-58993-0 (eBook)
DOI 10.1007/978-3-319-58993-0

Library of Congress Control Number: 2017952058

Printed on acid-free paper

This Springer imprint is published by Springer Nature
The registered company is Springer International Publishing AG
The registered company address is: Gewerbestrasse 11, 6330 Cham, Switzerland

Contents

Contributors

Yoella Bereby-Meyer Psychology Department, Ben-Gurion University of the Negev Beer Sheva, Israel

Shoham Choshen-Hillel Jerusalem School of Business Administration and the Federmann Center for the Study of Rationality, The Hebrew University of Jerusalem, Jerusalem, Israel

Jeff DeWitt Department of Psychology, Rutgers University, New Brunswick, NJ, USA

Karen S. Fulk Department of Anthropology, Boise State University, Boise, ID, USA

Delaney Glass Department of Anthropology, Boise State University, Boise, ID, USA

Tom Gordon-Hecker Psychology Department, Ben-Gurion University of the Negev Beer Sheva, Israel

Jordan Kiper Department of Anthropology, University of Connecticut, Storrs, CT, USA

Carolyn K. Lesorogol George Warren Brown School of Social Work, Washington University in St. Louis, St. Louis, MO, USA

Department of Anthropology, Washington University in St. Louis, St. Louis, MO, USA

Meng Li Department of Health and Behavioral Sciences, University of Colorado Denver, Denver, CO, USA

Govind Persad Berman Institute of Bioethics, Johns Hopkins University, Baltimore, MD, USA

Department of Health Policy and Management, Bloomberg School of Public Health, Johns Hopkins University, Baltimore, MD, USA

Alan Sanfey Donders Institute for Brain Cognition and Behavior, Radboud University Nijmegen, Nijmegen, The Netherlands

Shane A. Scaggs Department of Anthropology, Oregon State University, Corvallis, OR, USA

Shaul Shalvi Department of Economics, Center for Research in Experimental Economics and Political Decision Making (CREED), University of Amsterdam, Amsterdam, The Netherlands

Mark Sheskin Cognitive Science Program, Yale University, New Haven, CT, USA

Richard Sosis Department of Anthropology, University of Connecticut, Storrs, CT, USA

David P. Tracer Departments of Health & Behavioral Sciences and Anthropology, University of Colorado Denver, Denver, CO, USA

Jeroen van Baar Donders Institute for Brain Cognition and Behavior, Radboud University Nijmegen, Nijmegen, The Netherlands

Peter Vavra Donders Institute for Brain Cognition and Behavior, Radboud University Nijmegen, Nijmegen, The Netherlands

John P. Ziker Department of Anthropology, Boise State University, Boise, ID, USA

Chapter 1
An Introduction and Guide to the Volume

David P. Tracer and Meng Li

The notion that humans have a taste for fairness, equity, and justice is both profoundly empirically satisfying, and troublesome, theoretically. It is comforting to know that "from cooperative hunting to contributing to charitable causes to helping stranded motorists, humans in all societies, industrialized and small-scale alike, frequently engage in acts that benefit other unrelated individuals, often at a non-trivial cost to themselves" (Tracer, this volume); in other words, that humans are intensely prosocial creatures. But this same fact is at once problematic for theories of human motivation and behavior. Most theories of human behavior in the social sciences rely upon the premise that we are fundamentally self-regarding maximizers of personal gain. This is alternatively known as the "selfishness axiom" or the *Homo economicus* model of human behavior (Henrich et al., 2004). Are humans prosocial creatures or selfish maximizers? In this volume, we examine the concepts of fairness, equity, and justice from an interdisciplinary perspective. Before we proceed to the various perspectives from disciplines as diverse as neuroscience, psychology, bioethics, and anthropology, this chapter offers a brief introduction to and definition of the terms, concepts, and theories in which much of the work reported in this volume is grounded. It also provides a brief justification for approaching the concepts of fairness, equity, and justice from an interdisciplinary perspective, as well as a guide to the volume to illustrate how its individual chapters fit together to provide some answers to the enigma of human prosociality and our taste for fairness, equity, and justice.

D.P. Tracer (✉)
Departments of Health & Behavioral Sciences and Anthropology,
University of Colorado Denver, Denver, CO, USA
e-mail: david.tracer@ucdenver.edu

M. Li
Department of Health and Behavioral Sciences, University of Colorado Denver,
Denver, CO, USA
e-mail: meng.li@ucdenver.edu

M. Li, D.P. Tracer (eds.), *Interdisciplinary Perspectives on Fairness, Equity, and Justice*, DOI 10.1007/978-3-319-58993-0_1

Theoretical Considerations: *Homo economicus* and the Axiom of Selfishness

In their now classic book on behavioral ecology, Krebs and Davies (1981) concerned themselves with the question of why certain behaviors come to predominate among species occupying particular ecological contexts. They proposed that questions about behavior can best be answered using a "functionalist" orientation, that is, by understanding "how a particular behavior pattern contributes to an animal's chances of survival and its reproductive success" (1981:22). Like advantageous morphology or physiology, behaviors that promote survival and reproduction tend to be passed on at higher frequencies (either genetically or through analogous teaching or emulation practices) and will come to predominate until such time as the environment changes in ways that favor some other behavioral propensity. Krebs and Davies conclude by noting that the quest for survival and reproductive success necessarily means that "individuals are expected to behave in their own selfish interests" (1981:22). Similarly, in his now classic book on evolution and behavior, *The Selfish Gene,* evolutionary biologist Richard Dawkins noted that:

> we must expect that when we go and look at the behavior of baboons, humans, and all other living creatures, we shall find it to be selfish. If we find that our expectation is wrong, if we observe that human behavior is truly altruistic, then we shall be faced with something puzzling, something that needs explaining (1976).

Consequently, for almost the past half-century, the "selfishness axiom" has prevailed within the natural and life sciences in order to explain the evolution and maintenance of behaviors.

A theoretical orientation very similar to that of evolutionary biology has also been prevalent for a very long time in the social and behavioral sciences. For example, perhaps the best-known quote by any economist is that made by Adam Smith in his *Wealth of Nations:*

> It is not from the benevolence of the butcher, the brewer, or the baker that we expect our dinner, but from their regard to their own interest. We address ourselves, not to their humanity but to their self-love, and never talk to them of our own necessities but of their advantages (1776).

For Smith, services are provided not for the benefit of individual others or one's own group but in satisfaction of the service providers' own needs and necessities. This view has come to prevail in economics and is sometimes known as the "*Homo economicus*" model: "theoretical economists postulated a being called *Homo economicus*—a rational individual relentlessly bent on maximizing a purely selfish reward" (Fehr, Sigmund, & Nowak, 2002). It is worth noting that the "selfishness axiom" became pervasive in some schools of anthropology and psychology as well, most notably, in the evolutionary subareas of these disciplines (Henrich et al., 2005).

As useful as the selfishness axiom and *Homo economicus* model of human behavior are for theorizing about the roots of human strategic interaction, empirical evidence from multiple sources has cast doubt on whether humans truly behave in ways predicted by these paradigms.

Beyond Selfishness: Fairness, Equity, and Justice

Behavioral ecologists, psychologists, anthropologists, and economists have with increasing frequency employed experimental techniques, also referred to as "games," to measure human behavioral propensities both in the laboratory and in more naturalistic settings (Camerer, 2003; Gintis, 2000; Henrich et al., 2005; Ibuka, Li, Vietri, Chapman, & Galvani, 2014; Kagel & Roth, 1995; Tracer, 2003). These methods have also been used to gauge whether individuals seem to adhere to the selfishness axiom and maximize their own payoffs or deviate from it. One of the simplest games that has been conducted numerous times and in different geographic locations is the "ultimatum game." In this game, two individuals, a "proposer" and "responder," play anonymously with one another. The proposer specifies how a given sum of money will be divided between him and a responder who then has the opportunity to accept or reject the offer. If the offer is accepted, then the sum of money is divided as specified by the proposer; if it is rejected, then both individuals receive nothing. According to the selfishness axiom—that humans are expected to behave as self-regarding maximizers of absolute payoffs—it is relatively easy to predict how individuals should play the ultimatum game. Under this axiom, responders should accept any nonzero offer proposed, since this means that they leave with more than they started; for example, if n is the amount they started with and the proposal is x, by accepting they leave with $n + x$. By contrast, rejection means that they earn zero and simply leave with n, which should never be preferred by a self-regarding money maximizer over $n + x$. Moreover, knowing that responders should be willing to accept any nonzero offer, proposers are expected to offer them the smallest possible division of the nonzero sum in the game, generally 10% of the stake (such as $1 out of a $10 stake).

The results of a series of ultimatum games conducted 25 years ago by Roth, Prasnikar, Okuno-Fujiwara, and Zamir (1991) cross-culturally in the cities of Pittsburgh (USA), Tokyo (Japan), Ljubljana (Slovenia), and Jerusalem (Israel) deviated significantly from the predictions of the selfishness axiom and *Homo economicus* model presented above. The lowest possible nonzero proposals made up fewer than 1% of all proposals; modal offers by proposers were generally 50% of the total stakes; mean offers ranged from 37% (Israel) to 47% (USA), and rejections of nonzero offers by responders varied between 19% and 27%, with offers of 20% and less being rejected commonly (Roth et al., 1991). The deviations from predictions of the *Homo economicus* model, in particular the higher than expected offers and costly rejection of relatively low offers, have been interpreted by social scientists as indicating a taste for "fairness" among humans, as well as their tendency to punish those not showing similar tastes for fairness. Further experimental research over the ensuing 25 years has confirmed that only in a minority of cases do humans act as self-interested maximizers of personal gain. Instead, the burden of experimental, ethnographic, and neuroscientific data has shown that humans the world over have a distinct taste for deliberate "prosociality" and hold dear the values of fairness, equity, and justice (Camerer, 2013; Henrich & Henrich, 2007; Wilson, O'Brien, & Sesma, 2009).

Fairness is most often defined as the quality of treating people evenhandedly or in tit-for-tat fashion, or according to Rabin (1993), helping those who help you and hurting those who hurt you. Rabin's model also takes into account motivations—fairness being motivated by kind intentions whereas unfairness by hostile intentions—which are arguably much harder to model and certainly to ascertain empirically. Fehr and Schmidt (1999) define fairness in terms of self-regarding equity promotion or conversely as inequity aversion. Thus an equitable payoff for ego relative to others is regarded as fair and an inequitable payoff as unfair. This begs the question of what we mean exactly by equity.

Equity is often incorrectly used synonymously with equality. Equality means that payoffs for two actors are exactly the same. But equity need not imply equality. Instead, equity implies a payoff that is commensurate with an actor's initial investment (Gordon-Hecker et al., this volume), or can mean more for those who need or merit it and less for those who do not.

Finally, although justice can be used in a number of senses depending on the modifier used with it, e.g., distributive justice or social justice, in this volume we use the unmodified term in just two relatively simple senses. The first sense is as the outcome of behaving fairly or equitably broadly defined. A fair and equitable outcome is thus a just outcome. Secondly, Tracer (this volume) uses justice to mean an action that is employed to remediate an unfair or inequitable social outcome.

Precise definitions aside, the pervasive taste for fairness, equity, and justice that occurs in the human species forms the basis of our general tendency to behave prosocially and deviate from the selfishness axiom and *Homo economicus* model of behavior. Remarkably, some 17 years before he wrote *The Wealth of Nations*, none other than Adam Smith recognized, in *The Theory of Moral Sentiments*, the essentialness of fairness, equity, and justice to the maintenance of the social order:

> All men…abhor fraud, perfidy, and injustice and delight to see them punished…few men have reflected upon the necessity of justice to the existence of society (Smith 1759 in Ashraf, Camerer, & Loewenstein, 2005).

As noted above and will be illustrated abundantly throughout this volume, however, what exactly constitutes fairness, equity, and justice and how individuals construe these concepts may be profoundly affected by context. In other words, it is entirely possible for good, prosocial people to differ in their assessments of what constitutes the fairest, most equitable and just solutions to social dilemmas.

Why an Interdisciplinary Perspective?

When the great natural historian Charles Darwin returned from his famous 5-year scientific expedition circumnavigating the world aboard the HMS Beagle, he was faced with explaining the origin of the species diversity that he had observed. As a case in point, we use the well-known example of the Galapagos Island finches. These are varieties of obviously closely related but slightly different birds whose differences, particularly in the form of the beak, seem to render them well adapted to different environments and food resources. The finches made a strong impression upon the young Darwin and he surmised that "seeing this gradation and diversity of structure in one small, intimately related group of birds, one might really fancy that from an original paucity of birds in this archipelago, one species had been taken and modified for different ends" (Darwin, 1859). In trying to deduce the mechanism that produced this spectrum of variation, Darwin relied principally upon knowledge that he had garnered from reading outside the comfort of what could arguably be construed as his own disciplinary boundaries. This began with his reading of Charles Lyell's writings including his multi-volume *Principles of Geology* (1830). Lyell's writings were not about Darwin's area of concern, the biological world, but rather the geological world and it proposed what was to become known as "uniformitarianism"—the idea that natural processes acting in the past were the same as those currently observable and in operation in the present time. Thus the world's topography could be explained by the gradual impact of cycles of freezing and thawing, erosion from wind and rain, volcanism, and the like extrapolated back over vast amounts of time. This instilled in Darwin the notion that perhaps gradual uniform natural processes were the keys to understanding the biological world as well. But the biological species-generating mechanism(s) analogous to those in the geological world eluded Darwin until once again he referenced work outside of his own disciplinary area of interest—this time economics. In *An Essay on the Principle of Population* (1798), British economist Thomas Malthus sought to answer whether poverty and suffering were inevitable parts of the human condition. In short, his sad answer was that the fundamental inequity between the explosive power of population and inability of resources to increase at a level commensurate with population would indeed usually (except in exceptional cases where population might be curtailed by restraint from marriage) lead to a struggle over resources where the "losers" in the struggle would suffer poverty (until population was ultimately "checked" by disease, famine, and warfare). Darwin adapted Malthus' ideas about the economics of human suffering and ultimately applied them to the biological world, contributing what has since become the central theory underlying all of the natural sciences. As he is quoted by his son Francis Darwin who edited Charles Darwin's "Life and Letters" (Darwin, 1887):

> In October 1838, that is fifteen months after I had begun my systematic enquiry, I happened to read for amusement Malthus on Population, and being well prepared to appreciate the struggle for existence which everywhere goes on from long-continued observation of the habits of animals and plants, it at once struck me that under these circumstances favourable variations would tend to be preserved, and unfavourable ones to be destroyed. The result of this would be the formation of a new species. Here, then, I had at last got a theory by which to work (Darwin, 1887).

This is just one example, and many could be given, but the lesson is clear; reading outside one's disciplinary area has the potential to yield valuable insights not available to ones constrained within their own disciplinary silos.

According to Vugteveen, Lenders, and Van den Besselaar (2014), research that is truly interdisciplinary has two main characteristics: (1) its questions are engaged using information from a variety of disciplines and (2) results gleaned from the research diffuse back into and inform the various disciplines that engaged it to begin with. Research on prosociality has already taken place in disciplines as seemingly disparate as anthropology, biology, business, economics, neuroscience, philosophy, psychology, and business/management. But this research is largely housed in the academic journals of these individual disciplines. This volume seeks to gather together in one place research on fairness, equity, and justice by researchers from a wide variety of disciplines interested in similar questions of prosociality with the hope that its results will feedback across disciplinary boundaries and provide the added value and insights that emerge from this type of interdisciplinary enterprise.

Guide to the Volume

In putting this volume together, we have strived to provide a truly interdisciplinary perspective on fairness, equity, and justice. Thus the volume includes contributions from social psychologists, behavioral scientists, anthropologists, bioethicists, and neuroscientists. The order of the chapters has been arranged such that the volume considers fairness, equity, and justice beginning from more micro-levels like that of neural substrates to that of individuals and finally to cultural systems. Thus Chap. 2 explores how fairness may be encoded in the brain (Vavra et al.), Chap. 3 then moves on to consider the ontogeny of fairness and moral development in children (Sheskin). Chapter 4 discusses the ethics as well as public preferences in how resources should be allocated across the population, particularly in the domain of allocating scarce and potentially lifesaving medical resources (Persad), Chaps. 5 and 6 consider how adults presented with such allocation problems are sensitive to contextual factors and how such problems are framed (Li and DeWitt; Gordon-Hecker et al.). And finally moving on to anthropological perspectives, Chaps. 7–10 include research bearing on the issue of how macro-level forces like cultural contexts affect individuals' propensities to behave prosocially (Kiper and Sosis; Lesorogol; Tracer; Scaggs et al.).

Each chapter is written as a complete piece of research that can be read on its own, but at the same time, compliments and enhances perspectives from others in the volume in unique ways. Thus in keeping with our assertion that there is much to be gained from an interdisciplinary perspective, we believe that the volume will yield its most important and helpful insights when considered in its entirety.

References

Ashraf, N., Camerer, C. F., & Loewenstein, G. (2005). Adam Smith, behavioral economist. *The Journal of Economic Perspectives, 19*(3), 131–145.

Camerer, C. F. (2003). *Behavioral game theory: Experiments in strategic interaction*. New York, NY: Russell Sage Foundation.

Camerer, C. F. (2013). Experimental, cultural, and neural evidence of deliberate prosociality. *Trends in Cognitive Sciences, 17*(3), 106–108.

Darwin, C. (1859). *On the origin of species*. New York, NY: Penguin Classics.

Darwin, F. (1887). *The life and letters of Charles Darwin*. London: John Murray.

Dawkins, R. (1976). *The selfish gene*. London: Oxford University Press.

Fehr, E., & Schmidt, K. M. (1999). A theory of fairness, competition, and cooperation. *The Quarterly Journal of Economics, 114*(3), 817–868.

Fehr, E., Sigmund, K., & Nowak, M. A. (2002). The economics of fair play. *Scientific American, 286*, 82–87.

Gintis, H. (2000). *Game theory evolving: A problem-centered introduction to modeling strategic interaction*. Princeton, NJ: Princeton University Press.

Henrich, J., Boyd, R., Bowles, S., Camerer, C., Fehr, E., & Gintis, H. (Eds.). (2004). *Foundations of human sociality: Economic experiments and ethnographic evidence from fifteen small-scale societies*. Oxford: Oxford University Press.

Henrich, J., Boyd, R., Bowles, S., Camerer, C., Fehr, E., Gintis, H., … Tracer, D. (2005). "Economic man" in cross-cultural perspective: Behavioral experiments in 15 small-scale societies. *Behavioral and Brain Sciences, 28*(6), 795–815.

Henrich, N., & Henrich, J. P. (2007). *Why humans cooperate: A cultural and evolutionary explanation*. Oxford: Oxford University Press.

Ibuka, Y., Li, M., Vietri, J., Chapman, G. B., & Galvani, A. P. (2014). Free-riding behavior in vaccination decisions: An experimental study. *PLoS One, 9*(1), e87164.

Kagel, J. H., & Roth, A. E. (1995). *The handbook of experimental economics*. Princeton, NJ: Princeton university press.

Krebs, J. R., & Davies, N. B. (1981). *An introduction to behavioural ecology*. London: Blackwell Scientific Publications.

Lyell, C. (1830). *Principles of geology*. Chicago, IL: University of Chicago Press.

Malthus, T. (1798). *An essay on the principle of population*. New York, NY: Penguin Classics.

Rabin, M. (1993). Incorporating fairness into game theory and economics. *The American Economic Review, 83*(5), 1281–1302.

Roth, A. E., Prasnikar, V., Okuno-Fujiwara, M., & Zamir, S. (1991). Bargaining and market behavior in Jerusalem, Ljubljana, Pittsburgh, and Tokyo: An experimental study. *American Economic Review, 81*(5), 1068–1095.

Smith, A. (1776). An inquiry into the nature and causes of the wealth of nations. *Library of Economics and Liberty*. Retrieved from http://www.econlib.org/library/Smith/smWN1.html

Tracer, D. (2003). Selfishness and fairness in economic and evolutionary perspective: An experimental economic study in Papua New Guinea. *Current Anthropology, 44*(3), 432–438.

Vugteveen, P., Lenders, R., & Van den Besselaar, P. (2014). The dynamics of interdisciplinary research fields: The case of river research. *Scientometrics, 100*(1), 73–96.

Wilson, D. S., O'Brien, D. T., & Sesma, A. (2009). Human prosociality from an evolutionary perspective: Variation and correlations at a city-wide scale. *Evolution and Human Behavior, 30*(3), 190–200.

Chapter 2
The Neural Basis of Fairness

Peter Vavra, Jeroen van Baar, and Alan Sanfey

Introduction

Recent laboratory research in cognitive neuroscience has begun to explore paradigms that offer fruitful avenues to examine how processes involving a sense of fairness may be encoded in the human brain. Most of this research is embedded within the field of Decision Neuroscience (also known as Neuroeconomics), an interdisciplinary effort to better understand the fundamentals of human decision-making. Within this field, researchers endeavor to build accounts of decision-making that incorporate the psychological processes that influence decisions, that indicate how these processes are constrained by the underlying neurobiology of the brain, and at the same time developing formal models of these decisions, an approach extended from economics.

The emergence of this approach to examining interactive decision-making offers real promise for the development of such models. This nascent research field combines psychological insight and brain imaging with realistic decision tasks that allow for the exploration of fairness in a controlled laboratory environment. In contrast to standard behavioral studies, the combination of game theoretic models with online measurement of brain activity during decision-making allows for the discrimination and modeling of processes that are often hard to separate at the behavioral level. Within this approach, tasks have been designed that ask people to decide about monetary divisions in an interactive setting, with money used both as a reward in itself, and also as a proxy for other "rights" that affect cooperation (land, political power, etc.). These tasks (see Box 2.1) are well suited to be used in combination with brain imaging methods, and produce a surprisingly rich pattern of decision-making, which allows for a wide range of questions to be answered about the

P. Vavra • J. van Baar • A. Sanfey (✉)
Donders Institute for Brain Cognition and Behavior, Radboud University Nijmegen, Nijmegen, The Netherlands
e-mail: p.vavra@donders.ru.nl; j.vanbaar@donders.ru.nl; a.sanfey@donders.ru.nl

M. Li, D.P. Tracer (eds.), *Interdisciplinary Perspectives on Fairness, Equity, and Justice*, DOI 10.1007/978-3-319-58993-0_2

motivations that underlie fairness behavior. In this chapter, we review the work to date in understanding fairness from a Decision Neuroscience perspective, with particular interest paid to the brain regions that appear to be prominently involved when we consider whether outcomes or procedures are fair or not, and what actions we are willing to take to redress the balance. Exploring these fundamental mechanisms can provide valuable insight into the associated psychological processes, and ultimately can help us better understand the complex but important concept of fairness.

Box 2.1 Experimental Tasks

Tasks used to investigate fairness-related decision-making have their root in behavioral economics and game theory. In these games, typically two players are facing a decision situation. We briefly describe here four games that have often been used in the context of fairness and equity.

The Ultimatum Game (UG; Güth, Schmittberger, & Schwarze, 1982) is a two-player game where the players each make a decision sequentially. The first player, termed the proposer, is endowed with a sum of money. The proposer has to decide how much of this sum to offer the second player. Then, the second player, the responder, decides whether to accept or reject the offer. If the responder accepts, the two players split the money accordingly. If the responder rejects, however, neither player receives any money. The proposer's decision is seen as reflecting strategic decision-making—how much is the responder probably willing to accept?—as well as reflecting some form of consideration of fairness—what do I consider a fair split of money? The responder's decision to reject a low offer is seen as a canonical example of altruistic punishment: the willingness to forgo a (monetary) payoff in favor of enforcing a social norm of fairness. Indeed, most people reject low offers and consider them unfair (Camerer, 2003).

The Dictator Game (DG) and Impunity Game are closely related to the UG. In the DG, the only difference with the UG is that the responder doesn't have the opportunity to reject the offer. Instead, the allocation of money is realized after the first player, now called a dictator, decides how much to transfer to the recipient. Given that there is no risk here of rejection for the dictator, the motivation to transfer money in this game is seen as genuine generosity. In the Impunity Game, the responder does have the option to accept or reject an offer. However, in contrast to the UG, when rejecting an offer, only the responder receives nothing; the proposer still receives the rest of the money. That is, in the Impunity Game, there is also no risk of losing money for oneself.

The above games are all related to equity or, more narrowly, equality norms. However, fairness and justice also relate to reciprocity. One simple, two-player game used for investigating reciprocity is the Trust Game. The first player, termed the investor, is endowed with a sum of money. They can decide how much of their money to transfer to the second player, the trustee. Importantly,

(continued)

Box 2.1 (continued)
whatever amount is transferred is multiplied by a fixed factor, e.g., four. For example, the investor could transfer $5. Then, the trustee would receive $20 and can, in turn, decide how much of this latter amount to transfer back. Importantly, the trustee can also decide to not transfer any money at all. Thus, the decision of the investor is seen as a sign of trusting the second player to return some amount of money. The second player's decision to return any amount is seen as a sign of reciprocating trust. Note that for the trustee, the decision is structurally identical to a dictator's decision in the DG, except for the history of how the trustee arrived in the position of having any endowment at all.

In their most straightforward form, these games are played as one single round with a completely anonymous partner. However, for the purpose of neuroimaging studies, it is important to have multiple observations, so many studies employ so-called single-shot multi-round games: as a participant, one plays the game multiple times, on each round paired with a new partner. Alternatively, studies focusing on learning processes often employ repeated paradigms. For example, by playing with the same set of partners, one can learn to trust or distrust trustees in the TG based on how often, and how much, money they return. These simple yet powerful tasks allow researchers to employ computational models to quantify key theoretical variables. By using simple variations of these tasks, e.g., by playing for a third person instead of oneself, it is also possible to disentangle the contributions of different motivations to the decisions. In sum, these tasks are exceptionally well suited for the study of fairness and justice, because they provide a unique balance between experimental control, rich psychological processes, and formal modeling.

By employing functional neuroimaging (see Box 2.2) to examine a range of tasks that are rooted in behavioral economics, a network of brain regions has been identified that support a decision as to whether to behave fairly or unfairly in a given situation, as well what underlies the response to the fair or unfair behavior of others. A major effort in this regard has been to elucidate the psychological and computational roles each of these brain regions might play in this process. In this chapter, we highlight the brain systems (Fig. 2.1) that have been most consistently identified in these processes, and review the respective roles they may play in fairness-related decision-making.

Trading-Off Self-Interest Versus the Greater Good

In most of the experiments used to study fairness-related processing in the brain, participants face a trade-off between self-interest and adhering to a fairness norm of some type. It should be noted that these two motivations are often explicitly pitted against each other by the researcher. While self-interest and fairness regularly

Box 2.2 Functional Neuroimaging Techniques
Since the early twentieth century, humans have been capable of measuring neural activity in the living brain, without damaging underlying tissue. The first of these noninvasive functional neuroimaging techniques was the electroencephalogram (EEG). Building on the pioneering work of Hans Berger in 1920s Germany, modern EEG methods are capable of measuring electric field changes at up to 256 electrode sites on the scalp. These electric field changes are assumed to be caused by synchronized neural firing in the cerebral cortex. Given that EEG picks up on electric field changes, its temporal resolution is very high and limited only by the sampling frequency of the EEG equipment. For this reason, EEG is extremely useful in measuring the brain's response to rapidly developing stimuli, like chunks of spoken language. The spatial resolution of EEG is, however, quite low, as electric fields generated by the brain are smeared by the layers of soft and hard tissue that lie between the brain and the electrode cap. Furthermore, EEG favors measuring superficial brain structures over deep ones, as the electric field changes caused by deep structures may not even reach the scalp.

A neuroimaging method which is complementary to EEG is functional magnetic resonance imaging (fMRI). fMRI picks up on magnetic field changes inside the brain, which are caused by changes in the relative flow of oxygenated and deoxygenated blood to and from active brain tissue. As such, the fMRI signal is termed the *blood oxygenation level-dependent* response, or BOLD. Due to numerous advances in fMRI techniques since its inception in the early 1990s, the spatial resolution of this method is in the order of millimeters, allowing, for example, for precise functional parcellation of brain structures. It is equally powerful in measuring deep brain regions as it is in measuring superficial ones, as signals from different brain regions do not interfere with one another. As a limitation however, the temporal resolution of fMRI is relatively low, as the response of the blood flow to brain activity is slow: it takes between 6 and 10 s after a brain region is active for the blood flow response to reach its peak, and the entire response can take up to 30 s. Still, by systematically varying time intervals between experimental stimuli, it is possible to connect the brain response to individual stimuli, even if they are very close together in time. One major downside of fMRI is its cost, both in purchasing the equipment (in the order of millions of dollars) and running it (hundreds of dollars per hour).

A method that is sometimes heralded as having both high spatial and high temporal resolution is the magnetoencephalogram, or MEG. MEG capitalizes on the fact that, by the laws of electromagnetic induction, neuronal electrical activity in the brain ever so slightly changes the magnetic field that exists around the head of a participant. By placing many tiny superconducting sensors in an array around the head, one can sense these magnetic field changes at a high temporal resolution. Compared to fMRI, an important advantage of

(continued)

Box 2.2 (continued)

MEG is that, like EEG, it directly measures neuronal activity, and not a secondary measure like blood flow. Localizing the source of the magnetic field change (the active brain region) in MEG at the centimeter scale is more feasible than in EEG, as the magnetic field can easily pass through skull and scalp. Unfortunately, the MEG signal is, like EEG, dominated by neuronal activity in superficial brain areas. Therefore, MEG is still seldom used to investigate the activity of brain structures that are crucial in understanding fairness processing, such as the striatum and the insula. In addition, using MEG requires advanced shielding of the experimental environment to external magnetic fields—even the movement of an elevator in the building generates a magnetic field change much larger than that caused by brain activity.

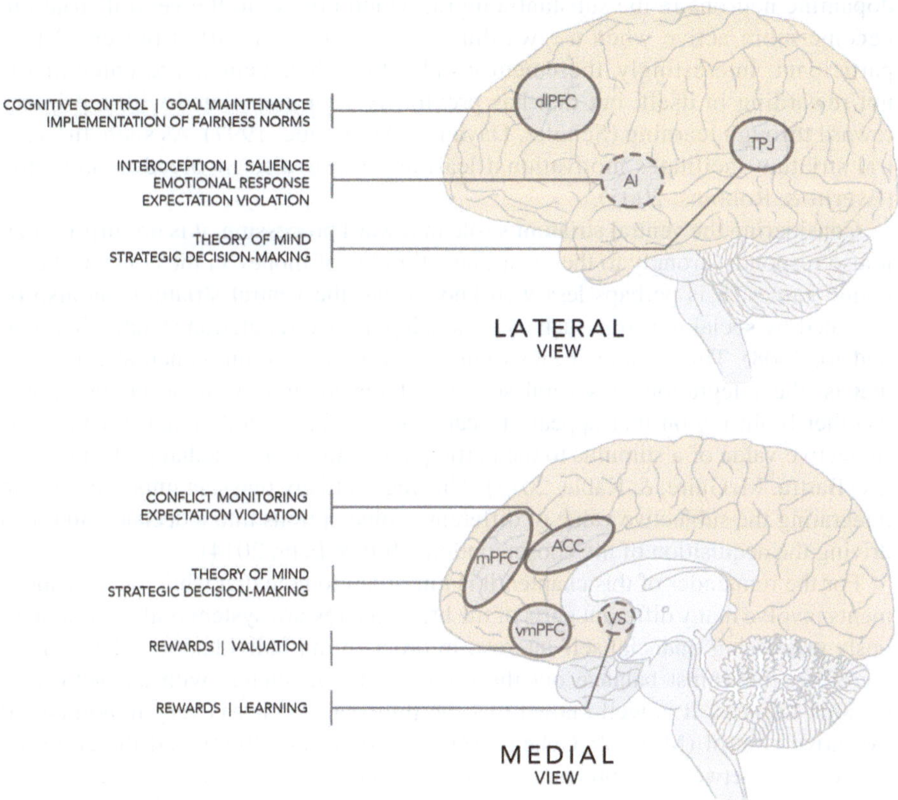

Fig. 2.1 Brain areas involved. Brain regions and their involvement in different processes during fairness-related decision-making, showing lateral (*top* panel) and medial (*bottom* panel) views of the human brain. *Solid lines* indicate surface structures, *dashed lines* indicate deep structures, *mPFC* medial prefrontal cortex, *TPJ* temporoparietal junction, *vmPCF* ventromedial prefrontal cortex, *ACC* anterior cingulate cortex, *dlPFC* dorsolateral prefrontal cortex, *VS* ventral striatum, *AI* anterior insula

motivate the same behavior in everyday situations (for example, when voting in support of wealth redistribution while being on the receiving end of such a measure), researchers are typically interested in isolating a single motivation. By pitting self-interest against fairness and observing subsequent behavior, they can deduce which motivation was the primary driver of the participants' decisions. This allows for careful study of the psychological and neural processes underlying fairness motivations. Note that in experimental practice, "unfair" decisions most often align with financially self-interested ones, while "fair" decisions usually serve the greater good (i.e., others' (financial) interests).

Turning to the brain, we first consider which neural systems instantiate self-interested behavior. The first structure that deserves mention in this respect is the ventral striatum, a collection of brain nuclei situated underneath the neocortex. It has long been known that the substructures of the ventral striatum play an important role in driving choice behavior. Ventral striatal structures are responsible for incentive salience (i.e., desire), pleasure, and learning. For example, dopamine neurons in the substantia nigra, which project to the ventral striatum, become more active when a rewarding stimulus (e.g., food) is presented to a participant. Interestingly, these neurons also fire when a cue is presented that is not rewarding in itself, but that has previously been associated with a primary reward through learning (Schultz, Dayan, & Montague, 1997). As such, the ventral striatum facilitates motivational learning, but is also involved in addiction (Everitt & Robbins, 2005).

Considering the ventral striatum's role in reward processing, it is no surprise that it also responds strongly to the rewarding stimulus of money in the context of economic games. It is perhaps less well-known that the ventral striatum can also be activated by social rewards, such as possessing a good reputation (Izuma, Saito, & Sadato, 2008). This finding speaks to the concept of a "common neural currency," that is, the integration of several sources of reward into a single neural signal. Another brain region that appears to carry a domain-general signal, tracking the subjective value of a stimulus to the participant, is the ventromedial prefrontal cortex (Bartra, McGuire, & Kable, 2013). This region likely plays an important role in integrating the subjective value of different choice options into a decision and then driving the acquisition of the chosen option (Ruff & Fehr, 2014).

For the remainder of this chapter, it is important to note that while fairness judgments involve many different parts of the brain, the reward system is also simultaneously processing financial self-interest. In order for an individual to behave fairly, therefore, they must balance out the impulse of self-interest with an inclination towards fairness. It is well-known that the prefrontal cortex is very important for executive control (Miller & Cohen, 2001; Seeley et al., 2007), and therefore the connections between the prefrontal cortex and the reward system are prime targets for the neurobiological study of fairness-related behavior. We will discuss these connections in more detail below.

On the fair, "greater good," side of the equation, it is useful to start by investigating what happens in the brain when someone observes both the fair and unfair behavior of another person.

Monitoring (Un)fairness: The Role of the Anterior Insula

Some of the earliest neuroscientific experiments concerning fairness implicated two brain regions whose involvement in fairness-probing tasks has been consistently replicated, these regions being the bilateral anterior insulae. The insula is a part of the cerebral cortex that is folded inward on the side of the brain, located between the frontal and temporal lobes. This region is broadly divided into a posterior part (towards the back of the brain) and an anterior part (towards the front).

From neuroimaging experiments using economic games, we know that the anterior insula becomes more active when processing the unfair behavior of their game partner. For example, in the Ultimatum Game, receiving a low, as compared to a high, offer is associated with increased anterior insula activity (see Feng, Luo, & Krueger, 2015 and Gabay, Radua, Kempton, & Mehta, 2014 for meta-analyses). Anterior insula activity has also been found to be correlated with the probability of subsequently rejecting an Ultimatum Game offer (Kirk, Downar, & Montague, 2011; Sanfey, Rilling, Aronson, Nystrom, & Cohen, 2003), suggesting that participants with a more responsive anterior insula were less likely to accept unfair behavior. However, this was not the case in all studies (e.g., Civai, Crescentini, Rustichini, & Rumiati, 2012; see also Gabay et al., 2014).

When playing a UG on behalf of others, Civai et al. (2012) showed that the anterior insula was more active for more unequal allocations, whether they are advantageous or disadvantageous for the person one is playing for. Simply receiving unfair offers without being able to reject them, i.e., when playing the Dictator Game, also recruits the insula (Grecucci, Giorgetta, Bonini, & Sanfey, 2013). Similarly, in a Trust Game experiment, Delgado, Frank, and Phelps (2005) reported increased activity in the insular cortex of the investor when they learned that the trustee defected. The anterior insula, thus, appears to respond to observed unfair behavior on the part of a game partner, independent of whether one can act on this unfairness, e.g., by punishing the perpetrator, or not, and also independent of whether oneself is the target of the unfairness or not.

These findings on the anterior insula raise the question as to when a game partner's behavior is actually deemed unfair. One way to approach this question is through the lens of inequity aversion (Fehr & Schmidt, 1999; see Box 2.3). Inequity aversion theory posits that participants derive negative utility (i.e., diminished subjective value) from an unequal distribution of resources between individuals. In the Ultimatum Game, then, a player is thought to balance the conflicting goals of making money and minimizing inequity. This explains why responders in the UG sometimes reject low offers: although accepting a low offer would yield more financial payoff than rejecting, acceptance would also bring about an undesirable degree of inequity. By responding to unfairness, therefore, the anterior insula may play an instrumental role in the neural implementation of inequity aversion. In line with this interpretation, Hsu, Anen, and Quartz (2008) find insular cortex activity to be correlated with trial-by-trial inequity when deciding between different allocations for other people (third-party allocation).

Box 2.3 Computational Approaches

Computational models have greatly risen in use in recent years in order to better understand decision-making. The main appeal of these approaches is that they allow the formal specification of theories and the decomposition of the underlying psychological processes into useful subcomponents. Conceptually, there are three distinct classes of formal models typically employed: Utility models, Learning models, and Process models. We will briefly highlight an example of each in the context of fairness-related decision-making.

Utility models: This class of models specifies which features of a situation influence the evaluation of the available options by the decision maker. The inequity-aversion (Fehr & Schmidt, 1999) and Expectation (Battigalli et al., 2015) models are prominent examples here. They propose that the utility of accepting an offer in, for example, the Ultimatum Game comprise two parts: the value of the money, and the (dis)utility from deviating either from an equal split (Inequity-Aversion) or from expectations. When making the decision itself, the utility for accepting the offer is compared to the utility for rejecting it. By formalizing these utilities, it is possible to look for neural correlates and shed light on the specific contributions of brain regions to this decision-making process. For example, Chang & Sanfey (2013) compared these two models and found that anterior insula and anterior cingulate cortex showed neural activity consistent with the Expectation model specifically.

Learning models: A rapidly growing amount of work focuses on how we update our utilities based on prior experience. Reinforcement learning models (Sutton & Barto, 1998), for example, propose that we compare an experienced reward to our previous expectation of that reward, resulting in a prediction error which has been linked to phasic dopamine firing of midbrain neurons (Schultz et al., 1999; Niv & Schoenbaum, 2008). In the context of the Ultimatum Game, Xiang et al. (2013) used a Bayesian Observer model to extend the abovementioned expectation model. They demonstrated that people dynamically updated their expectations based on their experience, and that their norm prediction errors correlate with the subjective emotional experience. Recent reviews highlight such learning models, as many observed neural correlates may be related to incidental learning, and can help in disentangling the specific contributions of different brain regions (e.g., Apps, Rushworth, & Chang, 2016; Lee & Seo, 2016).

Process models: Whereas utility models formalize which features of a situation affect subjective utilities, a third group of formal models propose how a single decision is reached. A prime example of such algorithmic models is the drift-diffusion model (DDM; Ratcliff & Mckoon, 2008; Smith & Ratcliff, 2004). In a DDM, the computation of a utility is modeled as an accumulation of a noisy signal, with a choice being made when this value signal reaches a certain threshold, that is, after enough "evidence" has accumulated in favor of

(continued)

Box 2.3 (continued)
one of the options. Importantly, such models do predict not only the decision itself, but also the associated reaction times. For example, Hutcherson, Bushong, and Rangel (2015) modeled the decision to choose either a selfish or a generous offer in a modified Dictator Game as a noisy calculation of a relative value signal. Hutcherson and colleagues proposed that the decision process needs to compare the value for oneself and the value for the other player, and that these values are calculated independently. Among other regions, they found that activity in the striatum was related to the value of the options for the self, while right TPJ activity was related to value for the other. Finally, activity in the vmPFC showed overlap for self and other utilities, consistent with the idea that the vmPFC integrates multiple attributes into a final value (Basten, Biele, Heekeren, & Fiebach, 2010).

Further, people who weigh inequity more strongly in their decisions also show a larger insula response to inequity (Hsu et al., 2008).

Crucially, the inequity aversion account implies that fairness norms are static and always favor a precisely even distribution of money. An alternative interpretation is that the evaluation of a game partner's behavior is made in comparison to one's expectations of the partner's behavior (Battigalli, Dufwenberg, & Smith, 2015). After all, what we find "fair" in everyday life is strongly dependent on both mitigating and aggravating circumstances, as well as dependent on our moral expectations of the individual we are dealing with—one may expect fairer behavior from a nun than from a convicted conman. In line with this view, there is evidence that the response of the responder's anterior insula to Ultimatum Game offers is proportional to the difference between the offer in question and that which was a priori expected (Chang & Sanfey, 2013; Xiang, Lohrenz, & Montague, 2013). In line with this dynamic view of fairness norms underlain by the cognitive expectations we generate, Fareri, Chang, and Delgado (2012) showed that the insular and cingulate brain response to prediction error after seeing the outcome of the trust game correlated with the participant's individual learning rate. That is, participants with a higher learning rate (who respond more sensitively to deviations from expectation) show a greater brain response in cingulate and insular cortex when being disappointed by a trustee.

One important question in the practice of cognitive neuroscience is: what is the participant experiencing subjectively while completing the experimental task? Measurements of brain activity can offer a window into this experience. For one, we know that the insular cortex plays an important role in emotion processing, especially of anger and disgust (Damasio et al., 2000; Phillips et al., 1997), and in the visceral experience of negative feelings (Critchley et al., 2004; Singer, Critchley, & Preuschoff, 2009). Therefore, the increased anterior insula activity in the Ultimatum Game is often interpreted as an emotional response to unfair behavior (Sanfey et al., 2003). In line with this interpretation, several studies show the importance of emotions in the UG. For example, Harlé, Chang, van't Wout, and Sanfey (2012) demonstrate that after watching a sad movie clip compared to a neutral one, people more often reject unfair UG offers. Importantly, the change in emotional state was accompanied by increased activity in the anterior insula, which was shown to mediate the relationship between the emotion condition and acceptance rate.

Even simply instructing participants to either up- or downregulate their emotional response can increase and decrease the rejection rate of unfair UG offers, respectively (Grecucci, Giorgetta, van't Wout, Bonini, & Sanfey, 2013). Importantly, the (posterior) insula activity decreased for downregulation and increased for upregulation of one's emotional arousal, in line with the changes in rejection rates. When playing the Dictator Game, that is, without having the opportunity to punish a low offer, insula activity is also affected by emotional reappraisal in the same pattern and is correlated with the subjective experience of anger (Grecucci, Giorgetta, Bonini, & Sanfey, 2013).

Nonetheless, the role of emotions and its link to the insula activity are less straightforward than these studies suggest. In a set of studies, Civai and colleagues compared playing the UG for oneself and playing it on behalf of a third party. When measuring emotional arousal using skin conductance response, Civai et al. (2010) found that participants had an increased emotional response to unfair offers only if playing for themselves, even though they would reject unfair offers as often as when playing for others. The anterior insula was associated with rejections in both contexts, and it was the mPFC which dissociated between the two situations (Corradi-Dell'Acqua, Civai, Rumiati, & Fink, 2013).

Therefore, to summarize, it has been known since the first neuroimaging experiments on fairness that the anterior insula responds to unfair behavior of oneself and others. This response is thought to reflect the difference between the observed behavior of others and one's prior expectations of this behavior. The result of this comparison, i.e., the deviation from expectations, may drive the emotional response as well as the decision to reject in some situations.

Conflict Monitoring and Cognitive Control in Economic Games

Aside from its role in emotion processing, the anterior insula is also thought to play a key role in the brain's salience network (Seeley et al., 2007). This ensemble of brain regions is thought to integrate sensory information with bodily cues from the autonomic nervous system, thereby enabling fast responding to the most homeostatically relevant events. This network additionally comprises, among other regions, the anterior cingulate cortex (ACC; Seeley et al., 2007). The ACC is hypothesized to monitor conflict in information processing, thereby triggering compensatory adjustments in cognitive control (Botvinick, Cohen, & Carter, 2004). In recent years, the role of the cognitive control system, and the role of the ACC in particular, in interactive decision-making has become clearer.

In the context of fairness and equity, the ACC has been related to several different psychological states. For example, in the Ultimatum Game, the ACC is more active when observing unfair as compared to fair offers (Feng et al., 2015; Gabay et al., 2014), and this activity is proportional to the deviation from fairness expectations (Chang & Sanfey, 2013), much like activity in the anterior insula (AI). Similarly, Haruno and Frith (2010) found that activity in ACC and AI tracked the difference between the payoffs of the participant and another person (i.e., inequity). Additionally, in the Trust Game, Baumgartner, Fischbacher, Feierabend, Lutz, and Fehr (2009) found increased activity in the ACC in trustees who were about to defect, breaking a promise they had previously made to their game partner, as compared to trustees who were about to keep their promise to reciprocate. A working hypothesis holds that ACC detects conflict between a norm (fairness, equity, etc.) and real or possible behavior (Chang, Smith, Dufwenberg, & Sanfey, 2011; Fehr & Krajbich, 2013).

Interestingly, however, contrary to the above findings, some research has found anterior cingulate cortex to be more active during reciprocation than during defection in Trust Games (Chang et al., 2011; Van Baar, Chang, & Sanfey, 2016). How to explain these seemingly contradictory findings? One should realize that many of these conflict detection operations can be carried out by ACC in the time it takes to acquire one snapshot of the brain with functional MRI. It may well be, for instance, that the increased ACC activity observed by Baumgartner et al. (2009) occurred in response to the participants' own decision to break their promise and defect, while the ACC activity observed by Chang et al. (2011) occurred in response to the participants merely considering defection. Strong ACC activity may have different effects on behavior when it occurs at different time points across the decision-making process.

Moreover, recent research points towards a subdivision of ACC into two regions with potentially distinct functions (e.g., Apps et al., 2016), as well as to multiple, but different, brain signals present in the same subregion of ACC (e.g., Kolling, Behrens, Wittmann, & Rushworth, 2016). Therefore, while intriguing thus far, more investigation of the location and time course of activity in ACC will be needed in order to clarify its role in fairness-related decision-making.

Other important nodes of the cognitive control network are dorsolateral prefrontal cortex (DLPFC) and supplementary motor area (SMA). Both have been found to be more active when trustees reciprocated in a Trust Game, thereby adhering to a fairness norm (Chang et al., 2011; Van Baar et al., 2016; van den Bos, van Dijk, Westenberg, Rombouts, & Crone, 2011). This evidence fits with the notion that cognitive control is required to overcome the temptation of making an unfair, though financially beneficial, decision. Fairness-based decisions can thus be likened to effortful actions: a prepotent (selfish) response needs to be overridden in order for an intentional (fair) action to occur. In line with this interpretation, it has been found that increased functional connectivity between the salience (AI and ACC) and central executive (DLPFC and posterior parietal cortex) networks is associated with increased reciprocity (Cáceda, James, Gutman, & Kilts, 2015).

There is currently a lively debate in experimental psychology as to whether prosocial behavior is prepotent and thereby intuitive, or alternatively requires overriding a prepotent selfish response and is thus deliberate. Using measurements of reaction time, Rand, Greene, and Nowak (2012) have made the case for intuitive cooperation—a typical prosocial behavior. They showed that faster responses in their task were on average more prosocial than slower responses. However, Krajbich, Bartling, Hare, and Fehr (2015) point out that it may in fact be strength-of-preference rather than selfishness that predicts longer reaction times. In response, Rand (2016) provided meta-analytic evidence that deliberation is associated with self-interested behavior in situations where prosocial behavior is not beneficial for the self, i.e., situations of "pure cooperation."

If we assume that "deliberation" maps onto DLPFC, there appears a contradiction between the aforementioned behavioral evidence and the available neuroscientific evidence about the role of DLPFC in social decision-making. Specifically, Knoch, Pascual-Leone, Meyer, Treyer, and Fehr (2006) temporarily disrupted neural function in the left and the right DLPFC using repetitive transcranial magnetic stimulation (TMS; see Box 2.4). They found that disrupting right (but not left) DLPFC reduced subjects' willingness to reject unfair offers in single-shot, anonymous Ultimatum Games. In other words, intact DLPFC function was associated with costly fair decisions on the part of the subjects, which suggests that deliberation can contribute to fair behavior. Interestingly, this stimulation method left the subjective unfairness ratings of the subjects unaffected. The researchers therefore concluded that the judgment of fairness was not supported by the right DLPFC, but rather the actions based on this judgment. Further, Baumgartner, Knoch, Hotz, Eisenegger, and Fehr (2011) showed that TMS stimulation decreased both activity in right DLPFC and functional connectivity between right DLPFC and ventromedial prefrontal cortex (valuation), and that this reduced connectivity could explain the change in offer acceptance rates. A working hypothesis is, therefore, that fairness judgments in the anterior insula are relayed to the DLPFC, which in turn inhibits the self-interested "greed" response in VMPFC to make costly fair behavior possible. This neuroscientific interpretation however is at odds with the intuitive cooperation findings of Rand and colleagues, and as such offers fruitful avenues for further research.

Much like with anterior insula, it is an open question how we should define the "fairness" that DLPFC appears to strive towards. Several different approaches have recently been proposed to help solve this question. First, Ruff, Ugazio, and Fehr (2013)) showed that increasing neural excitability in right lateral prefrontal cortex (LPFC) in Dictator Game Proposers, using anodal tDCS, led to decreased monetary transfers from the dictator to the receiver and thus, arguably, a decreased sense of fairness. When repeating this experiment with Ultimatum Game Proposers, however, upregulating LPFC with anodal tDCS now led to increased offer amounts from proposers to responders. As the only

Box 2.4 Brain Stimulation Techniques

To assess causal roles for brain regions in decision-making, two dominant noninvasive methods exist: transcranial magnetic stimulation (TMS) and transcranial current stimulation (tCS).

In TMS, researchers place a coil close to the skull. By running a brief, but strong, current though the coil, a transient magnetic field is created which in turn creates a secondary, induced, electric field inside the skull. This field can cause electrical currents in tissue and generate action potentials. When stimulating the primary motor cortex, for example, these impulses can lead to muscle contractions. For tCS, the researcher places two electrodes on the body, one electrode being the active electrode, i.e., positioned at the brain region one wants to stimulate, with the other being the reference electrode placed somewhere else. The reference electrode can be positioned either close by (e.g., only a one or two centimeters away) or far away, for example on a limb. By varying the size of the electrode itself, it is possible to vary the induced change in potential in the underlying tissue. The reference electrode is, thus, typically larger than the active electrode, causing less change to the tissue beneath it. One can use either direct current (tDCS) or alternating current (tACS) stimulation paradigms, with the former being more commonly used in the context of decision-making. The canonical interpretation for tDCS is that cathodal stimulation worsens performance (Stagg & Nitsche, 2011), while anodal improves it, but this dual-polarity effect is not always observed (e.g., Jacobson, Koslowsky, & Lavidor, 2012; Miniussi, Harris, & Ruzzoli, 2013).

There are two main types of paradigm for using noninvasive brain stimulation techniques: online or offline. Online paradigms use the stimulation at the time of the process itself. For example, by stimulating the dlPFC while playing the Ultimatum Game, it is possible to investigate how this stimulation alters the underlying neural processes (Knoch et al., 2008). In contrast, in offline paradigms one stimulates the brain region of interest first, up- or down-regulating its activity for several minutes, and only then is a task used to study the process of interest. Using TMS, this means that one uses a repetitive stimulation paradigm (rTMS) where pulses are created with typically 1 Hz frequency for several minutes. This is thought to cause a deactivation of the underlying brain region (Iyer, Schleper, & Wassermann, 2003). In decision-making research therefore, one first (de)activates a brain region of interest and then participants play, for example, the Ultimatum Game (e.g., Knoch et al., 2006; van't Wout, Kahn, Sanfey, & Aleman, 2005).

One strong limitation of all noninvasive brain stimulation techniques is the lack of spatial specificity. Although one might be interested in altering function in a single brain region (e.g., dlPFC), stimulation might affect even distant brain regions via neural connectivity. Indeed, it might be the connections themselves that are affected by the stimulation, such as dlPFC-vmPFC

(continued)

Box 2.4 (continued)
connectivity in the UG (Baumgartner et al., 2011). Thus, the conclusions that can be drawn from stimulation studies are greatly enhanced when conducted in conjunction with functional brain imaging. Alternatively, one can add multiple control conditions, using varied stimulation sites to show spatial specificity and a collection of tasks to assess cognitive specificity of the employed stimulation intervention. A more practical limitation is that only superficial brain regions can be targeted directly. Unfortunately, therefore it is difficult to stimulate for example the anterior insula, an especially important brain region for understanding fairness. Despite these limitations, noninvasive brain stimulation techniques such as rTMS and tDCS are valuable tools for the investigation of fairness-related decision-making. An opportunity for future studies is to combine stimulation techniques and formal modeling to arrive at a better understanding of the respective processes and computations.

difference between the DG and the UG for the proposers is the "sanction threat" of not getting any money at all, Ruff and colleagues concluded that the right lateral PFC processes voluntary and sanction-induced "fairness" differently. Sanfey, Stallen, and Chang (2014) added another interpretation of this finding: it is possible that increased activity in LPFC places participants' behavior more in line with what they believe other people would do in the same situation (their "descriptive social norm"). That is, participants may believe that other people would transfer relatively little money in the Dictator Game but a greater amount in the (potentially sanctioned) Ultimatum Game, and if this is the case, upregulating LPFC activity with tDCS could stimulate behavior to align these descriptive social norms. In either case, the findings by Ruff and colleagues suggest that the norm for "fair" or "correct" behavior is dependent on social interactions, sanction threats, and neural activity in lateral prefrontal cortex.

In an interesting addition to this line of reasoning, Bereczkei, Deak, Papp, Perlaki, and Orsi (2013); Bereczkei et al. (2015) reported that Iterative Trust Game players who scored high on a scale for Machiavellian (manipulative) personality traits showed increased activity in left DLPFC when responding to a cooperative move of their game partner. As the high-Machiavellian subjects responded to this cooperative move by sending back less money (thus profiting more), in this case DLPFC activity was associated with reduced fairness behavior. It may well be, therefore, that brain systems involved in cognitive control are simply producing goal-directed behavior, whatever one's goal is. If one values fairness, these areas may override greedy impulses to facilitate fair behavior; if one values maximizing personal gains, these areas may override a cooperative response in favor of the exploitation of others. Indeed, this interpretation is in line with the role of the DLPFC in goal maintenance and cognitive control independent of fairness-related decisions (Miller & Cohen, 2001).

Fairness as Reward

To this point, we have discussed the role of the brain's reward system in facilitating financially self-interested behavior. That is, however, not the complete story. Tricomi, Rangel, Camerer, and O'Doherty (2010) reported observations that neural activity in ventromedial prefrontal cortex and ventral striatum increased when money was transferred from another player to the participant—but only if that other player had begun the experiment with a large monetary endowment. If the participant was the one who was endowed with money, the opposite pattern was observed: monetary transfers from self to the other player were associated with increased ventral striatal and VMPFC activity. Thus, Tricomi and colleagues argue for evidence for a reward-based neural implementation of inequity aversion, by which the receipt of money is only rewarding if it reduces inequity between game partners, in either direction. Whether this inequity-sensitivity in the brain's reward system is a function of DLPFC-VMPFC connectivity is still unknown.

These findings relate to an earlier report by Harbaugh, Mayr, and Burghart (2007). Here, the transfer of money from a participant to a charity of their choice elicited neural activity in the ventral striatum, both when those transfers were voluntary (similar to real-world donation) and when they were mandatory (similar to real-world taxation). In addition, it seems that the ventral striatum also responds to reward receipt of others although this response is diminished by social distance to the other person (Mobbs et al., 2009). In sum, the role of the reward system in fairness-related decision-making is complex and deserves further inquiry.

The Link Between Theory of Mind and Fairness

Humans may have an intrinsic need for justice (Decety & Yoder, 2015), but can also act strategically in social interactions (Lee & Seo, 2016). One core ability underlying such strategic choices is that of theory of mind, i.e., the skill of maintaining a mental model of others' minds. Brain systems that facilitate theory of mind, such as medial prefrontal cortex (MPFC; Denny, Kober, Wager, & Ochsner, 2012; Van Overwalle & Baetens, 2009) and the temporoparietal junction (TPJ), have often been mentioned in the context of economic games, and their role in fairness-related decisions is potentially important.

The medial PFC is proposed to integrate emotional, deliberative, and social information (Amodio & Frith, 2006), especially when social interests are in conflict with self-interest (Koban, Pichon, & Vuilleumier, 2014). Indeed, in the UG, the mPFC plays a crucial role in rejecting offers. By comparing how people play for themselves versus play for others, Corradi-Dell'Acqua et al. (2013) showed that people reject unfair offers equally often, but recruit the mPFC more strongly when playing for themselves. Importantly, the insula shows a similar response in both situations. Civai, Miniussi, and Rumiati (2015) expand on this finding by manipulating mPFC activity using tDCS, demonstrating a causal role: when playing for oneself, decreasing mPFC activity using cathodal stimulation leads to fewer unfair offers being rejected; however, when playing for a third party, the same stimulation does not affect the rejections of unfair offers, but instead leads to more fair offers being rejected. Together these findings suggest that the insular cortex evaluates the fairness of the allocation, while the mPFC integrates this with the direct impact for oneself.

Hutcherson et al. (2015) let participant play a DG as the proposers, and found that TPJ and vmPFC signals correlated with the value for the other. Since the vmPFC activity was also correlated with the value for oneself, they proposed that the TPJ represents the valuation for the other, while the vmPFC integrates this information with the amount for the self. This interpretation is in line with extensive work in nonsocial decision-making, where the vmPFC seems to integrate value-information of different choice options (Hare, Camerer, & Rangel, 2009; Kable & Glimcher, 2009).

In a recent study of third-party punishment, Feng et al. (2016) compared participants' willingness to punish when they were either alone or as part of a larger group of (potential) third-party players. They found that participants punished more when alone and that in the group condition, the dmPFC activity modulated the activity in vmPFC and AI.

In the Trust Game, multiple studies have found medial prefrontal cortex (MPFC) to be more active when trustees defected than when they reciprocated (Chang et al., 2011; Van Baar et al., 2016; van den Bos, van Dijk, Westenberg, Rombouts, & Crone, 2009; van den Bos et al., 2011). This may mean that trustees process the other's mental state when they decide to behave unfairly. In line with this interpretation, Van Baar et al. (2016) observed increased activity in posterior superior temporal sulcus (pSTS), another important region for theory of mind, when participants did not reciprocate trust. On the other hand, increased activity in TPJ was found by Chang et al. (2011) when participants reciprocated. We can, therefore, not simply state that the theory of mind network contributes either positively or negatively to fair behavior.

It may prove more fruitful to investigate not simply brain activity but rather functional and effective connectivity between brain regions. If the activity in two brain regions is strongly correlated, they may be influencing one another; if the strength of this correlation changes with task demands, the two regions are said to be "effectively" connected (Friston et al., 1997). When investigating the neural signals from the trustee through this lens, Van Baar et al. (2016) found that functional connectivity between TPJ (theory of mind) and VMPFC (valuation) is stronger in guilt-averse trustees than in inequity-averse subjects. That is, there were trustees who appeared to behave perfectly fairly, yet reached that fair behavior by reasoning only from the investor's expectations and not from their own norms about fair behavior. These participants showed strong functional connections between the theory of mind and valuation systems, whereas other participants, who made their decisions based on their own fairness norms, did not have these functional connections. In line with this "individual differences" interpretation, Van den Bos et al. (2009) found that the right TPJ and precuneus were more responsive to defection in participants who were, in general, more prosocial. Just like the salience network, therefore, the theory of mind network may be flexibly activated during reciprocity decisions based on the personal preferences of the trustee. One should therefore be mindful of such personal differences in social preferences when studying the neural correlates of fairness.

Influencing Fairness Using Neuropharmacology

One final avenue for studying fairness-related behavior is via the use of pharmacological manipulations. By administering hormones like oxytocin and testosterone, or using procedures like acute tryptophan depletion, researchers are able to directly affect the nervous system and observe the behavioral outcomes.

The influence of several neuromodulators has been investigated in the context of the Ultimatum Game. In a series of studies, Crockett and colleagues studied how serotonin influences the behavior of the responder. Specifically, Crockett, Clark, Tabibnia, Lieberman, and Robbins (2008) showed that people with lower serotonin levels reject more unfair offers, independent of the stake size. Importantly, the manipulation of serotonin levels did not affect self-reported mood, nor what proportion of the stake participant considered a fair split. However, those participants for whom lower serotonin levels led to more rejections also became more impatient, as measured using a temporal discounting task in which participants have to choose between a lower reward sooner (impatient choice) and a larger reward later (patient choice) (Crockett, Clark, Lieberman, Tabibnia, & Robbins, 2010). In a follow-up study, Crockett, Clark, Hauser, and Robbins (2010) now increased serotonin levels with citalopram. Using the same paradigm with variable stake sizes, they found that increased levels of serotonin reduced rejection rates, without affecting fairness perceptions or self-reported mood. Based on additional tests, the authors proposed that serotonin might modulate how likely one is to cause harm to others. Finally, Crockett et al. (2013) combined these procedures with fMRI. The neuroimaging results showed that the activity in the dorsal striatum correlated with increased rejection rates under decreased levels of serotonin. These findings are indeed consistent with the interpretation that serotonin modulates the willingness to punish unfair behavior, without affecting the perception of fairness itself.

Other neuromodulators which have been proposed to play a role in social decision-making include testosterone and oxytocin. However, the relationship here with fairness and reciprocity is less clear. Increasing testosterone levels in women leads them to propose higher offers in the Ultimatum Game (Eisenegger, Naef, Snozzi, Heinrichs, & Fehr, 2010). However, this might be due to increased concerns for social status (Eisenegger, Haushofer, & Fehr, 2011), and not a concern for fairness in itself. The latter would imply that responders should reject unfair offers at a greater rate as well. However, there does not seem to be an effect of testosterone on the responder's behavior in the UG (Cueva et al., 2016; Zethraeus et al., 2009). Additionally, oxytocin has been linked to trust. Early studies (Kosfeld, Heinrichs, Zak, Fischbacher, & Fehr, 2005) showed that oxytocin increases transfers by investors in a Trust Game, or whether they adapted their investments after receiving feedback that the trustee did not reciprocate (Baumgartner, Heinrichs, Vonlanthen, Fischbacher, & Fehr, 2008). However, these findings have not been consistently replicated (Nave, Camerer, & McCullough, 2015).

Conclusion

As we have attempted to demonstrate, cognitive neuroscience can provide important biological constraints on the processes involved in decisions involving fairness, and indeed the research reviewed here is revealing that many of the processes underlying these complex social decisions may overlap with rather fundamental brain mechanisms, such as those involved in reward, punishment, and learning.

Though still occupying a small subfield, the cross-disciplinary nature of these studies is innovative, and combining insights from Psychology, Neuroscience, and Economics has the potential to greatly increase our knowledge about the psychological and neural basis of fairness. Participants in these studies are generally directly embedded in meaningful social interactions, and their decisions carry real weight in that their compensation is typically based on their decisions. Importantly, observed decisions in these tasks often do not conform to the predictions of classical game theory, and therefore more precise characterizations of both behavioral and brain mechanisms are important in adapting these models to better fit how decisions are actually made in an interactive environment. Further, the recent use of formal modeling approaches in conjunction with psychological theory and fMRI offers a unique avenue for the study of social dynamics, with the advantages of this approach being twofold. Firstly, it ensures that models of fairness are formally described, as opposed to the ad-hoc models that have been typically proposed. And secondly, by assessing whether these models are neurally plausible, it provides a more rigorous test of the likelihood that these models are good representations of how people are actually making decisions about fairness and equity.

Finally, as we mentioned earlier, there is the potential for this work to ultimately have a significant practical impact in terms of understanding how interactive decision-making works. More comprehensive knowledge of people's attitudes to fairness could usefully be employed to inform how policy decisions are taken, for example in relation to tax compliance, environmental behavior, and legal judgments. Typically, these policy decisions are based on the standard economic models of behavior that often do not accurately capture how individuals actually decide. The development of more accurate, brain-based, models of decision-making has the potential to greatly help with these policy formulations as they relate to our interactive choices. Knowing what signals commonly trigger both actions of fairness and unfairness can assist in designing policy to better achieve desired societal aims.

References

Amodio, D. M., & Frith, C. D. (2006). Meeting of minds: The medial frontal cortex and social cognition. *Nature Reviews Neuroscience, 7*(4), 268–277. http://doi.org/10.1038/nrn1884.

Apps, M. A. J., Rushworth, M. F. S., & Chang, S. W. C. (2016). The anterior cingulate gyrus and social cognition: Tracking the motivation of others. *Neuron, 90*(4), 692–707. http://doi.org/10.1016/j.neuron.2016.04.018.

Bartra, O., McGuire, J. T., & Kable, J. W. (2013). The valuation system: A coordinate-based meta-analysis of BOLD fMRI experiments examining neural correlates of subjective value. *NeuroImage, 76*(1), 412–427. http://doi.org/10.1016/j.neuroimage.2013.02.063.

Basten, U., Biele, G., Heekeren, H. R., & Fiebach, C. J. (2010). How the brain integrates costs and benefits during decision making. *Proceedings of the National Academy of Sciences of the United States of America, 107*(50), 21767–21772. http://doi.org/10.1073/pnas.0908104107.

Battigalli, P., Dufwenberg, M., & Smith, A. (2015). *Frustration & anger in games*. Working paper (pp. 1–44). http://doi.org/10.13140/RG.2.1.3418.4403.

Baumgartner, T., Fischbacher, U., Feierabend, A., Lutz, K., & Fehr, E. (2009). The neural circuitry of a broken promise. *Neuron, 64*(5), 756–770. http://doi.org/10.1016/j.neuron.2009.11.017.

Baumgartner, T., Heinrichs, M., Vonlanthen, A., Fischbacher, U., & Fehr, E. (2008). Oxytocin shapes the neural circuitry of trust and trust adaptation in humans. *Neuron, 58*(4), 639–650. http://doi.org/10.1016/j.neuron.2008.04.009.

Baumgartner, T., Knoch, D., Hotz, P., Eisenegger, C., & Fehr, E. (2011). Dorsolateral and ventromedial prefrontal cortex orchestrate normative choice. *Nature Neuroscience, 14*(11), 1468–1474. http://doi.org/10.1038/nn.2933.

Bereczkei, T., Deak, A., Papp, P., Perlaki, G., & Orsi, G. (2013). Neural correlates of Machiavellian strategies in a social dilemma task. *Brain and Cognition, 82*(1), 108–116. http://doi.org/10.1016/j.bandc.2013.02.012.

Bereczkei, T., Papp, P., Kincses, P., Bodrogi, B., Perlaki, G., Orsi, G., & Deak, A. (2015). The neural basis of the Machiavellians' decision making in fair and unfair situations. *Brain and Cognition, 98*, 53–64. http://doi.org/10.1016/j.bandc.2015.05.006.

Botvinick, M. M., Cohen, J. D., & Carter, C. S. (2004). Conflict monitoring and anterior cingulate cortex: An update. *Trends in Cognitive Sciences, 8*(12), 539–546. http://doi.org/10.1016/j.tics.2004.10.003.

Cáceda, R., James, G. A., Gutman, D. A., & Kilts, C. D. (2015). Organization of intrinsic functional brain connectivity predicts decisions to reciprocate social behavior. *Behavioural Brain Research, 292*, 478–483. http://doi.org/10.1016/j.bbr.2015.07.008.

Camerer, C. F. (2003). *Behavioral game theory: Experiments in strategic interaction*. Princeton, NJ: Princeton University Press.

Chang, L. J., & Sanfey, A. G. (2013). Great expectations: Neural computations underlying the use of social norms in decision-making. *Social Cognitive and Affective Neuroscience, 8*(3), 277–284. http://doi.org/10.1093/scan/nsr094.

Chang, L. J., Smith, A., Dufwenberg, M., & Sanfey, A. G. (2011). Triangulating the neural, psychological, and economic bases of guilt aversion. *Neuron, 70*(3), 560–572. http://doi.org/10.1016/j.neuron.2011.02.056.

Civai, C., Corradi-Dell'Acqua, C., Gamer, M., & Rumiati, R. I. (2010). Are irrational reactions to unfairness truly emotionally-driven? Dissociated behavioural and emotional responses in the Ultimatum Game task. *Cognition, 114*(1), 89-95. http://doi.org/10.1016/j.cognition.2009.09.001.

Civai, C., Crescentini, C., Rustichini, A., & Rumiati, R. I. (2012). Equality versus self-interest in the brain: Differential roles of anterior insula and medial prefrontal cortex. *NeuroImage, 62*(1), 102–112. http://doi.org/10.1016/j.neuroimage.2012.04.037.

Civai, C., Miniussi, C., & Rumiati, R. I. (2015). Medial prefrontal cortex reacts to unfairness if this damages the self: A tDCS study. *Social Cognitive and Affective Neuroscience, 10*(8), 1054–1060. http://doi.org/10.1093/scan/nsu154.

Corradi-Dell'Acqua, C., Civai, C., Rumiati, R. I., & Fink, G. R. (2013). Disentangling self- and fairness-related neural mechanisms involved in the ultimatum game: An fMRI study. *Social Cognitive and Affective Neuroscience, 8*(4), 424–431. http://doi.org/10.1093/scan/nss014.
Critchley, H. D., Wiens, S., Rotshtein, P., Ohman, A., Dolan, R. J., Öhman, A., & Dolan, R. J. (2004). Neural systems supporting interoceptive awareness. *Nature Neuroscience, 7*(2), 189–195. http://doi.org/10.1038/nn1176.
Crockett, M. J., Apergis-Schoute, A., Herrmann, B., Lieberman, M. D., Muller, U., Robbins, T. W., & Clark, L. (2013). Serotonin modulates striatal responses to fairness and retaliation in humans. *Journal of Neuroscience, 33*(8), 3505–3513. http://doi.org/10.1523/JNEUROSCI.2761-12.2013.
Crockett, M. J., Clark, L., Hauser, M. D., & Robbins, T. W. (2010). Serotonin selectively influences moral judgment and behavior through effects on harm aversion. *Proceedings of the National Academy of Sciences of the United States of America, 107*(40), 17433–17438. http://doi.org/10.1073/pnas.1009396107.
Crockett, M. J., Clark, L., Lieberman, M. D., Tabibnia, G., & Robbins, T. W. (2010). Impulsive choice and altruistic punishment are correlated and increase in tandem with serotonin depletion. *Emotion, 10*(6), 855–862. http://doi.org/10.1037/a0019861.
Crockett, M. J., Clark, L., Tabibnia, G., Lieberman, M. D., & Robbins, T. W. (2008). Serotonin modulates behavioral reactions to unfairness. *Science, 320*(5884), 1739. http://doi.org/10.1126/science.1155577.
Cueva, C., Roberts, R. E., Spencer, T. J., Rani, N., Tempest, M., Tobler, P. N., … Rustichini, A. (2016). Testosterone administration does not affect men's rejections of low ultimatum game offers or aggressive mood. *Hormones*. http://doi.org/10.1016/j.surfcoat.2016.08.074.
Damasio, A. R., Grabowski, T. J., Bechara, A., Damasio, H., Ponto, L. L., Parvizi, J., & Hichwa, R. D. (2000). Subcortical and cortical brain activity during the feeling of self-generated emotions. *Nature Neuroscience, 3*(10), 1049–1056. http://doi.org/10.1038/79871.
Decety, J., & Yoder, K. J. (2015). Empathy and motivation for justice: Cognitive empathy and concern, but not emotional empathy, predict sensitivity to injustice for others. *Social Neuroscience, 919*(January), 1–14. http://doi.org/10.1080/17470919.2015.1029593.
Delgado, M. R., Frank, R. H., & Phelps, E. A. (2005). Perceptions of moral character modulate the neural systems of reward during the trust game. *Nature Neuroscience, 8*(11), 1611–1618. http://doi.org/10.1038/nn1575.
Denny, B. T., Kober, H., Wager, T. D., & Ochsner, K. N. (2012). A meta-analysis of functional neuroimaging studies of self- and other judgments reveals a spatial gradient for mentalizing in medial prefrontal cortex. *Journal of Cognitive Neuroscience, 24*(8), 1742–1752. http://doi.org/10.1162/jocn_a_00233.
Eisenegger, C., Haushofer, J., & Fehr, E. (2011). The role of testosterone in social interaction. *Trends in Cognitive Sciences, 15*(6), 263–271. http://doi.org/10.1016/j.tics.2011.04.008.
Eisenegger, C., Naef, M., Snozzi, R., Heinrichs, M., & Fehr, E. (2010). Prejudice and truth about the effect of testosterone on human bargaining behaviour. *Nature, 463*(7279), 356–359. http://doi.org/10.1038/nature08711.
Everitt, B. J., & Robbins, T. W. (2005). Neural systems of reinforcement for drug addiction: From actions to habits to compulsion. *Nature Neuroscience, 8*(11), 1481–1490. http://doi.org/10.1038/nn1579.
Fareri, D. S., Chang, L. J., & Delgado, M. R. (2012). Effects of direct social experience on trust decisions and neural reward circuitry. *Frontiers in Neuroscience, 6*(October), 148. http://doi.org/10.3389/fnins.2012.00148.
Feng, C., Deshpande, G., Liu, C., Gu, R., Luo, Y. J., & Krueger, F. (2016). Diffusion of responsibility attenuates altruistic punishment: A functional magnetic resonance imaging effective connectivity study. *Human Brain Mapping, 37*(2), 663–677. http://doi.org/10.1002/hbm.23057.
Feng, C., Luo, Y. J., & Krueger, F. (2015). Neural signatures of fairness-related normative decision making in the ultimatum game: A coordinate-based meta-analysis. *Human Brain Mapping, 36*(2), 591–602. http://doi.org/10.1002/hbm.22649.

Fehr, E., & Krajbich, I. (2013). Social preferences and the brain. In *Neuroeconomics: Decision making and the brain* (2nd ed.). Amsterdam: Elsevier. http://doi.org/10.1016/B978-0-12-416008-8.00011-5.

Fehr, E., & Schmidt, K. M. (1999). A theory of fairness, competition, and cooperation. *The Quarterly Journal of Economics, 114*(3), 817–868. http://doi.org/10.1162/003355399556151.

Friston, K. J., Buechel, C., Fink, G. R., Morris, J., Rolls, E., & Dolan, R. J. (1997). Psychophysiological and modulatory interactions in neuroimaging. *Neuroimage, 6*(3), 218-229. http://doi.org/10.1006/nimg.1997.0291.

Gabay, A. S., Radua, J., Kempton, M. J., & Mehta, M. A. (2014). The ultimatum game and the brain: A meta-analysis of neuroimaging studies. *Neuroscience and Biobehavioral Reviews, 47*, 549–558. http://doi.org/10.1016/j.neubiorev.2014.10.014.

Grecucci, A., Giorgetta, C., Bonini, N., & Sanfey, A. G. (2013). Reappraising social emotions: The role of inferior frontal gyrus, temporo-parietal junction and insula in interpersonal emotion regulation. *Frontiers in Human Neuroscience, 7*(September), 523. http://doi.org/10.3389/fnhum.2013.00523.

Grecucci, A., Giorgetta, C., Van't Wout, M., Bonini, N., & Sanfey, A. G. (2013). Reappraising the ultimatum: An fMRI study of emotion regulation and decision making. *Cerebral Cortex, 23*(2), 399–410. http://doi.org/10.1093/cercor/bhs028.

Güth, W., Schmittberger, R., & Schwarze, B. (1982). An experimental analysis of ultimatum bargaining. *Journal of Economic Behavior & Organization, 3*(4), 367–388. http://doi.org/10.1016/0167-2681(82)90011-7.

Harbaugh, W. T., Mayr, U., & Burghart, D. R. (2007). Neural responses to taxation and voluntary giving reveal motives for charitable donations. *Science, 316*(5831), 1622–1625. http://doi.org/10.1126/science.1140738.

Hare, T. A., Camerer, C. F., & Rangel, A. (2009). Self-control in decision-making involves modulation of the vmPFC valuation system. *Science, 324*, 646–648. http://doi.org/10.1126/science.1168450.

Harlé, K. M., Chang, L. J., van't Wout, M., & Sanfey, A. G. (2012). The neural mechanisms of affect infusion in social economic decision-making: A mediating role of the anterior insula. *NeuroImage, 61*(1), 32–40. http://doi.org/10.1016/j.neuroimage.2012.02.027.

Haruno, M., & Frith, C. D. (2010). Activity in the amygdala elicited by unfair divisions predicts social value orientation. *Nature Neuroscience, 13*(2), 160–161. http://doi.org/10.1038/nn.2468.

Hsu, M., Anen, C., & Quartz, S. R. (2008). The right and the good: Distributive justice and neural encoding of equity and efficiency. *Science, 320*(5879), 1092–1095. http://doi.org/10.1126/science.1153651.

Hutcherson, C. A., Bushong, B., & Rangel, A. (2015). A neurocomputational model of altruistic choice and its implications. *Neuron, 87*(2), 451–462. http://doi.org/10.1016/j.neuron.2015.06.031.

Iyer, M. B., Schleper, N., & Wassermann, E. M. (2003). Priming stimulation enhances the depressant effect of low-frequency repetitive transcranial magnetic stimulation. *Journal of Neuroscience, 23*(34), 10867–10872.

Izuma, K., Saito, D. N., & Sadato, N. (2008). Processing of social and monetary rewards in the human striatum. *Neuron, 58*(2), 284–294. http://doi.org/10.1016/j.neuron.2008.03.020.

Jacobson, L., Koslowsky, M., & Lavidor, M. (2012). tDCS polarity effects in motor and cognitive domains: A meta-analytical review. *Experimental Brain Research, 216*, 1–10.

Kable, J. W., & Glimcher, P. W. (2009). The neurobiology of decision: Consensus and controversy. *Neuron, 63*(6), 733–745. http://doi.org/10.1016/j.neuron.2009.09.003.

Kirk, U., Downar, J., & Montague, P. R. (2011). Interoception drives increased rational decision-making in meditators playing the ultimatum game. *Frontiers in Neuroscience, 5*(April), 1–11. http://doi.org/10.3389/fnins.2011.00049.

Knoch, D., Nitsche, M. A., Fischbacher, U., Eisenegger, C., Pascual-Leone, A., & Fehr, E. (2008). Studying the neurobiology of social interaction with transcranial direct current stimulation—The example of punishing unfairness. *Cerebral Cortex, 18*(9), 1987–1990. http://doi.org/10.1093/cercor/bhm237.

Knoch, D., Pascual-Leone, A., Meyer, K., Treyer, V., & Fehr, E. (2006). Diminishing reciprocal fairness by disrupting the right prefrontal cortex. *Science, 314*(5800), 829–832. http://doi.org/10.1126/science.1129156.

Koban, L., Pichon, S., & Vuilleumier, P. (2014). Responses of medial and ventrolateral prefrontal cortex to interpersonal conflict for resources. *Social Cognitive and Affective Neuroscience, 9*(5), 561–569. http://doi.org/10.1093/scan/nst020.

Kolling, N., Behrens, T. E. J., Wittmann, M. K., & Rushworth, M. F. S. (2016). Multiple signals in anterior cingulate cortex. *Current Opinion in Neurobiology, 37*, 36–43. http://doi.org/10.1016/j.conb.2015.12.007.

Kosfeld, M., Heinrichs, M., Zak, P. J., Fischbacher, U., & Fehr, E. (2005). Oxytocin increases trust in humans. *Nature, 435*(7042), 673–677. http://doi.org/10.1038/nature03701.

Krajbich, I., Bartling, B., Hare, T., & Fehr, E. (2015). Rethinking fast and slow based on a critique of reaction-time reverse inference. *Nature Communications, 6*(May), 7455. http://doi.org/10.1038/ncomms8455.

Lee, D., & Seo, H. (2016). Neural basis of strategic decision making. *Trends in Neurosciences, 39*(1), 40–48. http://doi.org/10.1016/j.tins.2015.11.002.

Miller, E. K., & Cohen, J. D. (2001). An integrative theory of prefrontal cortex function. *Annual Review of Neuroscience, 24*, 167–202. http://doi.org/10.1146/annurev.neuro.24.1.167.

Miniussi, C., Harris, J. A., & Ruzzoli, M. (2013). Modelling non-invasive brain stimulation in cognitive neuroscience. *Neuroscience Biobehavioural Review, 37*, 1702–1712.

Mobbs, D., Yu, R., Meyer, M., Passamonti, L., Seymour, B., Calder, A.J., Schweizer, S., Frith, C.D., & Dalgleish, T. (2009). A key role for similarity in vicarious reward. *Science, 324*(5929), 900-900. http://doi.org/10.1126/science.1170539.

Nave, G., Camerer, C., & McCullough, M. (2015). Does oxytocin increase trust in humans? A critical review of research. *Perspectives on Psychological Science, 10*(6), 772–789. http://doi.org/10.1177/1745691615600138.

Niv, Y., & Schoenbaum, G. (2008). Dialogues on prediction errors. *Trends in Cognitive Sciences, 12*(7), 265–272. http://doi.org/10.1016/j.tics.2008.03.006.

Phillips, M. L., Young, A. W., Senior, C., Brammer, M., Andrew, C., Calder, A. J., … David, A. S. (1997). A specific neural substrate for perceiving facial expressions of disgust. *Nature, 389*(October), 495–498. http://doi.org/10.1038/39051.

Rand, D. G. (2016). Cooperation, fast and slow: Meta-analytic evidence for a theory of social heuristics and self-interested deliberation. *Psychological Science, 27*(9), 1192–1206. http://doi.org/10.1177/0956797616654455.

Rand, D. G., Greene, J. D., & Nowak, M. A. (2012). Spontaneous giving and calculated greed. *Nature, 489*(7416), 427–430. http://doi.org/10.1038/nature11467.

Ratcliff, R., & Mckoon, G. (2008). The diffusion decision model: Theory and data for two-choice decision tasks. *Neural Computation, 20*(4), 873–922.

Ruff, C. C., & Fehr, E. (2014). The neurobiology of rewards and values in social decision making. *Nature Reviews Neuroscience, 15*(8), 549–562. http://doi.org/10.1038/nrn3776.

Ruff, C. C., Ugazio, G., & Fehr, E. (2013). Changing social norm compliance with noninvasive brain stimulation. *Science, 342*(6157), 482–484. http://doi.org/10.1126/science.1241399.

Sanfey, A. G., Rilling, J. K., Aronson, J. A., Nystrom, L. E., & Cohen, J. D. (2003). The neural basis of economic decision-making in the ultimatum game. *Science (New York, N.Y.), 300*(5626), 1755–1758. http://doi.org/10.1126/science.1082976.

Sanfey, A. G., Stallen, M., & Chang, L. J. (2014). Norms and expectations in social decision-making. *Trends in Cognitive Sciences, 18*(4), 172–174. http://doi.org/10.1016/j.tics.2014.01.011.

Schultz, W., Dayan, P., & Montague, P. R. (1997). A neural substrate of prediction and reward. *Science, 275*(5306), 1593–1599. http://doi.org/10.1126/science.275.5306.1593.

Schultz, W. (1999). The reward signal of midbrain dopamine neurons. *Physiology, 14*(6), 249-255.

Seeley, W. W., Menon, V., Schatzberg, A. F., Keller, J., Glover, G. H., Kenna, H., … Greicius, M. D. (2007). Dissociable intrinsic connectivity networks for salience processing and executive control. *Journal of Neuroscience, 27*(9), 2349–2356. http://doi.org/10.1523/JNEUROSCI.5587-06.2007.

Singer, T., Critchley, H. D., & Preuschoff, K. (2009). A common role of insula in feelings, empathy and uncertainty. *Trends in Cognitive Sciences, 13*(8), 334–340. http://doi.org/10.1016/j.tics.2009.05.001.

Smith, P. L., & Ratcliff, R. (2004). Psychology and neurobiology of simple decisions. *Trends in Neurosciences, 27*(3), 161–168. http://doi.org/10.1016/j.tins.2004.01.006.

Stagg, C. J., & Nitsche, M. A. (2011). Physiological basis of transcranial direct current stimulation. *The Neuroscientist, 17*(1), 37–53. http://doi.org/10.1177/1073858410386614.

Sutton, R. S., & Barto, A. G. (1998). *Reinforcement learning*. Cambridge, MA: MIT Press.

Tricomi, E., Rangel, A., Camerer, C. F., & O'Doherty, J. P. (2010). Neural evidence for inequality-averse social preferences. *Nature, 463*(7284), 1089–1091. http://doi.org/10.1038/nature08785.

Van Baar, J. M., Chang, L. J., & Sanfey, A. G. (2016). *Separating guilt aversion and inequity aversion in Trust Game reciprocity*. Poster presented at the Annual Meeting of the Society for Neuroeconomics, Berlin, Germany.

van den Bos, W., van Dijk, E., Westenberg, M., Rombouts, S. A. R. B., & Crone, E. A. (2009). What motivates repayment? Neural correlates of reciprocity in the Trust Game. *Social Cognitive and Affective Neuroscience, 4*(3), 294–304. http://doi.org/10.1093/scan/nsp009.

van den Bos, W., van Dijk, E., Westenberg, M., Rombouts, S. A. R. B., & Crone, E. A. (2011). Changing brains, changing perspectives: The neurocognitive development of reciprocity. *Psychological Science, 22*(1), 60–70. http://doi.org/10.1177/0956797610391102.

Van Overwalle, F., & Baetens, K. (2009). Understanding others' actions and goals by mirror and mentalizing systems: A meta-analysis. *NeuroImage, 48*(3), 564–584. http://doi.org/10.1016/j.neuroimage.2009.06.009.

van't Wout, M., Kahn, R. S., Sanfey, A. G., & Aleman, A. (2005). Repetitive transcranial magnetic stimulation over the right dorsolateral prefrontal cortex affects strategic decision-making. *Neuroreport, 16*(16), 1849–1852. http://doi.org/10.1097/01.wnr.0000183907.08149.14.

Xiang, T., Lohrenz, T., & Montague, P. R. (2013). Computational substrates of norms and their violations during social exchange. *The Journal of Neuroscience, 33*(3), 1099–1108. http://doi.org/10.1523/JNEUROSCI.1642-12.2013.

Zethraeus, N., Kocoska-Maras, L., Ellingsen, T., von Schoultz, B., Hirschberg, A. L., & Johannesson, M. (2009). A randomized trial of the effect of estrogen and testosterone on economic behavior. *Proceedings of the National Academy of Sciences of the United States of America, 106*(16), 6535–6538. http://doi.org/http://dx.doi.org/10.1073/pnas.0812757106.

Chapter 3
The Evolution of Moral Development

Mark Sheskin

The Evolution of Moral Development

Fairness is a central part of both moral judgment and moral behavior. In moral judgment, people are so committed to fairness that they often prefer situations with *lower* overall welfare but a *higher* degree of fairness. For example, people typically judge that a new medicine should not be introduced if it will decrease cure rates for a small group of people, even if it also increases cure rates for a large group of people, and therefore causes an overall increase in cure rates (Baron, 1994). In moral behavior, fairness motivates people to sacrifice their own welfare. For example, in many settings, people will share resources they could instead choose to keep (e.g., in the dictator game; Kahneman, Knetsch, & Thaler, 1986), and will reject unfair behavior from others, even when doing so is costly (e.g., in the ultimatum game; Güth, Schmittberger, & Schwarze, 1982).

The goal of this chapter is to explore the developmental origins of adult fairness. In doing so, I will situate the development of fairness within a larger framework of the evolution of moral development. Thus, I will begin by characterizing human moral psychology and the role of fairness within it (section "Human Moral Psychology"). I will then argue for a particular view of the evolution of morality that places fairness in the center (section "The Evolution of Morality, Especially Fairness"). This view accounts for the peculiar features of how fairness emerges over development, most notably a "knowledge-behavior gap" in which children understand many features of fairness before they are motivated to behave in compliance with those features (section "The Development of Morality, Especially Fairness"). Finally, I will discuss implications for other areas of research and future directions based on this account (section "Implications and Future Directions").

M. Sheskin (✉)
Cognitive Science Program, Yale University, New Haven, CT, USA
e-mail: msheskin@gmail.com

M. Li, D.P. Tracer (eds.), *Interdisciplinary Perspectives on Fairness, Equity, and Justice*, DOI 10.1007/978-3-319-58993-0_3

Human Moral Psychology

There is controversy over the structure of human moral psychology. One set of approaches suggests that all moral concerns fall into a discrete number of foundations, and that people around the world show moral concerns in each of the foundations (Haidt, 2012; Haidt & Joseph, 2004; Shweder, Much, Mahapatra, & Park, 1997). Early work suggested the three foundations of "Community," "Autonomy," and "Divinity" (Shweder et al., 1997), with violations of fairness being part of the "Autonomy" foundation. More recent expansions have separated out a distinct "fairness" foundation from either four (e.g., Haidt & Joseph, 2004) or five (e.g., Haidt, 2012) others: harm, hierarchy, in-group, purity, and liberty.

Other approaches to morality do not divide it among discrete foundations. For example, one approach suggests that all moral judgments are about harm (e.g., Gray & Schein, 2016) and that our moral judgments follow a "template" that includes (1) a moral agent (2) causing harm to (3) a moral patient (Gray, Schein, & Ward, 2014). Of particular interest for the current chapter, some approaches place fairness (rather than harm) at the center (e.g., Baumard, Boyer, & Sperber, 2010), and others argue for the presence of both harm and fairness, but identify fairness as a particularly important and defining feature of human morality (compared to social behavior in other species; Tomasello, 2016).

The ongoing debate about the structure of morality, and the role of fairness in it, may be due to morality being an "artificial kind" rather than a "natural kind." This distinction comes from philosophy (Bird & Tobin, 2016), and separates out groupings that reflect the true nature of reality, versus groupings that represent human interests. For example, "hydrogen" is a natural kind that picks out all atoms of a particular set, whereas "pets that are good choices for a small apartment" is an artificial kind that picks out individuals for a particular human purpose. An example of applying this distinction to morality comes from Greene (2015), who argues that morality is not natural kind in human cognition, but is instead unified at the functional level. He provides an analogy with the concept of "vehicle" and explains that:

> At a mechanical level, vehicles are extremely variable and not at all distinct from other things. A motorcycle, for example, has more in common with a lawn mower than a with a sailboat, and a sailboat has more in common with a kite than with a motor cycle. One might conclude from this that the concept VEHICLE is therefore meaningless, but that would be mistaken. Vehicles are bound together, not at the mechanical level, but at the functional level. I believe that the same is true of morality.

This way of thinking about morality, as a concept that is useful for picking out a collection of aspects of human cognition, suggests that we might benefit from abandoning the idea that "morality" is a unified phenomenon that will have a systematic structure, underlain by a bounded set of proximate mechanisms and with a unified evolutionary explanation. Instead, depending on specific research goals, morality must be "fractionated into a set of biologically and psychologically cogent traits" (McKay & Whitehouse, 2015).

Applying this analysis of morality in general to fairness in particular, we might conclude that fairness itself is an artificial rather than a natural kind. That is, although fairness judgments and behaviors may have natural foundations, there may be multiple distinct capacities that we artificially group together when we speak as though there is just one capacity called "fairness." To the extent that there is a unified domain of fairness, it will be a *functional* unity—a set of judgments and behaviors that are directed towards a particular human goal. Thus, in this chapter, I will discuss the development of multiple types of fairness judgments and behaviors, as well as the development of several proximate mechanisms related to these judgments and behaviors.

The Evolution of Morality, Especially Fairness

Within the set of topics that people study when they refer to "morality" (a term for which there are very many definitions), certain elements of human moral behavior are well understood, especially when they are continuous with behaviors found across a wide variety of species. For example, mothers typically provide high levels of benefits for their offspring, fitting the textbook definition of altruism: an individual acts in a way that makes herself worse off and another better off. The explanation of such "kin altruism" is in the logic of "Hamilton's Rule," which states that kin selection will lead to the increase of genes that conform to "$C < Br$," meaning that the costs to the acting individual are less than the benefits to the recipient of the action, discounted by the relatedness between the actor and recipient (Hamilton, 1964). Although it is possible to find debate on the technical details (e.g., Nowak, Tarnita, & Wilson, 2010; reply by Abbot et al., 2011), this well-established feature of evolution applies broadly, and the kin selection paradigm has been used to investigate a wide range of phenomena (West, Griffin, & Gardner, 2008).

On the other hand, many aspects of human morality may require human-specific explanations. This is clearly apparent for many of the specifics of our moral lives—there are no other animals that have a moral judgment regarding the outcome of US presidential elections—but it may also be true of many features of human morality that could plausibly apply to nonhuman animals. Specifically, there is mounting evidence that fairness may be both a unique feature of humans compared to other species (Sheskin & Santos, 2012) and a core part of human morality (Baumard & Sheskin 2015).

The claim that fairness is unique to humans is controversial. Starting with a seminal 2003 paper by Sarah Brosnan and Frans de Waal, one line of research has highlighted potential continuities between human fairness and precursors in non-human primates, especially regarding the potential that individuals may react negatively to receiving less than a conspecific (e.g., Brosnan, Talbot, Ahlgren, Lambeth, & Schapiro, 2010; Fletcher, 2008). Other researchers have even added non-primates to the list of species that might react negatively to unfairness, including dogs (Range, Horn, Viranyi, & Huber, 2009) and corvids (Wascher & Bugnyar, 2013).

On the other hand, many labs have failed to replicate these results (e.g., Sheskin, Ashayeri, Skerry, & Santos, 2014; Silberberg, Crescimbene, Addessi, Anderson, & Visalberghi, 2009).

A reasonable consensus position is that nonhuman animals show *at most* limited concerns about fairness. For example, a recent review that was generally sympathetic to nonhuman fairness concerns nonetheless concluded that "inequity responses are not developed to the same degree in other species as in humans" (Talbot, Price, & Brosnan, 2016). This experimentally derived conclusion that nonhumans show limited concerns about fairness (or maybe no concerns with fairness) is corroborated by theoretical arguments about *why* humans are concerned with fairness. As we will see, the likely evolutionary account of human fairness predicts that it will be characteristic of humans, but not of other species.

Why is fairness so important to humans? Humans cooperate with each other in a wide variety of contexts, and have a high degree of freedom to choose partners for mutually beneficial tasks. This creates a "biological market" in which people who have a reputation for being good collaborators gain benefits by being preferred as partners, while those with lesser reputations are not selected for group tasks and miss out on the benefits of collaboration (e.g., Noë & Hammerstein, 1994). The competition for a good moral reputation might lead to "competitive altruism," in which each person takes very high costs to establish the best possible reputation (e.g., Barclay & Willer, 2007), but it will often lead to fairness instead (Debove, André, & Baumard, 2015). Specifically, people benefit from having a reputation for putting in at least their fair share of effort (and taking no more than their fair share of the rewards), but the symmetry of many situations (i.e., each person can be in both the position of choosing a partner and the position of being chosen as a partner) leads to "meeting in the middle" exactly at fairness.

Importantly, this explanation is specific to humans. As argued by Tomasello (2016), "early humans were forced into a niche of obligate collaborative foraging" in which they "knew that they were being evaluated by others." Although there is collaboration in nonhuman species, "humans' last common ancestor with other apes…did not create enough of the right kind of interdependence (individuals could opt out and still do fine)." Thus, due to the extreme importance of being selected for joint tasks and of judiciously selecting others for joint tasks, humans (and not other animals) have a strong interest in being known as a trustworthy cooperator rather than as a cheat, and for tracking the reputations of others as trustworthy cooperators or as cheats.

Recently, this partner-choice framework has been applied to moral development (Sheskin, Chevallier, Lambert, & Baumard, 2014). If one of the major benefits of costly prosocial behavior is establishing a good reputation to be included in mutually beneficial joint tasks, then such behavior should be less common at younger ages. Specifically, very young children are provisioned by adult caregivers (e.g., Meehan, Quinlan, & Malcom, 2013), reducing the marginal utility of additional benefits gained by collaboration with others. Furthermore, even if the additional benefits from collaboration were worthwhile, very young children are not skilled at most collaborative tasks (e.g., hunting; Gurven, Kaplan, & Gutierrez, 2006), reducing the chances that a good reputation could lead to being selected for a task. These doubly decreased benefits of a good moral reputation mean that, for young children, costly prosocial behavior will often not be paid back by benefits from collaboration. Thus, natural selection may have produced a default developmental timeline for fair behavior that tracks the typical importance of a good moral reputation at different ages (i.e., low when young, but increasing with age).

Although this framework is focused on the species-typical developmental timeline for fairness, it also accounts for certain systematic individual and situational differences. This is because the claim that a system is the product of natural selection is *not* the claim that it develops identically in each individual or that it is insensitive to environmental variation. To the contrary, "plasticity in developmental systems that interact with more changing or variable aspects of the environment (e.g., social status, predatory threats) should be favored by selection" (Bjorklund & Ellis, 2014).

For example, the current framework suggests that a collaborative context might be especially conducive to fair behavior, even in young children. Consistent with this, Hamann, Warneken, Greenberg, and Tomasello (2011) found that 3-year-old children (but not adult chimpanzees) share more equally with each other when the resources are the result of collaborating on a joint task, compared to when the resources are either "free" or the result of working in parallel.

The Development of Morality, Especially Fairness

Infant Social Evaluation

The developmental origins of human fairness begin in early infancy. Although infants are unable to engage in most moral actions, research over the last decade has revealed that infants do engage in sophisticated social evaluation of interactions between third parties. Building off of classic work by Heider and Simmel (1944), which found that adults will interpret motives and social roles when watching animated geometric shapes (e.g., a bully chasing a victim), Kuhlmeier, Wynn, and Bloom (2003) found that 12-month-old infants prefer to see an animated triangle approach a shape that has previously helped it climb a hill, rather than one that has hindered that goal. Extending this result to the infants' own preferences, Hamlin, Wynn, and Bloom (2007) found that 6-month-olds will reach for a helper over a hinderer. These evaluations can be stunningly complex: 10-month-olds discriminate between a helper who is aware of an agent's preferences and knowingly helps to fulfill them, and a helper who is unaware of an agent's preferences and accidentally helps to fulfill them (Hamlin, Ullman, Tenebaum, Goodman, & Baker, 2013).

Infants react to more than just helping and hindering—they show a sophisticated understanding of fairness. Infants prefer agents who distribute fairly (Geraci & Surian, 2011; see also Meristo & Surian, 2013). They also expect that agents will typically provide equal numbers of resources to recipients: For example, Sloane,

Baillargeon, and Premack (2012) found that infants will look longer (indicating surprise) at a "2 and 0" distribution compared to a "1 and 1" distribution. Furthermore, this is a specifically social effect, rather than (e.g.,) a symmetry preference, as the infants show no difference in looking time when the distributions are to inanimate recipients. Even more impressively, infants expect that unequal effort merits unequal reward, expecting that a recipient who has worked harder on a task deserves more reward (see also Schmidt & Sommerville, 2011; Sommerville, Schmidt, Yun, & Burns, 2013).

The sophistication of infant social evaluation is consistent with the evolutionary account detailed in the previous section. Unlike costly prosocial behavior, merely observing and judging others is nearly costless, and it can have important benefits. This is because, from early in infancy, humans observe and learn from others. The same can be said of many species, and there is some overlap between the ways humans learn from each other and the ways animals learn from each other, but it remains the case that some features of social learning are specific to humans (for a recent review, see Heyes, 2016). As described by Csibra and Gergely (2009), "human communication is specifically adapted to allow the transmission of generic knowledge between individuals. Such a communication system, which we call 'natural pedagogy', enables fast and efficient social learning of cognitively opaque cultural knowledge that would be hard to acquire relying on purely observational learning mechanisms alone."

The strong effects of pedagogy can be seen clearly in situations where it leads to "poor" performance by children trusting adults who are giving them incorrect or incomplete information. For example, children assume that an adult demonstrating how to use an object demonstrates all relevant functions, and so are less likely to explore and discover novel features (Bonawitz et al., 2011). Likewise, human children engage in "overimitation" (Lyons, Young, & Keil, 2007): when shown how to open a puzzle box to retrieve a reward inside, children faithfully copy all demonstrated actions, even ones that seem unrelated to opening the box. Other species do not overimitate, including our closest evolutionary relatives (chimpanzees; Horner & Whiten, 2005) and species that have been bred to work closely with us (domesticated dogs; Johnston, Holden, & Santos, 2016).

The standard explanations for phenomena like those above (not exploring actions that are left out of instruction, but overimitating unnecessary steps when they are included in instruction) are that they are crucial for the cumulative learning of human culture (Legare & Nielsen, 2015). For example, a child will benefit from trusting adults that we should wash our hands before we eat, even if the reasons are not completely clear.

Given that adults sometimes disagree, and some may have malevolent intentions, it would be bad to learn equally from everyone. Fortunately, infants and children do not learn indiscriminately from all sources (for a review, see Poulin-Dubois & Brosseau-Liard, 2016). They learn selectively based on information ranging from previous accuracy (Koenig, Clément, & Harris, 2004) to features of the informant such as likely group membership (e.g., language; Liberman, Woodward, & Kinzler, 2016) and overall benevolence (Johnston, Mills, & Landrum, 2015).

In sum, even very young infants show sophisticated social evaluation. This is likely because the costs are lower than the benefits: such capacities are relatively cheap to implement (i.e., although it requires that attention to be paid to adult behavior, and the cognitive abilities to evaluate and remember these behaviors, it requires no overt behavior), and social evaluation is important for determining which adults to affiliate with and learn from.

The Emergence of Costly Fairness Behavior

In contrast with the presence of social evaluation even in infancy, costly fairness behavior—along with costly prosocial behavior in general—emerges slowly over development. This does not mean that young children never show prosocial behavior; it is possible to design tasks on which even the youngest children will take costs to help others (e.g., Warneken, Hare, Melis, Hanus, & Tomasello, 2007; Warneken & Tomasello, 2006), and it is possible to design tasks on which even older children will show some limitations on their prosocial behavior (e.g., Sheskin et al., 2016). And, of course, adults do not always show perfectly moral behavior; indeed, we are struck by the oddness of people who commit themselves fully to moral causes with no privileging of their own welfare (MacFarquhar, 2015).

However, when a task does show strong differences across ages, it is typically in the direction of showing more willingness to take costs with increasing age (e.g., Fehr, Bernhard, & Rockenbach, 2008; but see also House et al., 2013). For example, Benenson, Pascoe, and Radmore (2007) implemented a "Dictator Game" with 4- and 9-year-old children, in which one child decided how to divide ten stickers between self and other. Whereas 4-year-olds allocated the majority of stickers to themselves, and nearly half took all of the stickers, 9-year-olds were significantly fairer on both of these dependent measures. Similar results showing increasingly fair splits of resources with increasing age are well established in the literature, going back at least to a 1952 study in which Uğurel-Semin asked 4- to 16-year-olds in Istanbul to divide odd numbers of nuts between self and other.

This slow emergence of moral behavior, compared to the relatively earlier emergence of social evaluation in infants, has been called the "knowledge-behavior gap" (Blake, McAuliffe, & Warneken, 2014). A particularly striking demonstration of the gap comes from the work of Smith, Blake, and Harris (2013), in which 3-year-olds report that they *should* act fairly but decline to follow through and act fairly. Most strikingly, this is not a case of planning to be fair and then lacking the inhibitory control to give resources to another, as the 3-year-olds in this study predicted that they would behave selfishly.

Whereas the previous section explored the "ultimate" evolutionary explanation (based on costs and benefits) for this gap, in this section we will further explore the specific developmental timeline of fairness behavior, and the development of the proximate mechanisms that underlie it (Tinbergen, 1963). By what age do children act fairly, and when are they willing to take costs to avoid unfairness? The answer is very different depending on whether the potential unfairness puts the child at a disadvantage or an advantage.

Disadvantageous inequality aversion (DIA), consisting of negative reactions to receiving relatively less than someone else, emerges quite early in childhood. For example, children as young as 3 years old will react negatively to receiving a lesser number of stickers compared to another child (LoBue, Nishida, Chiong, DeLouache, & Haidt, 2011). When they are allowed to decide whether to accept or reject an experimenter-provided distribution, children between the ages of 3 and 7 years old will typically reject receiving one candy while another child will receive four candies, preferring that both children receive nothing (Blake & McAuliffe, 2011).

On the other hand, advantageous inequality aversion (AIA), consisting of negative reactions to receiving relatively *more* than someone else, emerges later. In the study by LoBue et al. (2011), the children who received unfairly more rarely complained. In the study by Blake and McAuliffe (2011), children below the age of 8 typically accepted receiving four while another child receives one (though 8-year-olds did sometimes reject these advantageous distributions).

The exact age at which each of these behaviors is seen varies depending on the exact method. For example, Shaw and Olson (2012) found advantageous inequality aversion in 6-year-olds, 2 years younger than the result from Blake and McAuliffe (2011). In the study by Shaw and Olson, the experimenter distributed four erasers evenly, and then observed "Uh oh! We have one left over" and asked "Should I give this eraser to you, or should I throw it away?" It could be that, by asking what the experimenter should do (as opposed to, e.g., what the child wanted), 6-year-olds were more likely to select the fair option than they might be otherwise. Indeed, other research has found that asking children "should" vs. "want" questions leads to differences in fairness behavior (e.g., Sheskin et al., 2016).

The emergence of AIA and DIA at different times, and the variability depending on study design, suggests that our concern with fairness may not be a unified phenomenon that emerges at a single precise time. Certainly, even if we do have cognitive mechanisms specialized for fairness (e.g., Baumard, André, & Sperber, 2013), our behavior is multiply determined. When faced with a potential payoff of (e.g.,) "2 for self and 3 for other" our motivations can be quite wide-ranging, including (1) selfishly maximizing our absolute welfare with no reference to the other person's welfare, (2) generously maximizing the other person's welfare with no reference to our own welfare, (3) an "efficiency" preference to maximize the total welfare, with no reference to the specific amounts received by either person, (4) a "fairness" preference to minimize the difference between people's welfare, and (5) a "social comparison" preference to maximize our own welfare compared to other people.

It could be, for example, that even very young children have a general motivation to behave fairly, but that the strength of this preference is relatively weaker than other preferences. Thus, a 5-year-old might reject disadvantageous inequality due to a fairness preference that is buttressed by a social comparison motivation that is likewise against being at a relative disadvantage, but the same 5-year-old might accept advantageous inequality because that same fairness preference is undermined by the social comparison motivation seeking a relative advantage. Indeed, given a strong enough social comparison motivation, a child might act spitefully: Sheskin, Bloom, and Wynn (2014) found that 5-year-olds will often choose a low-but-advantageous payoff of "1 for self and 0 for other" over a higher-and-fair payoff of "2 each."

Proximate Mechanisms

Reflecting the multitude of motivations involved in developing fairness behavior, there are likewise many potential proximate mechanisms. Some of these proximate mechanisms may appear in a person's awareness as motivations towards particular goals (e.g., empathy towards those who are treated unfairly leading to actions that reduce unfairness), whereas other proximate mechanisms may be unrelated to motivations. For example, numerical ability is important for many areas of human life, only one of which is supporting fair division of discrete, sharable resources. However, given that the motivation to share resources equally is impotent without the ability to match equal numbers, it is reasonable to assume that children's fairness behavior would increase with increasing numerical abilities. Recent research reveals exactly this connection (Chernyak, Sandham, Harris, & Cordes, 2016).

Likewise, understanding others' mental states is important for far more than fairness (e.g., it is important when trying to strategize against an opponent), but many researchers have suggested that theory-of-mind (ToM) may be important for prosocial behavior, and that increases in the former allow increases in the latter. For example, in adults, activity in a region of the brain associated with ToM (the dorsomedial prefrontal cortex) predicts prosocial behavior amount of money shared and amount of time spent helping another person (Waytz, Zaki, & Mitchell, 2012). Developmentally, 3- to 5-year-olds who pass a common test of ToM ability (the "Sally-Anne task") provide fairer divisions than children who do not (Takagishi, Kameshima, Schug, Koizumi, & Yamagishi, 2010; but see contrary results in Cowell, Samek, List, & Decety, 2015). Thus, many of the proximate mechanisms involved in fairness may be general cognitive capacities that are not specific to fairness.

Other proximate mechanisms are more specifically tied to fairness. For example, many researchers have highlighted the importance of reputational benefits for prosocial behavior, and some approaches (e.g., the partner-choice framework described in the previous section) build their entire view of morality around it. Thus, a developing sensitivity to reputation may be linked to the development of fairness behavior. Importantly, several research designs have provided converging evidence that young children are sensitive to cues to being watched (e.g., Piazza, Bering, & Ingram, 2011). With particular relevance to the claim that moral behavior is important for one's reputation with potential collaborators, "young children care more about their reputation with ingroup members and potential reciprocators" (Engelmann, Over, Herrmann, & Tomasello, 2013).

Likewise, empathy may be involved in increasing motivations for fairness. There is a long tradition of research on the "empathy-altruism" link (e.g., Batson, Duncan, Ackerman, Buckley, & Birch, 1981), and recognizing and then empathizing with people's distress at being treated unfairly may motivate fairness. In line with this prediction, empathy is associated with fairness at many ages (e.g., Edele, Dziobek, & Keller, 2013). On the other hand, empathy is a "spotlight" that is typically evoked by specific targets, and is therefore not well suited to governing complicated decisions about how to fairly value multiple targets (Bloom, 2016).

This section on proximate mechanisms is not intended to be a complete list. Indeed, the claim that fairness (and morality) are not unified phenomena implies that a complete list would be impossible. Thus, as a final example, consider how simple reinforcement learning might account for some of the increases in fair behavior. To the extent that children's initially weak motivations towards fairness lead to good outcomes (e.g., praise from adults, being included rather than shunned by peers), this may strengthen the behavior. Importantly, this idea is separate from the idea that the child is explicitly taught that one should act in certain ways, and is instead focused on children's internally motivated behavior becoming associated with positive outcomes. This idea has been explored by multiple researchers (e.g., Chater, Vlaev, & Grinberg, 2008), and, despite the simplicity of the learning mechanisms involved, it may lead to context-sensitive behavior in which people are intuitively fair in cooperative environments but intuitively selfish in noncooperative environments (Nishi, Christakis, Evans, O'Malley, & Rand, 2016; Rand, Greene, & Nowak, 2012).

Implications and Future Directions

This chapter has argued for an approach to fairness as a complicated phenomenon composed of many contributing mechanisms, but unified by the function of gaining a reputation as a valuable collaborator who will put in an appropriate proportion of effort on a joint task, and take an appropriate proportion of the resultant rewards. Given that increasing age is associated with increases in the importance of benefits from joint tasks, and with increases in the ability to contribute to joint tasks, fairness increases over development. This may be due to a default timeline for development determined by the average features of our ancestral environment, as well as individual learning over each person's lifespan. Even if there is an independent preference for fairness, our actual behavior (fair or not) is determined by a wide range of factors. This final section explores implications of this account for cross-cultural research, comparative research, and developmental research.

Implications for Cross-Cultural Research

Several studies have explored the extent to which fairness concerns are cross-culturally universal (Henrich et al., 2006; Hsu, Anen, & Quartz, 2008; Wright et al., 2012; though see criticisms of some methods in Dana, Cain, & Dawes, 2006; List,

2007; Winking & Mizer, 2013), and the extent to which they vary. For example, Henrich et al. (2010) studied dictator game behavior across 15 diverse populations, from the nomadic and foraging Hadza in Tanzania, to wageworkers in Missouri. They found that the degree to which a population engaged in an economic market (as measured by the percent of calories an average individual purchased) was correlated with offers in the dictator game. It is not possible to determine causation from their data (Delton, Krasnow, Cosmides, & Tooby, 2010), and one salient alternative is that participants use their experience in daily life to interpret the unusual situation presented to them in the economic game (Baumard et al., 2010).

This analysis suggests that the cross-cultural differences may reflect *not* the extent to which fairness norms are present in a culture, but the extent to which they are applied to an economic game played with a stranger: people who engage in frequent mutually beneficial economic exchanges with strangers (i.e., in societies with high market integration) import these interaction norms into the game, whereas people who do not engage in as much market activity with strangers do not import their (potentially equally strong) fairness norms into the game.

Future cross-cultural research might investigate how people apply fairness norms in economic games played against a wider range of individuals, ranging from anonymous strangers (as in Henrich et al., 2010) to face-to-face interactions with close friends. It could be that people in societies with low market integration show just as strong fairness norms with close friends as people in societies with high market integration. In fact, given the importance of collaborating with these known others, it is possible that the correlation between market integration and fairness would reverse. Indeed, such results would be consistent with research showing surprisingly high levels of egalitarianism in hunter-gatherer societies (Pennisi, 2014). Once more is known about adult patterns of behavior, it will be important to investigate how the common initial state in infancy diverges across cultures into the adult patterns. There are already interesting cross-cultural studies of the development of fairness (e.g., Blake et al., 2015; House et al., 2013), but (as with adults) we know little about how children apply fairness differentially with wide ranges of individuals.

Implications for Nonhuman Research

Currently, much of the literature on nonhuman behaviors related to morality are focused on identifying whether or not individuals show a nonzero level of behavior that seems related to a human capacity (e.g., the debate over nonhuman fairness described earlier in this chapter). However, if moral behavior is (largely) for gaining reputational benefits so that one is chosen as a participant in cooperative activities with others, then nonhuman species should be expected to show quite limited "moral" behavior. It is useful to be clear about how this claim is different from the previous section's analysis of cross-cultural variation. That claim was about how individual humans flexibly apply characteristically human fairness concerns depending on their environment; this section is about why nonhuman species *as a group* might be expected not to show much "moral" behavior.

One approach for moving the discussion forward comes from recent work comparing multiple species within a single paradigm (e.g., Claidière et al., 2015). For example, Burkart et al. (2014) tested prosocial behavior across 15 primate species, and found that prosocial motivation was associated with cooperative breeding. Similarly, it could be that fairness is only present to the extent that there is partner choice for collaborative tasks. More generally, hypotheses about the likely distribution of behavior across species, and then unified experimental designs applied across a wide range of species within a single paper, allows for more systematic testing than piecemeal results about whether ("$p < 0.05$") each particular species shows nonzero evidence of a behavior. This is especially true since, as is common throughout psychology, positive results are more likely to be reported than negative results (see Bones, 2012).

Future Directions for the Development of Fairness

Building off of the discussion on cross-cultural differences, a major question for future research on the development of fairness is how children come to acquire culturally specific behaviors about the scope of fairness. Progress on this question can build on work in a wide range of disciplines, from evolutionary developmental biology (e.g., adaptive developmental plasticity; Nettle & Bateson, 2015) to research on adults' valuation of others' welfare (e.g., "welfare tradeoff ratios," Tooby, Cosmides, Sell, Lieberman, & Sznycer, 2008). Most notably, the partner-choice framework (in accordance with common moral intuitions) suggests that it is appropriate for me to treat friends differently than strangers, but there is individual variation in judgments of how much more people should weigh the welfare of socially close versus socially distant others.

Reflecting the complexity of fairness judgments, future developmental research should also proceed with greater attention paid to the specific capacities being tested with various methods. When multiple approaches are included in one study (e.g., predictions vs. behaviors in Smith et al., 2013; "should" vs. "want" in Sheskin et al., 2016), it can reveal large differences in fairness behavior. This is likely true for a wide range of additional factors (whether the recipient is present or absent, whether the study is in a public park with onlookers or in a private testing room in a lab, etc.). Individual studies that explore a specific set of features can certainly be informative, but larger-scale studies that systematically test the impact of such features can be additionally informative (compare with the similar point made about animal research in the previous subsection).

In sum, much is known about the emergence of fairness behavior over childhood development. There is strong evidence for evaluation of others' fairness behavior even by young infants (e.g., Sloane et al., 2012), but there is an initially weak willingness to take costs to behave fairly (e.g., Smith et al., 2013), with the motivation increasing over time (e.g., Benenson et al., 2007). This "knowledge-behavior gap" (Blake et al., 2014) may be explained by an analysis of the typical costs and benefits of moral judgment and behavior at different ages (Sheskin, Chevallier, Lambert, & Baumard, 2014), and this framework may be useful for future work looking at the development not just of our general capacity for fairness, but also for individual and cross-cultural differences in how this capacity is *applied* across ecologies and to different people.

References

Abbot, P., Abe, J., Alcock, J., Alizon, S., Alpedrinha, J. A., Andersson, M., … Zink, A. (2011). Inclusive fitness theory and eusociality. *Nature, 471*(7339), E1–E4; author reply E9–E10. doi:10.1038/nature09831

Barclay, P., & Willer, R. (2007). Partner choice creates competitive altruism in humans. *Proceedings of the Royal Society B: Biological Sciences, 274*(1610), 749–753. doi:10.1098/rspb.2006.0209.

Baron, J. (1994). Nonconsequentialist decisions. *Behavioral and Brain Sciences, 17*(01), 1–10.

Batson, C. D., Duncan, B. D., Ackerman, P., Buckley, T., & Birch, K. (1981). Is empathic emotion a source of altruistic motivation? *Journal of Personality and Social Psychology, 40*(2), 290–302.

Baumard, N., André, J. B., & Sperber, D. (2013). A mutualistic approach to morality: The evolution of fairness by partner choice. *The Behavioral and Brain Sciences, 36*(1), 59–78. doi:10.1017/S0140525X11002202.

Baumard, N., Boyer, P., & Sperber, D. (2010). Evolution of fairness: Cultural variability. *Science, 329*(5990), 388–389.

Baumard, N., & Sheskin, M. (2015). Partner choice and the evolution of a contractualist morality. In J. Decety & T. Wheatley (Eds.), *The moral brain* (pp. 35–48). Cambridge, MA: MIT Press.

Benenson, J. F., Pascoe, J., & Radmore, N. (2007). Children's altruistic behavior in the dictator game. *Evolution and Human Behavior, 28*(3), 168–175. doi:10.1016/j.evolhumbehav.2006.10.003.

Bird, A., & Tobin, E. (2016). Natural kinds. In E. N. Zalta (Ed.), *The Stanford encyclopedia of philosophy* (Spring 2016 ed.). Stanford, CA: Stanford University. http://plato.stanford.edu/archives/spr2016/entries/natural-kinds/.

Bjorklund, D. F., & Ellis, B. J. (2014). Children, childhood, and development in evolutionary perspective. *Developmental Review, 34*(3), 225–264. doi:10.1016/j.dr.2014.05.005.

Blake, P. R., & McAuliffe, K. (2011). "I had so much it didn't seem fair": Eight-year-olds reject two forms of inequity. *Cognition, 120*(2), 215–224.

Blake, P. R., McAuliffe, K., Corbit, J., Callaghan, T. C., Barry, O., Bowie, A., … Warneken, F. (2015). The ontogeny of fairness in seven societies. *Nature, 528*(7581), 258–261. doi:10.1038/nature15703

Blake, P. R., McAuliffe, K., & Warneken, F. (2014). The developmental origins of fairness: The knowledge-behavior gap. *Trends in Cognitive Sciences, 18*(11), 559–561. doi:10.1016/j.tics.2014.08.00.

Bloom, P. (2016). *Against empathy: The case for rational compassion*. New York, NY: Ecco Press.

Bonawitz, E., Shafto, P., Gweon, H., Goodman, N. D., Spelke, E., & Schulz, L. (2011). The double-edged sword of pedagogy: Instruction limits spontaneous exploration and discovery. *Cognition, 120*(3), 322–330. doi:10.1016/j.cognition.2010.10.001.

Bones, A. K. (2012). We knew the future all along: Scientific hypothesizing is much more accurate than other forms of precognition—A satire in one part. *Perspectives on Psychological Science, 7*(3), 307–309. doi:10.1177/1745691612441216.

Brosnan, S. F., & de Waal, F. B. (2003). Monkeys reject unequal pay. *Nature, 425*(6955), 297–299. doi:10.1038/nature01963.

Brosnan, S. F., Talbot, C., Ahlgren, M., Lambeth, S. P., & Schapiro, S. J. (2010). Mechanisms underlying responses to inequitable outcomes in chimpanzees, pan troglodytes. *Animal Behaviour, 79*(6), 1229–1237. doi:10.1016/j.anbehav.2010.02.019.

Burkart, J. M., Allon, O., Amici, F., Fichtel, C., Finkenwirth, C., Heschl, A., ... van Schaik, C. P. (2014). The evolutionary origin of human hyper-cooperation. *Nature Communications, 5*, 4747. doi:10.1038/ncomms574

Chater, N., Vlaev, I., & Grinberg, M. (2008). A new consequence of simpson's paradox: Stable cooperation in one-shot prisoner's dilemma from populations of individualistic learners. *Journal of Experimental Psychology: General, 137*(3), 403–421. doi:10.1037/0096-3445.137.3.403.

Chernyak, N., Sandham, B., Harris, P. L., & Cordes, S. (2016). Numerical cognition explains age-related changes in third-party fairness. *Developmental Psychology, 52*(10), 1555–1562.

Claidière, N., Whiten, A., Mareno, M. C., Messer, E. J., Brosnan, S. F., Hopper, L. M., ... McGuigan, N. (2015). Selective and contagious prosocial resource donation in capuchin monkeys, chimpanzees and humans. *Scientific Reports, 5*, 7631. doi:10.1038/srep07631

Cowell, J. M., Samek, A., List, J., & Decety, J. (2015). The curious relation between theory of mind and sharing in preschool age children. *PloS One, 10*(2), e0117947. doi:10.1371/journal.pone.0117947.

Csibra, G., & Gergely, G. (2009). Natural pedagogy. *Trends in Cognitive Sciences, 13*(4), 148–153. doi:10.1016/j.tics.2009.01.005.

Dana, J., Cain, D. M., & Dawes, R. M. (2006). What you don't know won't hurt me: Costly (but quiet) exit in dictator games. *Organizational Behavior and Human Decision Processes, 100*(2), 193–201. doi:10.1016/j.obhdp.2005.10.001.

Debove, S., André, J. B., & Baumard, N. (2015). Partner choice creates fairness in humans. *Proceedings of the Royal Society B: Biological Sciences, 282*(1808), 20150392. doi:10.1098/rspb.2015.0392.

Delton, A. W., Krasnow, M. M., Cosmides, L., & Tooby, J. (2010). Evolution of fairness: Rereading the data. *Science, 329*(5990), 389–389.

Edele, A., Dziobek, I., & Keller, M. (2013). Explaining altruistic sharing in the dictator game: The role of affective empathy, cognitive empathy, and justice sensitivity. *Learning and Individual Differences, 24*, 96–102.

Engelmann, J. M., Over, H., Herrmann, E., & Tomasello, M. (2013). Young children care more about their reputation with ingroup members and potential reciprocators. *Developmental Science, 16*(6), 952–958. doi:10.1111/desc.12086.

Fehr, E., Bernhard, H., & Rockenbach, B. (2008). Egalitarianism in young children. *Nature, 454*(7208), 1079–1083. doi:10.1038/nature07155.

Fletcher, G. E. (2008). Attending to the outcome of others: Disadvantageous inequity aversion in male capuchin monkeys (cebus apella). *American Journal of Primatology, 70*(9), 901–905. doi:10.1002/ajp.20576.

Geraci, A., & Surian, L. (2011). The developmental roots of fairness: Infants' reactions to equal and unequal distributions of resources. *Developmental Science, 14*(5), 1012–1020. doi:10.1111/j.1467-7687.2011.01048.x.

Gray, K., & Schein, C. (2016). No absolutism here: Harm predicts moral judgment 30× better than disgust-commentary on Scott, Inbar, & Rozin (2016). *Perspectives on Psychological Science: A Journal of the Association for Psychological Science, 11*(3), 325–329. doi:10.1177/1745691616635598.

Gray, K., Schein, C., & Ward, A. F. (2014). The myth of harmless wrongs in moral cognition: Automatic dyadic completion from sin to suffering. *Journal of Experimental Psychology: General, 143*(4), 1600.

Greene, J. D. (2015). The rise of moral cognition. *Cognition, 135*, 39–42. doi:10.1016/j.cognition.2014.11.018.

Gurven, M., Kaplan, H., & Gutierrez, M. (2006). How long does it take to become a proficient hunter? Implications for the evolution of extended development and long life span. *Journal of Human Evolution, 51*(5), 454–470. doi:10.1016/j.jhevol.2006.05.003.

Güth, W., Schmittberger, R., & Schwarze, B. (1982). An experimental analysis of ultimatum bargaining. *Journal of Economic Behavior and Organization, 3*(4), 367–388.
Haidt, J. (2012). *The righteous mind: Why good people are divided by politics and religion.* New York, NY: Penguin.
Haidt, J., & Joseph, C. (2004). Intuitive ethics: How innately prepared intuitions generate culturally variable virtues. *Daedalus, 133*(4), 55–66.
Hamann, K., Warneken, F., Greenberg, J. R., & Tomasello, M. (2011). Collaboration encourages equal sharing in children but not in chimpanzees. *Nature, 476*(7360), 328–331. doi:10.1038/nature10278.
Hamilton, W. D. (1964). The Genetical evolution of social behaviour. *Journal of Theoretical Biology, 7*(1), 1–16.
Hamlin, J. K., Ullman, T., Tenenbaum, J., Goodman, N., & Baker, C. (2013). The mentalistic basis of core social cognition: Experiments in preverbal infants and a computational model. *Developmental Science, 16*(2), 209–226. doi:10.1111/desc.12017.
Hamlin, J. K., Wynn, K., & Bloom, P. (2007). Social evaluation by preverbal infants. *Nature, 450*(7169), 557–559. doi:10.1038/nature06288.
Heider, F., & Simmel, M. (1944). An experimental study of apparent behavior. *The American Journal of Psychology, 57*(2), 243–259.
Henrich, J., Ensminger, J., Mcelreath, R., Barr, A., Barrett, C., Bolyanatz, A., … Ziker, J. (2010). Markets, religion, community size, and the evolution of fairness and punishment. *Science, 1480*(March 2010), 1480–1484. http://doi.org/10.1126/science.1182238
Henrich, J., McElreath, R., Barr, A., Ensminger, J., Barrett, C., Bolyanatz, A., … Ziker, J. (2006). Costly punishment across human societies. *Science (New York, N.Y.), 312*(5781), 1767–1770. doi:10.1126/science.1127333
Heyes, C. (2016). Who knows? Metacognitive social learning strategies. *Trends in Cognitive Sciences, 20*(3), 204–213.
Horner, V., & Whiten, A. (2005). Causal knowledge and imitation/emulation switching in chimpanzees (*Pan troglodytes*) and children (*Homo sapiens*). *Animal Cognition, 8*(3), 164–181. doi:10.1007/s10071-004-0239-6.
House, B. R., Silk, J. B., Henrich, J., Barrett, H. C., Scelza, B. A., Boyette, A. H., … Laurence, S. (2013). Ontogeny of prosocial behavior across diverse societies. *Proceedings of the National Academy of Sciences of the United States of America, 110*(36), 14586–14591. doi:10.1073/pnas.1221217110.
Hsu, M., Anen, C., & Quartz, S. R. (2008). The right and the good: Distributive justice and neural encoding of equity and efficiency. *Science (New York, N.Y.), 320*(5879), 1092–1095. doi:10.1126/science.1153651.
Johnston, A. M., Holden, P. C., & Santos, L. R. (2016). Exploring the evolutionary origins of overimitation: A comparison across domesticated and non-domesticated canids. *Developmental Science, 20*(4). doi:10.1111/desc.12460
Johnston, A. M., Mills, C. M., & Landrum, A. R. (2015). How do children weigh competence and benevolence when deciding whom to trust? *Cognition, 144*, 76–90. doi:10.1016/j.cognition.2015.07.015.
Kahneman, D., Knetsch, J. L., & Thaler, R. (1986). Fairness as a constraint on profit seeking: Entitlements in the market. *The American Economic Review, 76*(4), 728–741.
Koenig, M. A., Clément, F., & Harris, P. L. (2004). Trust in testimony: Children's use of true and false statements. *Psychological Science, 15*(10), 694–698.
Kuhlmeier, V., Wynn, K., & Bloom, P. (2003). Attribution of dispositional states by 12-month-olds. *Psychological Science, 14*(5), 402–408.
Legare, C. H., & Nielsen, M. (2015). Imitation and innovation: The dual engines of cultural learning. *Trends in Cognitive Sciences, 19*(11), 688–699.
Liberman, Z., Woodward, A. L., & Kinzler, K. D. (2016). Preverbal infants infer third-party social relationships based on language. *Cognitive Science, 41*(Suppl 3), 622–634.
List, J. A. (2007). On the interpretation of giving in dictator games. *Journal of Political Economy, 115*(3), 482–493.

LoBue, V., Nishida, T., Chiong, C., DeLoache, J. S., & Haidt, J. (2011). When getting something good is bad: Even three-year-olds react to inequality. *Social Development, 20*(1), 54–170. http://doi.org/10.1111/j.1467-9507.2009.00560.x.

Lyons, D. E., Young, A. G., & Keil, F. C. (2007). The hidden structure of overimitation. *Proceedings of the National Academy of Sciences of the United States of America, 104*(50), 19751–19756. doi:10.1073/pnas.0704452104.

MacFarquhar, L. (2015). *Strangers drowning: Grappling with impossible idealism, drastic choices, and the overpowering urge to help*. New York, NY: Penguin Press HC.

McKay, R., & Whitehouse, H. (2015). Religion and morality. *Psychological Bulletin, 141*(2), 447–473. doi:10.1037/a0038455.

Meehan, C. L., Quinlan, R., & Malcom, C. D. (2013). Cooperative breeding and maternal energy expenditure among aka foragers. *American Journal of Human Biology: The Official Journal of the Human Biology Council, 25*(1), 42–57. doi:10.1002/ajhb.22336.

Meristo, M., & Surian, L. (2013). Do infants detect indirect reciprocity? *Cognition, 129*(1), 102–113. doi:10.1016/j.cognition.2013.06.006.

Nettle, D., & Bateson, M. (2015). Adaptive developmental plasticity: What is it, how can we recognize it and when can it evolve? *Proceedings of the Royal Society B: Biological Sciences, 282*(1812), 20151005. doi:10.1098/rspb.2015.1005.

Nishi, A., Christakis, N. A., Evans, A. M., O'Malley, A. J., & Rand, D. G. (2016). Social environment shapes the speed of cooperation. *Scientific Reports*, 6.

Noë, R., & Hammerstein, P. (1994). Biological markets: Supply and demand determine the effect of partner choice in cooperation, mutualism and mating. *Behavioral Ecology and Sociobiology, 35*(1), 1–11.

Nowak, M. A., Tarnita, C. E., & Wilson, E. O. (2010). The evolution of eusociality. *Nature, 466*(7310), 1057–1062. doi:10.1038/nature09205.

Pennisi, E. (2014). Our egalitarian Eden. *Science, 344*(6186), 824–825.

Piazza, J., Bering, J. M., & Ingram, G. (2011). "Princess Alice is watching you": Children's belief in an invisible person inhibits cheating. *Journal of Experimental Child Psychology, 109*(3), 311–320. doi:10.1016/j.jecp.2011.02.003.

Poulin-Dubois, D., & Brosseau-Liard, P. (2016). The developmental origins of selective social learning. *Current Directions in Psychological Science, 25*(1), 60–64.

Rand, D. G., Greene, J. D., & Nowak, M. A. (2012). Spontaneous giving and calculated greed. *Nature, 489*(7416), 427–430. doi:10.1038/nature11467.

Range, F., Horn, L., Viranyi, Z., & Huber, L. (2009). The absence of reward induces inequity aversion in dogs. *Proceedings of the National Academy of Sciences of the United States of America, 106*(1), 340–345.

Schmidt, M. F., & Sommerville, J. A. (2011). Fairness expectations and altruistic sharing in 15-month-old human infants. *PloS One, 6*(10), e23223. doi:10.1371/journal.pone.00232283.

Shaw, A., & Olson, K. R. (2012). Children discard a resource to avoid inequity. *Journal of Experimental Psychology: General, 141*(2), 382–395.

Sheskin, M., & Santos, L. (2012). The evolution of morality: which aspects of human moral concerns are shared with nonhuman primates? In J. Vonk & T. K. Shackelford (Eds.), The Oxford handbook of comparative evolutionary psychology (pp. 434–450). New York, NY: Oxford University Press.

Sheskin, M., Ashayeri, K., Skerry, A., & Santos, L. R. (2014). Capuchin monkeys (Cebus apella) fail to show inequality aversion in a no-cost situation. *Evolution and Human Behavior, 35*(2), 80–88. http://doi.org/10.1016/j.evolhumbehav.2013.10.004.

Sheskin, M., Bloom, P., & Wynn, K. (2014). Anti-equality: Social comparison in young children. *Cognition, 130*(2), 152–156. doi:10.1016/j.cognition.2013.10.008.

Sheskin, M., Chevallier, C., Lambert, S., & Baumard, N. (2014). Life-history theory explains childhood moral development. *Trends in Cognitive Sciences, 18*(12), 613–615. doi:10.1016/j.tics.2014.08.004.

Sheskin, M., Nadal, A., Croom, A., Mayer, T., Nissel, J., & Bloom, P. (2016). Some equalities are more equal than others: Quality equality emerges later than numerical equality. *Child Development, 87*(5), 1520–1528. doi:10.1111/cdev.12544.

Shweder, R. A., Much, N. C., Mahapatra, M., & Park, L. (1997). The "big three" of morality (autonomy, community, divinity) and the "big three" explanations of suffering. In A. Brandt & P. Rozin (Eds.), *Morality and health*. New York, NY: Routledge.
Silberberg, A., Crescimbene, L., Addessi, E., Anderson, J. R., & Visalberghi, E. (2009). Does inequity aversion depend on a frustration effect? A test with capuchin monkeys (cebus apella). *Animal Cognition, 12*(3), 505–509. doi:10.1007/s10071-009-0211-6.
Sloane, S., Baillargeon, R., & Premack, D. (2012). Do infants have a sense of fairness? *Psychological Science, 23*(2), 196–204. doi:10.1177/0956797611422072.
Smith, C. E., Blake, P. R., & Harris, P. L. (2013). I should but I won't: Why young children endorse norms of fair sharing but do not follow them. *PloS One, 8*(3), e59510. http://doi.org/10.1371/journal.pone.0059510.
Sommerville, J. A., Schmidt, M. F. H., Yun, J.-E., & Burns, M. (2013). The development of fairness expectations and prosocial behavior in the second year of life. *Infancy, 18*(1), 40–66. doi:10.1111/j.1532-7078.2012.00129.x.
Takagishi, H., Kameshima, S., Schug, J., Koizumi, M., & Yamagishi, T. (2010). Theory of mind enhances preference for fairness. *Journal of Experimental Child Psychology, 105*, 130–137. doi:10.1016/j.jecp.2009.09.005.
Talbot, C. F., Price, S. A., & Brosnan, S. F. (2016). Inequity responses in nonhuman animals. In C. Sabbagh & M. Schmitt (Eds.), *Handbook of social justice theory and research* (pp. 387–403). New York, NY: Springer.
Tinbergen, N. (1963). On aims and methods of ethology. *Zeitschfrift Fur Tierpsycologie, 20*, 410–433.
Tomasello, M. (2016). *A natural history of human morality*. London: Harvard University Press.
Tooby, J., Cosmides, L., Sell, A., Lieberman, D., & Sznycer, D. (2008). *15 internal regulatory variables and the design of human motivation: A computational and evolutionary approach, Handbook of approach and avoidance motivation* (Vol. 251). Mahwah, NJ: Lawrence Erlbaum.
Uğurel-Semin, R. (1952). Moral behavior and moral judgment of children. *The Journal of Abnormal and Social Psychology, 47*, 463–474. doi:10.1037/h0056970.
Warneken, F., Hare, B., Melis, A. P., Hanus, D., & Tomasello, M. (2007). Spontaneous altruism by chimpanzees and young children. *PLoS Biology, 5*(7), 1414–1420. doi:10.1371/journal.pbio.0050184.
Warneken, F., & Tomasello, M. (2006). Altruistic helping in human infants and young chimpanzees. *Science (New York, N.Y.), 311*(5765), 1301–1303. doi:10.1126/science.1121448.
Wascher, C. A., & Bugnyar, T. (2013). Behavioral responses to inequity in reward distribution and working effort in crows and ravens. *PloS One, 8*(2), e56885. doi:10.1371/journal.pone.0056885.
Waytz, A., Zaki, J., & Mitchell, J. P. (2012). Response of dorsomedial prefrontal cortex predicts altruistic behavior. *The Journal of Neuroscience: The Official Journal of the Society for Neuroscience, 32*(22), 7646–7650. doi:10.1523/JNEUROSCI.6193-11.2012.
West, S. A., Griffin, A. S., & Gardner, A. (2008). Social semantics: How useful has group selection been? *Journal of Evolutionary Biology, 21*(1), 374–385. doi:10.1111/j.1420-9101.2007.01458.x.
Winking, J., & Mizer, N. (2013). Natural-field dictator game shows no altruistic giving. *Evolution and Human Behavior, 34*(4), 288–293. doi:10.1016/j.evolhumbehav.2013.04.002.
Wright, N. D., Hodgson, K., Fleming, S. M., Symmonds, M., Guitart-Masip, M., & Dolan, R. J. (2012). Human responses to unfairness with primary rewards and their biological limits. *Scientific Reports, 2*, 593. doi:10.1038/srep00593.

Chapter 4
Public Preferences About Fairness and the Ethics of Allocating Scarce Medical Interventions

Govind Persad

Introduction

When there are not enough medical resources to go around, society faces the question of how to fairly allocate them. And when these resources are not only scarce but essential to treat a potentially deadly condition, fair allocation becomes a question of—as *Life* magazine once put it—deciding "who lives, who dies" (Alexander, 1962). These questions have prompted attention and reflection from medical professionals, ethicists, theologians, and the general public.

Some scholars, frequently social scientists, have conducted survey or focus-group research on various groups' preferences regarding how scarce medical resources should be allocated. My focus in this chapter is to examine how social-scientific research on public preferences bears on the ethical question of how those resources should in fact be allocated, and explain how social-scientific researchers might find an understanding of work in ethics useful as they design mechanisms for data collection and analysis. I proceed by first distinguishing the methodologies of social science and ethics. I then provide an overview of different approaches to the ethics of allocating scarce medical interventions, including an approach—the complete lives system—which I have previously defended, and a brief recap of social-scientific research on the allocation of scarce medical resources. Following these overviews, I examine different ways in which public preferences could matter to the ethics of allocation. Last, I suggest some ways in which social scientists could learn from ethics as they conduct research into public preferences regarding the allocation of scarce medical resources.

G. Persad (✉)
Berman Institute of Bioethics, Johns Hopkins University, Baltimore, MD, USA

Department of Health Policy and Management, Bloomberg School of Public Health, Johns Hopkins University, Baltimore, MD, USA
e-mail: gpersad@jhu.edu

M. Li, D.P. Tracer (eds.), *Interdisciplinary Perspectives on Fairness, Equity, and Justice*, DOI 10.1007/978-3-319-58993-0_4

Normative Versus Empirical Methodologies

The allocation of scarce medical resources, such as transplantable organs or vaccines in a pandemic, involves answering both normative and descriptive questions. Answering descriptive questions involves determining what *is* happening in the world, or what *will* likely happen as a result of certain choices. For example, allocating antiviral medication during an influenza pandemic involves answering the descriptive question of whether allocating medication to the people who are sickest right now is likely to save the most lives. In this chapter, the descriptive questions discussed will primarily involve research into people's values or preferences: whether the general public, or subgroups such as influenza patients, will approve of a policy that allocates that medication to the people who are sickest right now. Even though this research solicits opinions regarding what *should* happen, it is fundamentally descriptive rather than normative, because it does not try to answer the question of what in fact should happen, but instead reports individuals' preferences regarding what should happen. Such research fits the model described by Daniel Sulmasy and Jeremy Sugarman as "descriptive ethics," which "asks empirical questions such as, How do people think they ought to act in this particular situation of normative concern? What facts are relevant to this particular ethical inquiry? How do people actually behave in this particular circumstance of ethical concern?" (2001). What Sulmasy and Sugarman call "descriptive ethics" encompasses the identification both of what social scientists call *descriptive* norms, which refer to what people actually do, and *prescriptive* norms, which refer to what people believe they ought to do. Even when social scientists study prescriptive norms, they are describing what those norms and thereby making claims about how the world is, rather than making claims about how the world should be. Descriptive questions—in Sulmasy and Sugarman's sense—are typically answered using a scientific or social-scientific methodology.

In contrast, normative questions concern what outcomes *should* happen—for instance, whether we should allocate antiviral medication in ways that saves the most lives, or should instead allocate it on a first-come, first-served basis—and are addressed using methodologies within ethics rather than within the social sciences. Rather than identifying descriptive norms (what people actually do) or prescriptive norms (what people believe they should do), answering normative questions involves determining what people in fact should do. Familiar normative questions we answer for ourselves in daily life include whether we ought to help one person rather than another, or whether we are permitted to deceive someone for the sake of the greater good. In a medical context, an example of a normative question is whether we should allocate antiviral medication in a way that saves the most lives, or should instead allocate it in a way that gives everyone an equal chance of receiving medication.

Ethics offers a variety of approaches to answering normative questions. Utilitarianism, for instance, simply asks us to add up the benefits and burdens produced by a given intervention, and then tells us that we should do whatever produces the best balance of benefits over burdens. Other prominent approaches in biomedical ethics include principlism (which evaluates outcomes in terms of how well they realize beneficence, non-maleficence, autonomy, and justice), reflective equilibrium (which begins with our intuitive ethical responses to cases and then asks us to consider how well they cohere with one another upon reflection), and virtue ethics (which evaluates outcomes by comparing them to the decisions that a virtuous person would reach) (Sulmasy & Sugarman, 2001).

Ethical approaches often agree in many ways—for instance, most agree that we should avoid killing innocent people. However, there are also important points of disagreement. For instance, utilitarian approaches are more willing than many other approaches to countenance harming a smaller number of people in order to promote the good of a greater number of people. It may appear that ethics stands apart from the social sciences in its lack of consensus on methodology. However, disagreements about the proper methodology for answering normative questions are not so different from disagreements about the proper social-scientific method for answering certain descriptive questions, such as disagreements between Bayesian and frequentist statisticians (Malakoff, 1999) or disagreements between economists and sociologists.

Much social-scientific research on the allocation of scarce medical interventions makes tacit assumptions about normative questions: for instance, that maximizing a certain outcome (such as lives saved) is morally desirable, or that we ought to allocate scarce medical resources in ways that the general public approves of. Social scientists often do not examine these assumptions in depth. Part of this chapter's project is to identify and investigate these normative assumptions, as well as to explain what role descriptive research into public preferences can play in answering normative questions.

Ethical Principles for Fairly Allocating Scarce Medical Resources

In a prior article, I and two coauthors discussed several ethical principles proposed for the allocation of scarce medical resources (Persad, Wertheimer, & Emanuel, 2009). I adopt the same division of those principles here: maximizing total benefit, treating people equally, helping the worst-off, and promoting and rewarding usefulness.

Two ways of maximizing total benefit are to aim at saving the most lives, and to aim at saving the most life-years. While these goals sometimes go together, they can come apart: one article notes that "in the case of pandemic influenza, it is clear that unless vaccines are so plentiful that transmission can be completely or nearly halted, policies to minimize total mortality may differ from those to minimize years of life lost or disability-adjusted years of life lost" (Lipsitch, et al., 2011). Another study observes that bilateral lung transplantation (i.e., transplanting two lungs into a single person) can sometimes save more future life-years, even while transplanting lungs singly enables more people to receive transplants and thus saves more lives (Munson, Christie, & Halpern, 2011). Of course, the goal of minimizing deaths is ultimately unachievable, since everyone dies in the end (Chappell, 2016). The choice between maximizing lives saved and life-years saved is ultimately between providing a lesser number of life-years to a larger number of people and a greater number of life-years to a smaller number of people.

The two most prominent ways of treating people equally are random selection and first-come, first-served selection. Random selection ensures each person has the exact same chance of receiving the benefit. One way of conducting random selection is to conduct a lottery in which each person is assigned a number at random and then scarce interventions are provided to individuals with certain numbers. It is also possible to use other socially insignificant identifiers to implement random selection, such as the day of the week someone was born or the last digit of their social security number. First-come, first-served selection is often regarded as a way of treating people equally without random selection. However, some aspects of first-come, first-served selection suggest that it does not genuinely treat people equally, including time wasted in queuing and unfairness to individuals who lack the time to wait in line or who die while waiting. The latter unfairness threatens the ability of first-come, first-served allocation to genuinely treat people equally.

Another common value is helping the worst-off, which I understand to mean those who will be worst-off if they do not receive interventions. Some believe that those who are the sickest right now (i.e., most likely to die if they do not receive scarce resources) are the worst-off. However, if we take a lifetime rather than a momentary perspective on disadvantage, those who are in the greatest danger of dying right now are frequently not the worst-off when we consider their lives as a whole. For example, because living to only 25 is worse than living to 75, a 24-year-old who will die in a year unless she receives a scarce resource is worse off than a 74-year-old who will die tomorrow if she does not receive that resource. While sickest-first allocation can make sense when scarcity is only short term, it is less attractive when scarcity will persist for a long time. Accordingly, when scarcity is persistent, those who are in danger of dying early in life should receive priority over those who have already enjoyed many years of life but are in danger of dying soon if not helped. As the human rights scholar Alicia Yamin (2009) puts it, "An adequate rights framework must take account of intergenerational equity including the equal opportunity of younger people to live as long as older people already have" (p. 5).

Allocation according to instrumental value (usefulness) prioritizes individuals who have been helpful contributors to society in the past, or who are likely to be helpful contributors in the future. Unlike the prior principles discussed, allocation according to future contribution does not regard the set of resources available as a fixed quantity: rather, it allocates more to some people in order to achieve a larger total quantity of the scarce intervention or of other social goods. An example would be allocating antiviral medication preferentially to front-line health care workers responding to a viral pandemic, as was done during the recent Ebola outbreak (Rid & Emanuel, 2014). This allocation was justifiable because these workers could help many more patients once recovered. However, individuals who are most able to effectively contribute to society are also likely to be better-off in other ways, which means that allocation according to future contribution could exacerbate inequality, particularly if skilled health care workers are favored over family members who provide care. Meanwhile, allocation according to past conduct can be justified on the basis that it will encourage individuals to contribute to society, but also on the basis that past contributors acquire a reciprocity-based moral entitlement (or disentitlement) to assistance. One question posed by allocation according to past conduct involves defining what counts as a helpful contribution: does leading a healthy or law-abiding lifestyle count as a helpful contribution, and should it entitle people to priority?

One prominent principle we did not discuss is ability-to-pay allocation, where people can purchase access to scarce medical resources by outbidding others for those resources. Economic theory might appear to support ability-to-pay allocation as an effective way of eliciting individuals' capacity to benefit, on the principle that people who stand to benefit more from a resource will be willing to pay more for that resource. However, while ability-to-pay allocation has some merit for heterogeneous goods that are not immediately lifesaving, such as foodstuffs or clothing, it is a poor way of allocating lifesaving medical resources such as antiviral medications or transplantable organs. Most importantly, ability to pay reflects prior wealth, which is a poor proxy for ability to benefit, and which entrenches and amplifies existing social divisions. Additionally, those with poor prospects of benefiting from a scarce, lifesaving resource are unlikely to have a lower willingness to pay for the resource, since they will be dead without the resource (and so unable to use the money they saved). For this reason, ability-to-pay allocation is unattractive where the stakes of receiving an intervention are great and resources are absolutely scarce. Ability to pay is more appealing, though still controversial, for physician, pharmaceutical, and hospital services where no scarcity exists and the stakes, while significant, are lower (Krohmal & Emanuel, 2007). Some national health care systems, like that in the United States, are friendlier to ability-to-pay allocation, while others are less so.

Another principle we dismissed as morally untenable is identity-based allocation, where people receive scarce resources based on their membership in identity categories such as race, gender, national origin, or religion. These criteria have all the benefit-maximization disadvantages of pure lottery allocation, and, much more seriously, entrench societal divisions and threaten civic equality.

Ultimately, none of the principles we discuss are likely to be sufficient on their own for a fair allocation of resources. This suggests the attractiveness of approaches that combine one or more of the principles, such as the approach we call the "complete lives system." This system includes both benefit-maximizing principles (saving the most lives and saving the most life-years). However, it includes the other principles (giving priority to the worst-off, treating people equally, and promoting usefulness) only in specified ways: it favors the worst-off through a modified youngest-first system that weights age in a way that gives highest priority to children and adolescents; excludes first-come, first-served allocation; and allows promotion of usefulness only when the beneficiaries are front-line medical workers. Real-world approaches to allocating medical resources also balance different principles against one another: as an example, current rules for lung allocation balance the urgency of a problem against the medical benefit of that problem (Egan et al., 2006).

Though the general strategy of adopting a multi-principle approach to allocation has met little resistance, some specifics of the complete lives system have been criticized by commentators. Some have argued that more priority should be given to very young children, rather than adolescents (Gamlund, 2016). Others have argued that we should replace the principle of saving the most life-years with a principle that considers quality of life (McMillan & Hope, 2010; Norheim, 2010; Ottersen, 2013). Still others argue that we should understand the worst-off to be the people who are sickest right now rather than those in danger of dying young (Kerstein & Bognar, 2010). Some have also defended first-come, first-served allocation as equal to or better than a lottery (McMillan & Hope, 2010).

Though we continue to defend our view, many of the critics' emendations would also generate reasonable systems for allocation. It would be reasonable to adjust the degree of priority given to very young children upward or downward, or to give greater weight to saving the most life-years than to saving lives. It might also be reasonable to employ a first-come, first-served allocation approach rather than a lottery approach if first-come, first-served can be designed to prevent serious unfairness.

However, the inclusion of certain principles—many of which are popular in real-world politics—would lead to allocation systems that are seriously deficient. The most important example is the inclusion of sickest-first principles, which come close to being a simple mistake of fact if they assume that those who are less sick will be saved later on. Another change that would lead to a deficient system would be the exclusion of any priority for younger individuals. Even though the precise degree and scope of that priority can reasonably be debated, the importance of saving more life-years and protecting the worst-off—those who will die young if not helped—both favor giving priority to younger people. From a perspective of fairness to individuals, ability-to-pay and identity-based allocation must also be rejected.

Public Attitudes Regarding the Allocation of Scarce Medical Resources

Social scientists have employed a variety of methodologies to assess public preferences regarding the allocation of scarce medical resources. Some have circulated surveys to laypeople (Krütli, Rosemann, Tornblom, & Smieszek, 2016; Tong et al., 2010, 2012, 2013), while others have surveyed medical professionals (Strech, Synofzik, & Marckmann, 2008). Still others have conducted qualitative research, based on transcripts from focus groups or deliberative fora (Irving et al., 2013; Vawter et al., 2010; Vawter, Gervais, & Garrett, 2007). Other researchers have attempted to identify the neurological processes underlying decision-making about the allocation of scarce medical resources, or have studied whether psychological influences cause judgments about allocation to shift (Lenton, Blair, & Hastie, 2006; Smith, Anand, Benattayallah, & Hodgson, 2015). Most research focuses on the allocation of specific scarce resources, such as transplantable organs, intensive care unit beds, or vaccines in a pandemic, though some research focuses on public preferences for resource allocation more generally.

Surveys have found a wide range of public preferences though they generally agree on certain points. There is some preference for allocation to individuals who start off being more severely ill or otherwise worse-off; to younger patients rather than older ones; to individuals with dependents; and to those who are not perceived to have been culpable for their own ill health.

How Are Public Attitudes Relevant to Ethical Questions?

The social-scientific research briefly described in the prior section attempts to answer a descriptive question: what are people's beliefs about how medical resources should be allocated? However, society is ultimately interested not only in empirical surveys of how its members believe medical interventions should be allocated, but also in answers to the normative question of how medical resources should be allocated. This section will examine what bearing the answer to the descriptive question might have on the answer to the normative question.

Public Attitudes as an Answer to the Normative Question: Relativism

Some have suggested that answering questions such as "How should society allocate scarce medical resources?" simply involves determining how most people in the relevant society would answer those questions. On this understanding, normative questions can be answered using descriptive, survey-based methods.

This approach faces two serious problems. First, it cannot explain how societies can make moral mistakes or progress morally. For instance, when slavery was legal in the United States, it is plausible that individuals would have believed that slaves should not have received scarce medical resources. However, these beliefs—while understandable given the context of their time—were mistaken, and their abandonment was a form of moral progress. An approach that equates ethical correctness with popular acceptance cannot explain these facts. Second, it is inconsistent with its own methodology. When respondents in surveys or focus groups answer the normative question "How should society allocate scarce medical resources?" they do so not by looking to surveys of others' attitudes, but rather by engaging in some form of moral deliberation. In this respect, research on public attitudes is just as limited a methodology for answering normative questions as it is for answering factual questions in the sciences and social sciences. Asking people whether infant mortality is falling, or whether sea levels are rising, is the wrong approach to answering those factual questions.

Ultimately, while social-scientific research is an effective methodology for collecting public attitudes regarding normative questions, its very design concedes that moral deliberation—not surveys of public attitudes—is the correct methodology for answering normative questions. As Sulmasy and Sugarman observe, "The opinion survey, a commonly used empirical technique in medical ethics, should *never* be construed to give 'the answer.' ...The mere fact that almost everyone says that something is proper, or that almost everyone acts in a certain way, does not make it proper to act that way" (2001, pp. 8–9).

Expert Attitudes as an Answer to the Normative Question: Scientism

Another approach to answering normative questions is to treat surveys of experts, rather than surveys of the general public, as normatively authoritative. Where questions of technical expertise are at issue, such as which immunosuppressants are most likely to prevent an organ from being rejected, there is a clear difference between the weight we should give to surveys of medical professionals and surveys of laypeople. However, the question of how society should allocate scarce medical resources is not a technical question whose answers can be discovered via the methods of laboratory science: it is a question of values (Hope, Sprigings, & Crisp, 1993).

Some might object that medical professionals are not merely technical experts, but also experts in the craft or activity of medicine—an activity that also involves considering questions of value. However, it is doubtful that medical professionals have special expertise in the sorts of value questions involved in the allocation of scarce medical resources. Medical professionals, indeed, are often discouraged from thinking about value questions at a societal level and instead encouraged to see themselves as obliged to look out for the interests of individual patients.

Public Attitudes as an Entry Point for Moral Inquiry

That research on either public or expert attitudes cannot tell us the answer to normative questions might suggest that such research is irrelevant to normative questions. The ethicist Frances Kamm displays this attitude when she suggests:

> In general, the approach to deriving moral principles that I adopt may be described as follows: Consider as many case-based judgments of yours as prove necessary. Do not ignore some case-based judgments, assuming they are errors, just because they conflict with simple or intuitively plausible principles that account for some subset of your case-based judgments. Work on the assumption that a different principle can account for all the judgments. Be prepared to be surprised as to what this principle is. Remember that this principle can be simple, even though it is discovered by considering many complex cases…Then, consider the principle on its own, to see if it expresses some plausible value or conception of the person or relations between persons. This is necessary to justify it as a *correct* principle, one that has normative weight, not merely one that makes all the case judgments cohere…I say, consider your case-based judgments, rather than do a survey of everyone's judgments. This is because I believe that much more is accomplished when one person considers her judgments and then tries to analyze and justify their grounds than if we do mere surveys (2007, p. 5).

Skepticism about surveys as a basis for ethical claims is not unique to Kamm and others who share her non-consequentialist, case-based methodology for answering questions of value. Many consequentialist moral philosophers, who reach conclusions diametrically opposite from Kamm's, also reject the claim that surveys tell us what is valuable. They instead contend that certain basic claims are morally obvious—such as the idea that we should extend lives as much as possible—and that claims about how scarce medical resources should be allocated must build on these obvious facts.

Kamm and others are correct that surveys do not tell us what is right and wrong. As Allen Alvarez puts it, "Empirical investigation, e.g., surveys or ethnographies, can be methodologically appropriate in determining what people actually value. But in understanding, analyzing, solving, and communicating moral problems, the most appropriate approach would be philosophical reasoning or reflection" (2001, p. 518).

Even though public attitudes do not directly determine the solution to moral problems, empirical research into public attitudes can be useful in a variety of ways. By showing which beliefs are popular among the public, or which beliefs are points of division, empirical research can help to focus moral inquiry on those claims or beliefs, thereby ensuring that philosophical reasoning is relevant to real-world problems. Furthermore, even though popularity does not constitute correctness, the unpopularity of a normative position can justify placing it under scrutiny. The idea that an unpopular position is less likely to be correct is bolstered by the Condorcet Jury Theorem, which suggests that individuals forming beliefs independently who are each more likely to get things right than not are highly likely, as a large group, to get things right. This theorem depends in its original form on the assumption—frequently falsified in practice—that individuals form beliefs independently of one another, although some have suggested that it can hold even if there is some interdependence as well (Estlund, 1994). Lastly, research that elucidates not only people's beliefs but their reasons for holding those beliefs can help in developing arguments in favor of certain allocation systems.

How Are Public Attitudes Relevant to the Implementation of Allocation Systems?

Even though public attitudes have only an indirect role with respect to the question of how scarce medical resources should be allocated, they have a greater role in discussions of how allocation systems should be implemented. This section reviews three ways in which public attitudes can be relevant to implementation: as constraints on justice, as requirements of public reason, or as requirements for implementability.

Public Preferences as Constraints on Justice

Even if a proposed allocation policy appears normatively attractive, certain allocation policies may be practically difficult or impossible to implement because people will be unable or unwilling to go along with the policies. This raises a question about the interplay between the normative question of rightness and the empirical question of what is possible for individuals in society to achieve.

John Rawls is notable for defending the view that a just policy must be one that is implementable given empirical facts about human capacities, including psychological capacities. For Rawls (1999), part of justice is attainability, and if a policy could only be adopted and sustained by superhuman individuals—for instance, if it requires unlimited altruism or sociability—then it is not just but instead beyond justice. In contrast, G.A. Cohen has argued that fairness should be evaluated without reference to individuals' capacity to do what is fair. Considering human capacities should be done at a later stage, and should not be part of normative inquiry into what is just (Cohen, 2009).

If Rawls's account of justice is correct, empirical research into public attitudes can be relevant in helping to establish the limits of attitudes—such as altruism—that are necessary for allocation systems to function. In contrast, if Cohen's account is correct, Rawls's concerns about human capacities are really concerns about the implementability of justice (discussed later in this section), not about justice itself.

Public Attitudes as Constraints on Implementation: Public Reason

Rawls is also well known for his idea of "public reason." On Rawls's (2005) view, legislative judgments regarding "constitutional essentials and matters of basic justice"—a set which likely includes judgments about the allocation of scarce medical resources—must be justified by appeal to public reasons. Rawls defines public reasons as reasons that the decisionmaker proffering them can reasonably expect that others will reasonably accept. On a Rawlsian view, even if a decisionmaker believes that allocating medical resources in a certain way is morally right, she needs to be able to frame that allocation in a way that appeal to public reasons and values. Public reason approaches will make empirical research into public attitudes more relevant, because alternative allocation systems that are reasonable and widely popular will need to be addressed in public debate by those favoring other systems they believe are morally best.

In contrast, some reject public reason in favor of the view that individuals in charge of making decisions in society should simply do what is morally correct, even if others could not be expected to understand or accept those choices. These are often termed *perfectionist* or *comprehensive* approaches. On these approaches, empirical research into public attitudes will only be relevant if it affects what is morally correct: once we have determined what to do, we should do it even if it conflicts with reasonable public attitudes. So, for instance, if using a lottery to allocate scarce medical resources turns out to be morally correct, decisionmakers should use lotteries even if the public strongly prefers first-come, first-served allocation and is reasonable in holding to its preference.

Public Preferences as Implementation Constraints: Real-World Implementability

Even if a system of allocation is morally correct, publicly reasonable, and achievable for individuals, public endorsement may still matter in order for the system to be effectively implementable. For instance, even if it turned out that people with certain diseases should be ineligible for organ transplants because their prospect of benefit is too poor, a policy of entirely excluding these people might produce a backlash from their family members that renders the entire policy less effective. Even if the exclusion really would be morally best, a second-best policy may be the only one that is achievable.

Considerations of implementability might be used to justify adding principles that would not be judged best after philosophical deliberation. To return to an example discussed above, Greg Bognar and Samuel Kerstein argue in favor of sickest-first allocation on the basis that "Ignoring the present suffering of patients is likely to be hard for the public to accept especially in life-and-death cases, regardless of scarcity" (2010, p. 39). Similarly, a recent survey argues that "decisions in a democracy will not be sustainable in the long run unless legitimized by a majority" (Krütli, Rosemann, Tornblom, & Smieszek, 2016). However, even though public preferences matter to implementability, balancing the implementability of an allocation system against its moral desirability can present difficult questions. An easily implementable but morally flawed system may not be preferable, all things considered, to a morally meritorious but difficult-to-implement system.

How Ethics Can Inform Social-Scientific Research on Fairness

Surveys of public attitudes about fair allocation will be most relevant to normative questions if they ask respondents about allocation proposals that are compelling options from the standpoint of normative inquiry. However, most survey researchers receive little education in the methods of normative inquiry, just as most bioethicists receive little education in survey methods. Ethics education for survey researchers generally focuses on ensuring that survey participants give informed consent to participation and on avoiding harm to survey participants. The emphasis is on the ethics of conducting survey research, rather than on conducting survey research about ethics.

When surveys ask about normative questions, as opposed to factual questions, it is important for the surveys to reflect both expertise in the empirical methods of good survey design and expertise in thinking about and conceptualizing questions of value. Empirical expertise is important in ensuring that the surveys produce interpretable data, have sufficient statistical power, and can be conducted at reasonable cost. Ethical expertise is important in ensuring that the surveys are clear about which normative questions they are asking, and in analyzing the responses of qualitative interviewees and mapping them onto the normative landscape.

Qualitative Research and the Elucidation of Normative Justifications

Moral philosophers generally want to know not merely *that* people offer certain answers to questions of value, but *why* they offer those answers. Eliciting people's reasons and justifications for their answers is often more easily done using qualitative research methodologies, such as focus groups, document analysis, or ethnography, than by using quantitative surveys. However, quantitative surveys can also ask people about their justifications, even though they may be unable to bring out as much fine nuance as in-depth discussions.

One impressive, though dated, piece of empirical social science regarding fairness and allocation is the work of the Harvard political scientist Jennifer Hochschild. Hochschild (1981) begins her *What's Fair?*, a work examining public preferences regarding economic distribution, by reporting quantitative data regarding actual economic distributions, as well as public preferences regarding what economic distribution would be desirable. However, Hochschild spends the bulk of the book analyzing the transcripts of interviews with 28 respondents. She reports that:

> This research method permitted respondents to reveal their convictions and uncertainties, their reasoning process and emotional reactions, their foci for passion and indifference, their expertise and ignorance. From the interviews, I was able to evaluate the content, complexity, and strength of individual beliefs about justice, as well as the circumstances in which they occurred and their effects on respondents' political and economic views (1981, p. 23).

Hochschild goes on to explain how her qualitative methodology can add detail to a quantitative report of individual attitudes:

> For example, polls show that most of the population usually does not support programs leading to the downward redistribution of wealth. Surveyors explain this finding through the correlation between wealth and support; the researcher interprets the relationship and infers that the rich do not support certain programs because these programs would hurt their economic position. Intensive interviewers explain this finding by discussing with respondents what they expect and how they would feel about the effect of redistributive programs on their lives. The researcher interprets respondents' statements to draw conclusions about what redistribution means to people in various economic positions (1981, p. 24).

Though Hochschild's research is not focused on the allocation of medical resources, but rather on distributive justice generally, the value of her methodology suggests the merit of similar research into individuals' justifications for their choices about the fair allocation of medical resources. It is also valuable to have extended and analyzed transcripts of some interviews—as Hochschild provides—rather than simply a coded summary of what the interviewer takes to be the respondent's reasons for her stated preferences.

Quantitative Research and Question Wording

Some quantitative studies have aimed to test the popularity of normative theories of medical ethics. For instance, one recent study attempted to provide quantitative data on the popularity of different principles for allocation among laypeople, general practitioners, and medical students (Krütli et al. 2016).

However, as the survey notes, its definition of "sickest first" allocation made comparison to the normative theory difficult, because it defined the sickest individuals as "those who need the organ most urgently" (Krütli et al. 2016). By building a concept of need into the definition of sickest-first, it may have implicitly taken a stance on the moral attractiveness of that principle.

The challenge of wording survey questions about normative issues in a way that is faithful to the moral theory under discussion suggests the desirability of increased work on perceptions of fairness by social scientists that integrates qualitative and quantitative methods and provides in-depth analysis of survey responses. Given the desirability of examining the ethical reasoning of survey respondents in depth, such research could be effectively conducted as a partnership between moral philosophers and social scientists.

Conclusion

The normative challenge of how to fairly allocate scarce medical resources is a perennial one. Advances in medicine have expanded our ability to save lives, and in so doing have turned unpreventable tragedies into moral dilemmas. Empirical research into public preferences for the allocation of scarce medical resources has tremendous value, both in illuminating questions and approaches for ethical analysis and in identifying strategies for making allocation systems implementable. While knowing what the public prefers does not entail an answer to how medical resources should be allocated, improved collaboration between bioethicists and empirical researchers could lead to more productive research programs both in ethics and in the social sciences.

Acknowledgements I am grateful to Ezekiel Emanuel, Alan Wertheimer, and Timo Smieszek for discussion of these issues, and to Meng Li, David Tracer, and an anonymous reviewer for their comments. Thanks to Kristen Miller for her help with the references.

References

Alexander, S. (1962). They decide who lives, who dies. *Life,* 102–125.

Alvarez, A. A. (2001). How rational should bioethics be? The value of empirical approaches. *Bioethics, 15*(5–6), 501–519.

Chappell, R. Y. (2016). Against 'saving lives': Equal concern and differential impact. *Bioethics, 30*(3), 159–164.

Cohen, G. A. (2009). *Rescuing justice and equality* (pp. 229–273). Cambridge, MA: Harvard University Press.

Egan, T. M., Murray, S., Bustami, R. T., Shearon, T. H., McCullough, K. P., Edwards, L. B., … Grover F. L. (2006). Development of the new lung allocation system in the United States. *American Journal of Transplantation, 6*(5 Pt 2), 1212–1227.

Estlund, D. M. (1994). Opinion leaders, independence, and Condorcet's jury theorem. *Theory and Decision, 36*(2), 131–162.

Kamm, F. M. (2007). *Intricate Ethics* (p. 5). Oxford: Oxford UP.

Gamlund, E. (2016). What is so important about completing lives? A critique of the modified youngest first principle of scarce resource allocation. *Theoretical Medicine and Bioethics, 37*(2), 113–128.

Hochschild, J. L. (1981). *What's fair?: American beliefs about distributive justice*. Cambridge, MA: Harvard University Press.

Hope, T., Sprigings, D., & Crisp, R. (1993). "Not clinically indicated": patients' interests or resource allocation? *BMJ, 306*(6874), 379–381.

Irving, M. J., Tong, A., Jan, S., Wong, G., Cass, A., Allen, R. D., et al. (2013). Community preferences for the allocation of deceased donor organs for transplantation: A focus group study. *Nephrology, Dialysis, Transplantation: Official Publication of the European Dialysis and Transplant Association - European Renal Association, 28*(8), 2187–2193.

Kerstein, S. J., & Bognar, G. (2010). Complete lives in the balance. *The American Journal of Bioethics, 10*(4), 37–45.

Krohmal, B. J., & Emanuel, E. J. (2007). Access and ability to pay: The ethics of a tiered health care system. *Archives of Internal Medicine, 167*(5), 433–437.

Krütli, P., Rosemann, T., Tornblom, K. Y., & Smieszek, T. (2016). How to fairly allocate scarce medical resources: Ethical argumentation under scrutiny by health professionals and lay people. *PloS One, 11*(7), e0159086.

Lenton, A. P., Blair, I. V., & Hastie, R. (2006). The influence of social categories and patient responsibility on health care allocation decisions: Bias or fairness? *Basic and Applied Social Psychology, 28*(1), 27–36.

Lipsitch, M., Finelli, L., Heffernan, R. T., Leung, G. M., Redd, S. C., & 2009 H1N1 Surveillance Group. (2011). Improving the evidence base for decision making during a pandemic: The example of 2009 influenza A/H1N1. *Biosecurity and Bioterrorism: Biodefense Strategy, Practice, and Science, 9*(2), 89–115.

Malakoff, D. (1999). Bayes offers a 'new' way to make sense of numbers. *Science, 286*(5444), 1460–1464.

McMillan, J., & Hope, T. (2010). Balancing principles, QALYs, and the straw men of resource allocation. *The American Journal of Bioethics, 10*(4), 48–50.

Munson, J. C., Christie, J. D., & Halpern, S. D. (2011). The societal impact of single versus bilateral lung transplantation for chronic obstructive pulmonary disease. *American Journal of Respiratory and Critical Care Medicine, 184*(11), 1282–1288.

Norheim, O. F. (2010). Priority to the young or to those with least lifetime health? *The American Journal of Bioethics: AJOB, 10*(4), 60–61.

Ottersen, T. (2013). Lifetime QALY prioritarianism in priority setting. *Journal of Medical Ethics, 39*(3), 175–180.

Persad, G., Wertheimer, A., & Emanuel, E. J. (2009). Principles for allocation of scarce medical interventions. *The Lancet, 373*(9661), 423–431.

Rawls, J. (1999). *A theory of justice*. Cambridge, MA: Harvard University Press.

Rawls, J. (2005). *Political liberalism* (pp. 212–254). New York, NY: Columbia University Press.

Rid, A., & Emanuel, E. J. (2014). Ethical considerations of experimental interventions in the Ebola outbreak. *The Lancet, 384*(9957), 1896–1899.

Smith, L. J., Anand, P., Benattayallah, A., & Hodgson, T. L. (2015). An fMRI investigation of moral cognition in healthcare decision making. *Journal of Neuroscience, Psychology, and Economics, 8*(2), 116.

Strech, D., Synofzik, M., & Marckmann, G. (2008). How physicians allocate scarce resources at the bedside: A systematic review of qualitative studies. *Journal of Medicine and Philosophy, 33*(1), 80–99.

Sulmasy, D. P., & Sugarman, J. (2001). The many methods of medical ethics (or, thirteen ways of looking at a blackbird). In J. Sugarman & D. P. Sulmasy (Eds.), *Methods in medical ethics* (2nd ed., pp. 3–18). Washington, DC: Georgetown University Press.

Tong, A., Howard, K., Jan, S., Cass, A., Rose, J., Chadban, S., ... Craig, J. C. (2010). Community preferences for the allocation of solid organs for transplantation: A systematic review. *Transplantation, 89*(7), 796–805.

Tong, A., Jan, S., Wong, G., Craig, J. C., Irving, M., Chadban, S., ... Howard, K. (2012). Patient preferences for the allocation of deceased donor kidneys for transplantation: A mixed methods study. *BMC Nephrology, 13*, 18.

Tong, A., Jan, S., Wong, G., Craig, J. C., Irving, M., Chadban, S., ... Howard, K. (2013). Rationing scarce organs for transplantation: Healthcare provider perspectives on wait-listing and organ allocation. *Clinical Transplantation, 27*(1), 60–71.

Vawter, D. E., Garrett, J. E., Gervais, K. G., Prehn, A. W., DeBruin, D. A., Tauer, C. A., ... Marshall, M. F. (2010). *For the good of us all: Ethically rationing health resources in Minnesota in a severe influenza pandemic*. Minneapolis, MN: Minnesota Center for Health Care Ethics and University of Minnesota Center for Bioethics.

Vawter, D. E., Gervais, K. G., & Garrett, J. E. (2007). Allocating pandemic influenza vaccines in Minnesota: Recommendations of the pandemic influenza ethics work group. *Vaccine, 25*(35), 6522–6536.

Yamin, A. E. (2009). Shades of dignity: Exploring the demands of equality in applying human rights frameworks to health. *Health and Human Rights, 11*(2), 1–18.

Chapter 5
Equality by Principle, Efficiency by Practice: How Policy Description Affects Allocation Preference

Meng Li and Jeff DeWitt

Policy issues are aggregates of individual practical problems. However, practical problems demand that we think about specific details, while aggregating such problems at the policy level entails that we think about more abstract principles. For example, in an individual case of organ allocation, we may need to decide whether to allocate the next organ to a 5-year-old boy or a 60-year-old woman; yet, on a policy level, this same decision is aggregated with many others and abstracted to issues about valuing "efficiency," "equal access," "age," "prognosis," etc. Can these different ways of conceptualizing the same problem affect a person's preference for how such decisions are made?

According to recent behavioral research on policy decisions, the context of a decision can systematically influence the construction of preferences (Li, Vietri, Galvani, & Chapman, 2010; Slovic, 1995; Ubel, Baron, & Asch, 2001). In the domain of healthcare policy, research shows that people often avoid prioritizing among lives (Greene, 2001; Tetlock, Kristel, Elson, Green, & Lerner, 2000), so much so that they are willing to save fewer total lives (sacrificing medical efficiency) in order to achieve a more equal allocation (Ubel, DeKay, Baron, & Asch, 1996; Ubel & Loewenstein, 1996; Ratcliffe, 2000). However, this preference has also been shown to shift systematically as a result of how information in the question is framed, such as grouping of recipients (Colby, DeWitt, & Chapman, 2015) and description of the range of individuals under consideration (Ubel et al., 2001).

Given the impact of information presentation on allocation preferences, it is plausible that these same preferences may shift when information in the question is

M. Li (✉)
Department of Health and Behavioral Sciences, University of Colorado Denver, Denver, CO, USA
e-mail: meng.li@ucdenver.edu

J. DeWitt
Department of Psychology, Rutgers University, New Brunswick, NJ, USA
e-mail: jeffdewitt7@gmail.com

M. Li, D.P. Tracer (eds.), *Interdisciplinary Perspectives on Fairness, Equity, and Justice*, DOI 10.1007/978-3-319-58993-0_5

presented at different levels of abstraction. For example, discussions about practical problems in concrete detail may activate different goals than debates about abstract principles in public policy would. To date, research has not yet explored such potential effects. The current work aims to help fill this gap by focusing on how the abstraction level of policy descriptions affects the public's policy preference, and specifically, preference in the trade-off between medical efficiency and equality in healthcare allocation.

The conflict between equality and efficiency in medical allocation: Age and waiting time

When allocating scarce healthcare resources such as transplant organs or vaccines, a policy that maximizes equality is often in conflict with one that maximizes efficiency. In the context of indivisible goods, such as medical procedures and organs, equality means providing everyone with equal access to the resource (Rawls, 1999), usually by giving everyone equal probability of access, or allocating on a first-come, first-served basis when the resource is scarce. Medical efficiency, on the other hand, means maximizing total benefit, usually in units such as the number of lives saved, number of life-years saved, or number of quality adjusted life years saved (Persad, Wertheimer, & Emanuel, 2009; Pliskin, Shepard, & Weinstein, 1980). The conflict between efficiency and equality can arise in a number of situations, and the current work focuses on age and waiting time as potential causes of this tension.

Age is a relevant factor in existing healthcare allocation policies, such as the allocation of transplant organs (Organ Procurement and Transplantation Network, 2015) and dialysis (Rutecki & Kilner, 1999). However, the principles of equality and efficiency lead to very different allocation strategies concerning age: While the *efficiency* principle entails that, on average, younger individuals should be prioritized to increase the total number of life-years saved, the *equality* principle stipulates that all ages should have equal access to the resource (Persad et al., 2009). Much research shows that public opinion favors efficiency over equality when it comes to age: People prefer to save younger individuals compared to older individuals by a large margin (Cropper, Aydede, & Portney, 1994; Johannesson & Johansson, 1997; Lewis & Charny, 1989; Tsuchiya, Dolan, & Shaw, 2003). However, one problem with this conclusion is that such "public opinions" were invariably obtained by asking participants to compare the lives of individuals in specific age groups, as in "*Program A will save 200 lives from diseases that kill 20-year-olds; Program B will save 200 lives from diseases that kill 60-year-olds, Which program would you choose?*" (Cropper et al., 1994). It is unclear whether people would really endorse the abstract principle behind Program A if it was spelled out as, for example "life-saving programs should prioritize young victims." So far, no research has attempted to answer this question.

Waiting time is another key factor in healthcare allocation. For example, it is standard practice in many nations to incorporate the "first-come, first-served" rule when designing organ allocation systems. Prioritizing recipients who have waited longer is good practice in terms of ensuring equal access to scarce organs. However, much research shows that the amount of time spent on dialysis while waiting for a kidney transplant (exceeding 6 months) is negatively correlated with kidney graft survival time post-transplant (Goldfarb-Rumyantzev et al., 2005; Kennedy, Mackie, Rosenberg, & McDonald, 2006; Meier-Kriesche & Kaplan, 2002; Meier-Kriesche et al., 2000). The longer one waits for an organ, the shorter one is expected to live post transplantation. Thus, from the perspective of medical efficiency, prioritizing recipients who have waited longer is bad practice because the total amount of benefit produced by a donor organ is not maximized. Unlike age, a recent review (Tong et al., 2010) reports that the majority of people prefer to prioritize recipients who have stayed longer on the waiting list, suggesting an overall preference for equality. Again, however, there has been no study to evaluate how preferences regarding waiting time may shift when organ allocation is framed as specific problems or abstract principles.

Psychological Theories of Abstraction and General vs. *Specific Descriptions*

Psychological theories of abstraction lend support to the hypothesis that the abstraction level of description can influence preferences regarding policy. According to Construal Level Theory (Trope & Liberman, 2010) and Action Identification Theory (Vallacher & Wegner, 1987), actions (e.g., calling a friend) are identified in a hierarchical system, where they can be abstracted to a higher level that focuses on "why" they are done (e.g., sustain a friendship) or construed at a lower level that includes greater details and focuses on "how" they are done (e.g., dialing the friend's number). Construal Level Theory (Trope & Liberman, 2010) predicts that these different levels of construal representation can affect a range of judgments, including those involving moral values (Agerström & Björklund, 2009; Eyal, Liberman, & Trope, 2008; Gong & Medin, 2012; Lammers, 2012; Zezelj & Jokic, 2014), and in particular, higher-level construal prompts people to focus on central values instead of practical concerns.

Americans seem to hold an unshakable moral principle that "all lives are equal": "All men are created equal" was written into the United States Declaration of Independence (Declaration of Independence, 1776) and is cited frequently by political leaders. For example, a large-scale survey of representative Americans showed an overwhelming desire for greater income equality (Norton & Ariely, 2011). Efficiency, on the other hand, rarely receives nearly as much attention as a moral value. If Americans hold equality as a central value to a greater extent than efficiency, Construal Level Theory would predict that a higher-level construal will promote a greater focus on equality versus efficiency. Applying this prediction to healthcare allocation, a higher-level construal should promote more equal allocation, weighing all age groups equally, and giving priority to longer waiting time.

The Current Research

Drawing on Action Identification Theory (Vallacher & Wegner, 1987), and the natural variations policy-relevant discussions, we manipulate construal level through different levels of abstraction in policy descriptions. That is, we describe allocation policies either in specific details (what) or in terms of the general principles behind the allocation (why), and examine whether people's preferences between equality and efficiency shift as a result of these descriptions. In line with Construal Level Theory (Trope & Liberman, 2010), we predict that general policy descriptions would steer allocation preferences towards equality, while specific descriptions would shift preference towards efficiency.

To test this hypothesis, we conducted 4 studies using various allocation scenarios involving age or waiting time. Study 1 and Study 2 demonstrated the basic preference reversal effect in the context of vaccine allocation among different age groups; Study 3 extended this finding to the allocation of transplant kidneys based on waiting time, and tested whether differences in goal activation mediate the effect; Study 4 explored whether the effect was related to the inclusion of numerical values in the description of allocation plans.

Study 1: Recipient Age

The purpose of Study 1 was to test for systematic discrepancies in people's allocation preferences when the issue is described in specific versus general terms. The specific condition described vaccine distribution plans that affected specific age groups, whereas the general condition explicitly described the general principles of allocation consistent with the options in the specific condition.

We used a within-subjects design and tested the effect of abstraction on preference in two parts (see Table 5.1): Study 1A measured preferences between equal

Table 5.1 Policy descriptions in studies 1A and 1B

Specific version	General version
Study 1A	
Policy 1: 500 20-year-old people will be saved	*N/A*
Policy 2: 500 60-year-old people will be saved	
(A) Policy 1 is better	(A) Younger people should be valued more
(B) Policy 2 is better	(B) Older people should be valued more
(C) They are equally good	(C) All lives should be valued equally, regardless of age
Study 1B	
Policy 1: 500 25-year-old people will be saved, all of whom have 5 more years to live, due to pre-existing health conditions	*N/A*
Policy 2: 500 50-year-old people will be saved, all of whom have 30 more years to live	
(A) Policy 1 is better	(A) Young people should be valued more, regardless of the number of years they have left to live
(B) Policy 2 is better	(B) People with greater number of years left to live should be valued more, regardless of age
(C) They are equally good	(C) Age and number of years left to live are equally important in evaluating whose lives are more important to save.

allocation and an allocation that prioritizes the young, and Study 1B further distinguished two rationales for pro-young allocations ("years-left" and "years-lived," which we explain later), since prioritizing young recipients does not always reflect efficiency concerns.

Study 1A: Prioritizing Young vs. Equality

Methods

Participants. Participants were 103 Internet survey panel members from Amazon Mechanical Turk (34 males, 69 females), ages 18–68 ($M = 34.28$, $SD = 12.32$), who received a small amount of monetary compensation for completing the survey.

Questionnaires. Each participant received both the general and specific descriptions on separate web pages, with the order counterbalanced and no option to alter responses on previous pages. The specific version read "*Suppose a NEW form of fatal Influenza (Flu) virus has emerged in this region and is extremely infectious. Everyone in the region is equally susceptible to infection, regardless of their age and health status. A vaccine is fully effective against this new form of flu. But there are not enough vaccines to save everyone from flu death.*" It then asked participants to "*consider the outcomes of 2 vaccine distribution policies*," where policy 1 would save 500 20-year-olds, and policy 2 would save 500 60-year-olds. Participants indicated whether policy 1 was better, policy 2 was better, or they were equally good (Table 5.1). The general version did not present the vaccine scenario, but instead asked participants to consider general allocation principles under scarcity, "*When distributing medical resources, it is sometimes necessary to set priorities among lives, especially when the medical resource is limited. How do you think lives should be valued in such situations?*" Participants then made a choice among three options describing general allocation principles that valued either younger people more, older people more, or valued all ages equally (Table 5.1). We predicted that participants would show a greater preference towards the young in the specific version (as saving younger individuals on average means saving more life-years, making it a more efficient way of allocating the scarce resource), but more preference for equality in the general version.

Results

As Fig. 5.1 A illustrates, in the specific version, the majority of participants favored young recipients (62%) and only 37% chose the equal option. In the general version, however, the majority favored the equal option (60%) while 40% favored the young. Only one participant favored the old victims, and it occurred in the specific version. The allocation option (young, old, or equal) × version (specific vs. general)

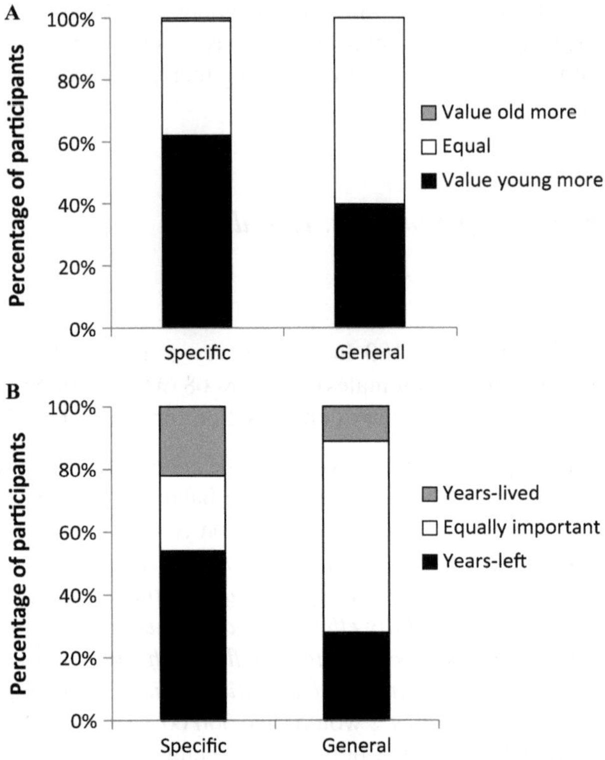

Fig. 5.1 Percentage of participants choosing each option in the specific and general versions in Study 1A (**A**) and 1B (**B**)

χ^2 test was significant,[1] McNemar's χ^2 (1, N = 102) = 16.70, $p < 0.001$, $\phi = 0.51$. Interestingly, there were no order effects.

We also examined the effect of participant's age and gender on choice. We conducted two logistic regressions, using age and gender to predict choice in the specific and general versions, respectively (we excluded the one participant who preferred to save older victims due to the lack of validity to draw conclusions based on one response; this leaves "pro-young" and "all lives equal" as the only options). In the specific version, participant age and gender were both significant predictors of choice: older participants and females were more likely to choose "all lives equal" over the "pro-young" option, $B = 0.06$, SE(B) = 0.02, OR = 1.06, 95% CI [1.03, 1.10], $p = 0.001$, and $B = 1.14$, SE(B) = 0.52, OR = 3.12, 95% CI [1.13, 8.60], $p = 0.03$, respectively. The pattern also held true in the general version, with age being a significant predictor, $B = 0.05$, SE(B) = 0.02, OR = 1.05, 95% CI [1.01, 1.10], $p = 0.01$, and female gender being a marginally significant predictor for

[1] We excluded one respondent in the specific version who favored the old. Including this data point would result in empty off-diagonal cells, rendering the McNemar's χ^2 tests invalid.

choosing "all lives equal" over the "pro-young" option, $B = 0.87$, SE(B) = 0.45, OR = 2.39, 95% CI [1.00, 5.77], $p = 0.05$. Thus, older participants and females showed greater preference for equal allocation in both versions. The age effect seems to demonstrate an egocentric bias, where participants are more sympathetic to victims closer to their own age.

Study 1B: "Years-Left" Metric vs. Equality

One limitation of Study 1A was the use of a preference for younger individuals to represent efficiency. Arguably, a preference to save younger people could reflect either one of two different reasons or a combination of both: One reason could be to save the greatest number of total life-years, that is, a "years-left" metric; another could be to prioritize younger people based on a "fair-innings" rationale regardless of their remaining life-years—younger people have not had the chance to live a full life, and therefore deserve the chance to survive more than someone who has lived a long life (Williams, 1997), which we call a "years-lived" metric. Only the "years-left" metric reflects medical efficiency, that is, to maximize medical benefit in the unit of live-years saved.

To distinguish the "years-left" metric from the "years-lived" metric, Study 1B reversed the assumption that younger people generally have more remaining life-years: It presented a scenario where the older vaccine recipients had more years left to live than the younger recipients (50-year-olds with 30 years left vs. 25-year-olds with 5 years left), with the difference in remaining life expectancy (25 years) equal to the age difference (25 years) (see Table 5.1). Thus, in Study 1B, a preference for saving the older targets with more remaining life-years would reflect a "years-left" metric, and indicates preference for medical efficiency, assigning equal value to all recipients would reflect preference for equality, while a preference for saving the younger targets with fewer remaining life-years would reflect "years-lived" metric, a preference that we do not consider to be either efficient or equal. We expected to replicate the results from Study 1A, where participants show a greater preference for efficiency in the specific version, but prefer equality more in the general version.

Method

Participants. Participants were 100 Internet survey panel members from Amazon Mechanical Turk (44 males, 56 females), ages 18–63 ($M = 32.13$, SD = 10.80), who received a small amount of monetary compensation for completing the survey.

Questionnaire. As in Study 1A, participants saw both the specific and the general versions, with order counterbalanced (Table 5.1). In the specific version, the same vaccine shortage scenario from Study 1A was presented, but in the description of the two policies: "*Policy 1: 500 25-year-old people will be saved, all of whom have*

5 more years to live, due to pre-existing health conditions" and "*Policy 2: 500 50-year-old people will be saved, all of whom have 30 more years to live.*" Choice options were the same as in Study 1A and included "policy 1 was better," "policy 2 was better" (indicating a preference for efficiency), and "they are equally good" (indicating a preference for equality).

The general version was the same as the general version in Study 1A, except the 3 options (Table 5.1): "*Young people should be valued more, regardless of the number of years they have left to live,*" "*People with greater number of years left to live should be valued more, regardless of age*" (indicating preference for efficiency), or "*Age and number of years left to live are equally important in evaluating whose lives are more important to save*" (a principle that would lead to the choice of the "equally good" option in the specific version, although true equality would dictate that neither age nor years left to live will be considered).

Results

Study 1B showed a preference reversal across versions of the survey similar to Study 1A. As illustrated in Fig. 5.1B, in the specific version, participants favored the option that prioritized older recipients with greater years left to live ("years-left" metric, 54%), and 24% judged it equally good to save the two groups ("equal"); in contrast, in the general condition, only 28% of the participants preferred to save older recipients with greater years left to live ("years-left" metric), but the majority of participants (61%) indicated that "years-lived" and "years-left" were equally important ("equal"). A minority (22% in the specific version and 11% in the general version) favored younger recipients with fewer years left to live ("years-lived" metric). The allocation option (3: years lived, years left, or equal) × version (2: specific vs. general) χ^2 test was significant, McNemar's χ^2 (3, $N = 100$) = 32.12, $p < 0.001$, Cramer's $V = 0.34$. Order had no effect.

We conducted two multinomial logistic regressions on choice in the specific and general versions, respectively. Predictors included participant age and gender, and the choice consistent with the "years-left" metric was the reference group in the outcome measure. Results show that, in either condition, gender had no effect on choosing either the "years-lived" metric or the equal option over the "years-lived" metric. Age was a negative predictor for choosing the "years-lived" metric (saving 25-year-old victims with 5 years left) over the "years-left" metric (saving 50-year victims with 30 years left) in the specific version, $B = -0.08$, SE(B) = 0.03, OR = 0.92, $p = 0.01$, but did not predict choice in the general version. Thus, in Study 1B, the egocentric age effect was only present in the specific condition, where the specific age of victims were clearly spelled out, and gender had no effect on choice.

Discussion

Studies 1A and 1B demonstrated that the public's allocation preference for scarce medical resources is influenced by the description of the allocation plans. When asked about allocation policies with regard to recipient groups in a specific case of allocation, participants assigned more value to young people (Study 1A) or people with a greater number of years left to live (Study 1B), both indicating preference for efficiency; however, when asked about general principles on how to evaluate lives in such situations, participants favored equality. This effect is particularly striking given that participants answered both types of questions in succession and that the difference persisted regardless of the order of the questions. Results on age effect suggest that participants' choices were influenced by a self-serving motivation: They were more likely to prioritize those closer to them in age. The inconsistent findings on gender effect (present in Study 1A but not Study 1B) demands further inquiry.

Admittedly, the general and specific versions of Studies 1A and 1B had many differences. For example, the specific version described a vaccine shortage scenario with life/death consequences, but the general version lacked a scenario that makes these consequences clear. In addition, the general version asked participants "*How do you think lives should be valued in such situations*," and such wording could be interpreted as an evaluation of the intrinsic value of the lives involved, instead of a question about the prioritizing that is necessary in situations of scarcity. A relatively minor issue was the fact that the specific version presented options based on two policies, but the general version did not. Study 2 addresses these issues and tests the robustness of our finding.

Study 2: Replication in Recipient Age

In Study 2, we addressed the limitations of Study 1 by making the general and specific versions of the survey more equivalent. In particular, we presented the same vaccine shortage scenario in both the general and the specific version of the survey. We also modified the question in the general version to make it clear that participants' evaluations of lives were only to set priorities for allocating vaccines. To further equate the general and specific measures, responses in both versions were recorded as a choice of favoring either one of two policies or a neutral option. Finally, Study 2 used a between-subjects design to test the robustness of the finding, in contrast to the within-subjects design in Study 1. As in Studies 1A and 1B, Study 2A measured preference between equal allocation and allocation that prioritizes the young, and Study 2B isolated number of years left from age.

Study 2A

Methods

Participants. In Study 2A, 148 participants (74 females) were recruited from campus bus stops at a large public university in exchange for a small snack, including 97% college students and 3% graduate students. Participant age ranged from 17 to 32, but only 5 participants were over the age of 25 ($M = 19.91$, SD = 2.13).

Questionnaire. Participants were randomly assigned to one of two between-subject conditions to receive either the specific or general version of the questionnaire. Both versions used the exact same vaccine shortage scenario, which we modified slightly from the specific version in Study 1A. In the specific version, we asked participants to "*consider the outcomes of 2 vaccine distribution policies*," and the policies were identical to those in Study 1A (see Table 5.2). In the general version, we asked participants to "*consider the following 2 policies on vaccine distribution, with regard to how lives of potential victims should be valued to set priorities in receiving the vaccine*," and the two policies included "*Policy 1: Younger people should be valued more*," and "*Policy 2: Older people should be valued more*" (Table 5.2). In both the specific and general versions, responses were recorded as a choice among three options: "*Policy 1 is better,*" "*Policy 2 is better,*" or "*They are equally good*." We predict that participants will demonstrate a greater preference towards the young in the specific version, but more preference for equality in the general versions.

Results

As illustrated in Fig. 5.2A, response patterns differed across the two conditions in Study 2A, Fisher's exact test = 9.16, $p = 0.006$. Specifically, 72% of the participants in the specific version favored young recipients and 27% indicated saving young and old recipients was equally good; in contrast, in the general version, the most

Table 5.2 Policy descriptions in studies 2A and 2B

Specific version	General version
Study 2A	
Policy 1: 500 20-year-old people will be saved	*Policy 1*: Younger people should be valued more
Policy 2: 500 60-year-old people will be saved	*Policy 2*: Older people should be valued more
Study 2B	
Policy 1: 500 25-year-old people will be saved, all of whom have 5 more years to live, due to pre-existing health conditions	*Policy 1*: Young people should be valued more, regardless of the number of years they have left to live
Policy 2: 500 50-year-old people will be saved, all of whom have 30 more years to live	*Policy 2*: People with greater number of years left to live should be valued more, regardless of age
Options: (A) policy 1 is better; (B) policy 2 is better; (C) they are equally good	

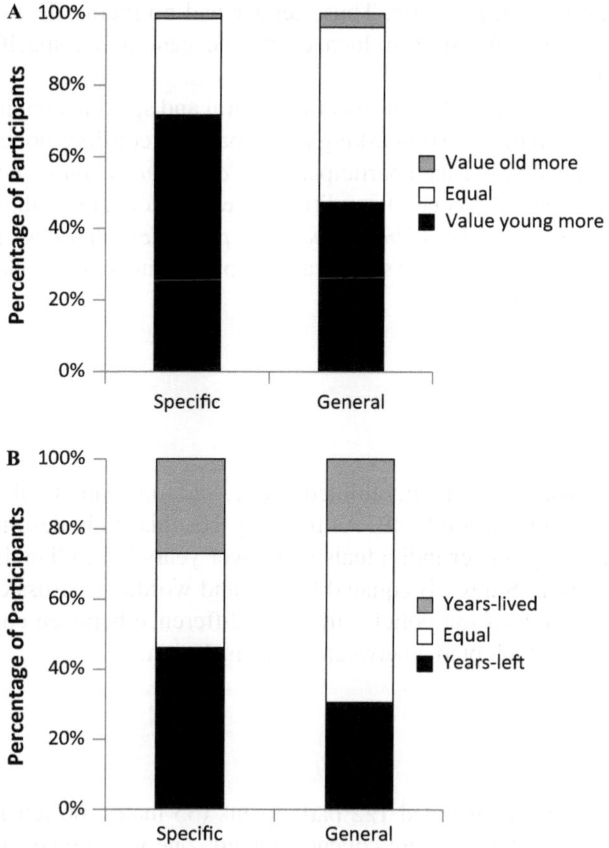

Fig. 5.2 Percentage of participants choosing each option in the specific and general versions in Study 2A (**A**) and 2B (**B**)

popular choice (49%) was the neutral option that indicated equality, while 47% of participants favored the young recipients. Thus, we replicated the response pattern observed in Study 1A using a between-subjects design. Also consistent with Study 1A, very few participants chose the "old" option in either the specific (one participant, or 1%) or the general (three participants, or 4%) conditions. Analysis excluding these four participants showed a similar significant effect, χ^2 (1, $N = 144$) = 8.23, $p = 0.004$, Cramer's $V = 0.24$.

Due to the extremely limited range of age among the mostly undergraduate participants, the effect of participant age was not tested. The effect of participant gender was tested in a logistic regression excluding the four participants who chose the "old" option (we cannot draw any valid conclusions based on such a small number of respondents). There was no main effect of gender on choice between the young and equal options, but gender had a marginal interaction with condition, whereby females were marginally more likely than males to shift from the pro-young choice in the specific condition to the equal choice in the general condition, $B = 1.27$, SE

(B) = 0.72, OR = 3.54, $p = 0.08$. Thus, gender had no main effect on choice, but females were marginally more influenced by the general vs. specific description than were males.

One limitation of Study 2A was that the general and specific conditions still used different wording in the question asking participants to consider policies: While the specific condition simply asked participants to "*consider the outcomes of 2 vaccine distribution policies*," the general condition asked participants to think about "*how lives of potential victims should be valued to set priorities in receiving the vaccine.*" Study 2B addressed this issue by simply asking participants to consider the distribution policies in both conditions.

Study 2B

To address the wording problem outlined above, and to isolate number of years left from age, we conducted Study 2B. As in Study 1B, this study described recipients in a context where younger individuals had fewer years left to live than older individuals. In addition, Study 2B equated format and wordings across conditions and made the description of the policies the only difference between conditions. Like Study 2A, Study 2B adopted a between-subjects design.

Method

Participants. Study 2B included 122 participants (55 males, 66 females, 1 missing gender information); 93.4% were college students, one was a graduate student, two were nonstudents, and two others provided no school information. Participant age ranged from 17 to 47, with only ten participants age 25 or older ($M = 20.76$, SD = 4.38).

Questionnaire. Participants were randomly assigned to receive either the specific or general version of the questionnaire. Both versions included the same vaccine shortage scenario as used in Study 2A, and both versions also used the same phrase, "*consider the outcomes of 2 vaccine distribution policies*," to ask participants about their opinions of the. These changes ensured that the only difference between the specific and general versions was their description of Policy 1 and Policy 2. As listed in Table 5.2, the specific version used the same specific description of allocation plans as presented in Study 1B, and the general version used the same general descriptions of allocation principles as presented in Study 1B, except now the first two options in Study 1B representing either the "years left" or "years lived" metric were described as "Policy 1" and "Policy 2." In both conditions, participants responded, "*Policy 1 is better,*" "*Policy 2 is better,*" and "*They are equally good.*" Compared to Study 1B, which used "*Age and number of years left to live are equally important in evaluating whose lives are more important to save*," as the neutral option, this third option "*They are equally good*" was a better representation of the concept of equality. Although admittedly, choosing the "*equally good*" option can still be interpreted as either a true preference for equality among all lives, or an equal weighting of age and number of years left.

Results

As predicted, Fig. 5.2B shows significantly different response patterns in the specific and general versions, $\chi^2(2, N = 122) = 6.44$, $p = 0.04$, Cramer's $V = 0.23$. While 46% of participants in the specific version favored the "years-left" metric and only 27% chose the equal option, this pattern was reversed in the general version, with 31% and 49% choosing the "years-left" and equal options, respectively, thus replicating the findings from Study 1B.

As in Study 2A, we did not test for effects of participant age. The effect of participant gender was tested in a multinomial logistic regression including all participants. When the reference choice option was younger victims who had fewer years left to live, gender had no effect on choosing either the option to favor older victims who had more years left to live, $B = -0.32$, $SE(B) = 0.66$, $OR = 0.73$, $p = 0.63$, or choosing the neutral option, "they are equally good," $B = 0.49$, $SE(B) = 0.67$, $OR = 1.63$, $p = 0.47$. Therefore, gender had no main or interaction effect on choice in Study 2B.

Discussion

Results from Studies 2A and 2B confirmed the findings from Studies 1A and 1B with a between-subjects design. When the general version was modified to be almost identical to the specific version, except for the descriptions of policies, general descriptions still resulted in greater preference for equal allocations, while specific descriptions led to greater preference for efficient allocations.

One common limitation of Studies 1 and 2 is that they both used age and vaccine allocation as the context that produced the conflict between efficiency and equality. To ensure the generalizability of the findings, Study 3 tested these effects in scenarios involving a different factor and a different type of scarce health resource: Waiting time and transplant organ allocation.

Study 3: Waiting Time

In Study 3, we tested the effect of abstraction on allocation preference in the context of transplant organs. As mentioned earlier, in the allocation of scarce transplant organs, the conflict between equality and efficiency can manifest itself in the consideration of waiting time: Prioritizing those who have waited longer for the organ is consistent with the equality principle, while prioritizing those who have waited a shorter amount of time promotes efficiency, since more timely transplants maximize the total life-years saved by the transplant. In Study 3, we explicitly presented this conflict to participants and measured their allocation preference concerning waiting time in two different conditions, one describing a general allocation policy issue and the other describing a specific allocation problem. As before, we predicted that participants would show a greater preference for equality in the general condition and a greater preference for efficiency in the specific condition.

Another goal of Study 3 was to understand whether the effect of abstraction is indeed due to a shift in concern for efficiency vs. equality, instead of just a preference shift in the isolated scenarios of allocation. Specifically, we tested whether abstraction affects the weight a person places on efficiency versus equality in the context of organ allocation, and whether this shift in goals mediates the shift in policy preference.

Method

Participants. Participants were 418 Internet survey panel members from Amazon Mechanical Turk (239 males, 167 females), ages 18–64 ($M = 31.72$, $SD = 10.75$), who received a small monetary compensation for completing the survey.

Questionnaire. We adopted a between-subjects design in Study 3. Participants were randomly assigned to either the general or specific condition. We explained to all participants that "*because the demand for kidney transplants currently exceeds the supply, the waiting list for such transplants is long. One practice is to assign available kidneys to those who have been waiting longer. This is like waiting in line for many other things. However, the longer someone has been on the waiting list for a kidney transplant, the more deteriorated his/her physical condition is, and therefore, the worse the outcome of the transplant will be. Thus, giving available kidneys to those who have been on the waiting list for a shorter amount of time will save the most total life-years*." We then told all participants "*Suppose there is a shortage of kidneys for transplantation within a state*", and "*This means there are not enough kidney transplants for all the people who need one. Please consider the following kidney transplant distribution plans on how to allocate a limited supply of kidneys*."

In the general condition, we described two general plans of how to allocate a limited supply of kidneys with regard to waiting time, Plan 1: "*People who have been on the waiting list for a shorter period of time should have priority in receiving the transplant*" and Plan 2: "*People who have been on the waiting list for a longer period of time should have priority in receiving the transplant*." In contrast, participants in the specific condition were told "*there are currently only 50 kidneys available for transplantation, but far more potential recipients*." and asked to consider how to allocate the limited supply of 50 kidneys, and saw to specific allocation plans, Plan 1: "*Allocate the kidney transplants to 50 people who have been on the waiting list for a kidney transplant for 1 year*" and Plan 2: "*Allocate the kidney transplants to 50 people who have been on the waiting list for a kidney transplant for 6 years.*" In both conditions, participants responded by choosing "*Plan 1 is better,*" "*Plan 2 is better,*" or "*They are equally good.*"

Note that in this study, choosing plan 1 indicates a preference for efficient allocation, as it is consistent with maximization of benefit, whereas choosing plan 2 indicates a preference for equal allocation, as it corresponds to a "first-come, first-served" principle. Choosing "they are equally good" is harder to interpret and perhaps indicates indifference or tendency to avoid making such a choice.

After selecting an allocation plan, participants responded to a follow-up question about their preference between the two conflicting goals: equality and efficiency. We described the conflict between efficiency and equality in decisions to distribute scarce medical resources again, by stating "*Equality means treating everyone the same. For example, giving everyone equal access or an equal chance to get a transplant kidney. Efficiency means getting the best health outcome out of the intervention. For example, maximizing the total number of life-years gained from the transplant kidneys available.*" and asked participants to divide 100 "points" between equality and efficiency to indicate the relative importance of efficiency and equality to them in making such choices.

Finally, we included a comprehension check question. We asked participants to indicate, based on the allocation scenario presented to them earlier, whether people who waited a longer or shorter amount of time would gain more life-years from a kidney transplant, or if waiting time did not influence life-years gained.

Results[2]

Among 417 participants, 12 (2.9%) did not answer the check question and 84 (20.8%) responded incorrectly, leaving 321 participants who answered the check question correctly (choosing that those waited a shorter amount of time would gain more life-years from a kidney transplant). Below we present results including only those who answered the check question correctly ($n = 321$). However, similar analyses performed among all participants produced the same conclusions.

As illustrated in Fig. 5.3, condition significantly influenced choice, χ^2 (2, $N = 321) = 16.18$, $p < 0.001$, Cramer's $V = 0.23$. Although most participants chose the longer waiting time option (equality) overall, participants were significantly more likely to choose shorter waiting time (efficiency) in the specific condition (35%) than in the general condition (16%); in contrast, they were more likely to choose longer waiting time in the general condition (60%) than in the specific condition (45%).

Participants in the specific condition ($M = 46.93$, SD = 20.97) also allocated significantly more points to "efficiency" (out of 100) than participants in the general condition ($M = 41.82$, SD = 20.69), t (319) = 2.20, $p = 0.03$, Cohen's $d = 0.25$.

[2]We conducted another study among 199 MTurk participants using scenarios almost identical to Study 3 (with a different set of follow-up questions) and a within-subjects design, which yielded similar results.

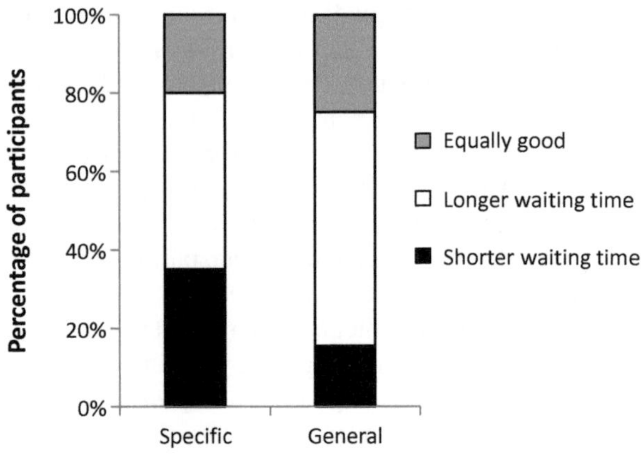

Fig. 5.3 Percentage of participants choosing each allocation plan in the general and specific conditions in Study 3

To confirm that this difference in the general weighting of equality and efficiency was responsible for the shift in policy choices, we conducted a mediation analysis with condition as the independent variable, choice between efficient and equal allocation (Plan 1 vs. Plan 2)[3] as the dependent variable, and points allocated to efficiency as the mediator. Based on the PROCESS Macro developed for SPSS by Hayes (2013, and using a bias-corrected bootstrapping method with 5000 resampling, the indirect effect was significant, $B = 0.54$, 95% CI [0.18, 0.95]. That is, the specific description (compared to general description) increased the weight participants placed on the efficiency goal, which in turn increased preference for the allocation plan that prioritized shorter waiting time.

We then conducted a multinomial logistic regression to examine the effect of participant age and gender, as well as their interaction with experimental condition, on choice. The reference category was the option for shorter waiting time (efficient option). Predictors included participant age, participant gender, and experimental condition, all centered on the mean. The results showed that, again, the general description led to a greater preference for the "longer waiting time" option (equality option), $B = 1.13$, $SE(B) = 0.31$, OR = 3.09, $p < 0.001$; gender was not significant, $B = 0.45$, $SE(B) = 0.32$, OR = 1.57, $p = 0.16$; age had no main effect, but had a marginally significant interaction with condition, $B = -0.06$, $SE(B) = 0.03$, OR = 0.95, $p = 0.06$, where older participants had a tendency to be less influenced by the general vs. specific description manipulation. Repeating this analysis among all participants regardless of their answer to the comprehension check question yielded similar results, except the gender effect became marginally significant, with females somewhat more likely to choose "longer waiting time," $B = 0.53$, $SE(B) = 0.30$, OR = 1.71, $p = 0.07$. Thus, females may have a greater tendency to prefer equality than males, consistent with our finding from Study 1A.

[3] We did not include participants who chose the option that the two plans were "equally good," as it does not indicate a clear preference for either equal or efficient allocation.

Discussion

Study 3 provides further evidence that specific compared to general descriptions of allocation policies can increase the public's preference for efficient allocation. These results are especially noteworthy as they indicate that the findings from Studies 1 and 2 extend to other domains beyond the consideration of age in vaccine allocations. More impressively, the effect of description was strong enough to move preferences towards prioritizing patients with shorter waiting times, even though actual organ allocation systems prioritize patients with longer waiting times (Organ Procurement and Transplantation Network, 2015). Thus, the public's opinion on the allocation of scarce health resources can be very different depending on the framing of the question: They are much more accepting of allocation plans intended to promote efficiency even at the cost of equality, when these plans are presented as a specific allocation case compared to general allocation principles.

The meditation analysis showed that manipulating policy description led to a change in the general weight placed on efficiency versus equality in organ allocation decisions, and that this general change in goals led to the change in preference among allocation plans. Thus, the effect of abstraction in description on choice was not restricted to the unique set of potential victims used in the scenario, but reflects a true shift in the value participants place on efficiency and equality in such allocations.

One potential limitation of Study 3 is the large proportion of participants who failed to correctly answer the check question although analyses including and excluding these participants produced the same results.

Study 4: The Role of Numbers

Studies 1–3 consistently demonstrated that when participants choose among general allocation principles, they show a stronger preference for equal allocation than when choosing among specific plans, in which they were more likely to favor efficient allocation. Study 4 asks a more practical question related to the application of such findings to policy decisions. That is, what aspects of the description are important in producing the effect? The answer to this question can provide practical guidance in understanding which policy descriptions in the real world would sway the public in a particular direction.

In Study 2, where we equated most of the language between conditions, a key difference between the general and specific descriptions was the use of numbers. In particular, the specific descriptions always included numbers (e.g., 500 20-year-olds, 500 60-year-olds; 50 people, 1 year, 6 years) and the general descriptions did not (e.g., younger people, older people; shorter period of time, longer period of time). The numbers in the specific descriptions may have helped keep the abstraction level low by highlighting the specific group of individuals affected by the policy, and by assigning a concrete index to categories such as "younger/older" or "shorter/longer." In contrast, the lack of numbers may elevate the level of abstraction by abstracting meaning from the numbers to semantic categories, and focusing participants' attention on general allocation principles. If this was true, the conspicuity of numbers in the description of allocation plans should influence people's allocation preferences.

Study 4 tested this hypothesis by creating an additional condition that lied in between the general and specific conditions used thus far. In particular, a *numerical words* condition was introduced which described groups of victims using words with numerical meaning, instead of numbers per se. Given that numerical words refer to numbers, but are less conspicuous than Arabic numbers, we expected this condition to yield a response pattern in between those from the general and specific conditions. However, complicating this prediction is the fact that individuals with varying levels of numerical competency respond to numerical information differently (Reyna, Nelson, Han, & Dieckmann, 2009). Therefore, it is likely that the effect of numerical presentation will be moderated by individual differences in numerical competency. Study 4 measured participants' numerical competency using a numeracy scale adapted from Lipkus, Samsa, and Rimer (2001).

Methods

Participants. Three hundred and one undergraduate students (125 males, 162 females, 4 missing gender information) at a large public university participated in the study in exchange for course credits.

Questionnaire. To simplify the design, Study 4 adopted the vaccine allocation scenario used in Studies 1A and 2A, where only age was differentiated among the options. In an online survey, participants were randomly assigned to one of three conditions: specific, numerical words, and general. The specific and general conditions were the same as those in Study 2A, while the numerical words condition replaced the numbers in the specific condition, "*500 20-year-old people/500 60-year-old people*," with the following numerical words: "*A large number of younger people/An equally large number of older people will be saved*" (Table 5.3). All participants were asked whether they favored Policy 1, Policy 2, or thought both policies were equally good.

Subsequently, we presented a scale to assess agreement with statements on equal or efficient allocation of scarce medical resources in general, which included five statements: (1) "*It's morally wrong to place priority on some*

Table 5.3 Policy descriptions in Study 4

Specific version	Numerical words version	General version
Policy 1: 500 20-year-old people will be saved	Policy 1: A large number of younger people will be saved	Policy 1: Younger people should be valued more
Policy 2: 500 60-year-old people will be saved	Policy 2: A large number of older people will be saved	Policy 2: Older people should be valued more
Options: (A) policy 1 is better; (B) policy 2 is better; (C) they are equally good		

people's lives over others," (2) "*I would feel guilty not giving everyone equal access to medical resources,*" (3) "*Everyone deserves equal chance in receiving medical resources, even if equal distribution of such resources results in fewer total life-years saved among potential victims (i.e., the total number of years they would live if they receive the resources, but will lose if they don't),*" (4) "*Healthcare policies must consider efficiency when allocating medical resources (one measure of efficiency is how many total life-years potential recipients would live if they receive such resources, but will lose if they don't),*" and (5) "*Health policies should focus on how to minimize cost and maximize benefit among the population.*" Participants indicated how much they agree with each statement on a 1–7 point scale.

In a prescreening survey battery administered in the beginning of the semester, and prior to the main study, participants also completed a 10-item numeracy scale adapted from Lipkus et al. (2001) to assess numerical competency, which included 10 simple questions asking participants to compute probabilities and convert between percentages and fractions, such as "*If the chance of getting a disease is 10%, how many people would be expected to get the disease out of 100? (A) 1, (B) 5, (C) 100, (D) 10*" or "*Imagine that we roll a fair, six-sided die 1000 times. Out of 1000 rolls, how many times do you think the die would come up even (2, 4, or 6)? (A) 500, (B) 450, (C) 200, (D) 750.*"

Results

As illustrated in Fig. 5.4, the proportion of participants who favored the young was 82%, 67%, and 55% in the specific, numerical words, and general conditions, respectively; in contrast, 14%, 23%, and 40% of the participants preferred equality in these conditions; very few participants favored older people in each condition. These differences were in line with our predictions and significant, χ^2 (4, $N = 301$) = 22.23, $p < 0.001$, Cramer's $V = 0.19$. In particular, separate chi-square analyses showed that the response pattern in the numerical words condition differed

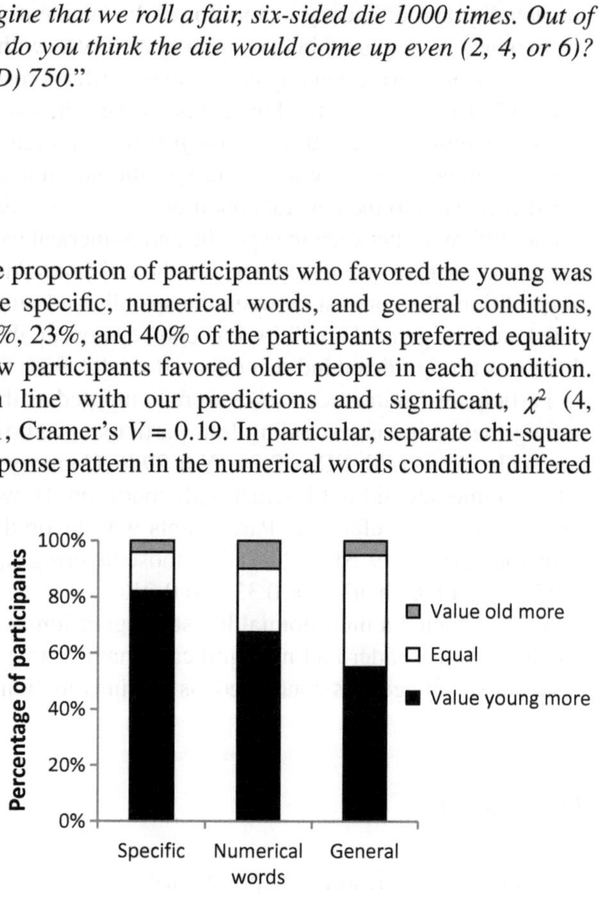

Fig. 5.4 Percentage of participants choosing each option in the three conditions in Study 4

Table 5.4 Factor loadings for each equality/efficiency statement on the equality and efficiency factors in Study 4

	Equality factor	Efficiency factor
Item 1 (morally wrong)	0.81	−0.02
Item 2 (guilty non-equal)	0.80	0.11
Item 3 (equal chance)	0.80	0.03
Item 4 (consider efficiency)	−0.11	0.83
Item 5 (maximize benefit)	0.21	0.78

Factor analysis was conducted with principle component extraction and varimax rotation, using the criterion of eigenvalue >1. The two factors explain 66% of the total variance

significantly from that in the specific condition, χ^2 (2, N = 201) = 6.06, $p < 0.05$, Cramer's $V = 0.17$, and the general condition, χ^2 (2, N = 201) = 7.62, $p = 0.02$, Cramer's $V = 0.19$.

Factor analysis on the ratings for the five equality/efficiency statements extracted an equality factor (loading: 0.80–0.81) and an efficiency factor (0.78–0.83) with principle component extraction and varimax rotation. Table 5.4 shows factor loadings on the equality and efficiency factors for each statement. Participants' factor scores on the two factors were used in two one-way ANOVAs with condition as the independent variable. Scores on the equality factor did not differ across conditions, $F\,(2, 295) = 0.82$, $p = 0.44$, partial $\eta^2 = 0.006$, but scores on the efficiency factor differed significantly across condition, F (2, 295) = 3.16, $p = 0.04$, partial $\eta^2 = 0.02$. Focused contrasts revealed higher efficiency scores in specific and numerical words conditions combined compared to the general condition, t (295) = 2.49, $p = 0.01$, Cohen's $d = 0.29$, but no difference between the specific and numerical words conditions, $p > 0.70$. In a mediation analysis, we tested whether the efficiency factor score mediated the effect of condition (the contrast between the specific and numerical words condition combined, and the general condition) on choice between the young and equal option, but there was no significant indirect effect, $B = 0.02$, 95% CI [−0.04, 0.15].

Participants' numeracy scores were computed as the number of correct answers among the ten items, excluding four participants who did not complete the numeracy scale (M = 7.78, SD = 2.21, N = 297). Contrary to our predicted moderation effect, numeracy did not interact with condition. However, there was a main effect of numeracy on preference: Participants who favored younger patients had higher numeracy ($M = 7.99$, SD = 2.04) than those favoring equality ($M = 7.26$, SD = 2.43), t (276) = 2.49, Cohen's $D = 0.32$, $p = 0.01$.

We conducted a multinomial logistic regression to examine the effect of gender on choice, but gender had no significant main or interaction effect with condition. No analysis on age was conducted, as age information was not available.

Discussion

In addition to replicating the preference shift found in Studies 1–3, Study 4 demonstrated that actual numbers such as "*500 20-year-olds/60-year olds*" led to a greater preference for efficiency, compared to numerical words such as "*a large number of younger/older people*," which still produced a greater preference for efficiency compared to general descriptions of allocation policy without numbers. These findings are consistent with the hypothesis that using more prominent numbers to describe potential recipients in allocation policies increases the preference for efficiency.

The results on agreement to the efficiency/equality statements showed that general vs. specific policy descriptions did not influence participants' opinions on the equality principle. However, descriptions including numbers or numerical words increased endorsement to the efficiency principle compared to general descriptions that lacked numerical information. Although such increased endorsement to efficiency did not mediate the effect of policy description on allocation preference, it indicates that rather than focusing less on equality in the specific condition, participants focused more on efficiency.

The lack of an interaction between numeracy and condition suggests that the effect of numerical presentation can persist across various numeracy levels. The positive correlation between numeracy and efficiency preference, however, may indicate a link between preferring efficiency and general cognitive style.

General Discussion

Real-world resource allocation problems are discussed both in conversations about specific details and in debates over abstract principles. Building on Construal Level Theory (Trope & Liberman, 2010), we have argued that these different levels of abstraction can prompt emphasis on different values and ultimately shift policy preferences. The current studies tested this effect explicitly by describing the same allocation situation either in terms of specific allocation outcomes or in terms of the general allocation principles consistent with such outcomes. The findings across four studies spanning different allocation domains (vaccines and transplant organs) and participant samples (young college students and a more diverse online panel) demonstrate a robust influence of abstraction level on allocation preference. When policies describe specific outcomes, especially with actual numbers, people lean towards medical efficiency—they prioritize recipients who are younger, who have a longer life expectancy, or who have a better prognosis. In contrast, when policies describe general principles of allocation, people gravitate towards equality—they avoid prioritization based on age or life expectancy, or support the first-come, first-served principle.

These findings add significant new insights to our understanding of the malleability of human preferences in resource allocation. Most research on preference reversals in the allocation of scarce medical resources has studied the effect of description valence (Goodwin & Landy, 2014; Kahneman, 2003; Li, Vietri, Galvani & Chapman, 2010). The current research explored abstraction level as a new factor that can systematically shift allocation preference. In addition, previous studies on the preference between efficiency and equality in medical allocation have focused on showing that people assign a nonzero weight to equality, even when equality comes at the cost of efficiency (Ubel et al., 1996; Ubel & Loewenstein, 1996).

Distinct from these studies, the current research went further in exploring how the weight people assign to equality versus efficiency can be malleable depending on the abstraction level of the policies' descriptions, even within the same person.

The current research also has practical implications for multiple domains. First, it raises important questions about the validity of public opinion polls that consistently rely on a particular type of description, such as polls that exclusively use specific age groups to gauge how the public values age in medical allocation (Cropper et al., 1994; Johannesson & Johansson, 1997; Lewis & Charny, 1989; Tsuchiya et al., 2003). Such polls may reflect a biased preference, or at least a preference that does not take into account people's consideration of general allocation principles.

Second, in the public discourse (e.g., communication and discussions in the media) about resource allocation policies, the abstraction level of language can have a powerful influence on people's opinions about the issue at hand. Due to its sheer volume of audience, such media influence may have large effects on public thinking about policy issues and in turn, public voting behavior should such issues become part of political campaigns.

Third, allocation preferences at different levels in the healthcare system may be inconsistent due to the different contexts in which they are constructed. We speculate that healthcare workers in hospitals or transplant centers may discuss allocation policies in a more specific fashion, as they have more exposure to the concrete outcomes of such policies on specific patients; on the other hand, policy makers may discuss the same scenarios using more abstract language involving bioethical principles. If this is true, allocation policies supported by policy makers may meet resistance from practitioners in individual cases partly because of the different contexts in which they form their preferences. More studies are needed to assess the effect of language abstraction on policy decisions across the healthcare system.

Fourth, this research provides some evidence that people may be self-serving in their allocation opinions, favoring recipients whose are to their own. This egocentric tendency in allocation has been demonstrated in previous research (Li et al., 2010). To avoid egocentric biases on part of policy makers, the best solution may be to avoid delegating the duty of policy making to a homogeneous group of policy makers, but instead, sample opinions from a wide range of age groups.

Finally, the current findings may have a wider application in areas outside of medical allocations. For instance, when we discuss tax policy, work compensation, or the allocation of household responsibilities, whether we use abstract principles or concrete examples may also affect how we view these issues. Further studies may extend our findings and explore the real-world impact of description abstraction on preference in a host of societal issues.

To conclude, the evidence presented here informs us that the public's policy preferences are quite malleable and shift systematically depending on the abstraction level of the description. Thus, policy makers need to think hard about which types of policy descriptions will elicit the most accurate depiction of the public's opinion if they are serious about developing policies that reflect those values. Likewise, the public needs to be cognizant of the influence of abstraction level on preference to better evaluate the policies presented to them by different sources (e.g., policy experts, media, persons directly instituting/affected by the policy, etc.). Finally, abstraction level can serve as a powerful piece of decision architecture to help policy makers garner greater public support, as long as such policy reflects prudent considerations of what is best for the public.

Acknowledgement Part of this research was Meng Li's doctoral dissertation. We thank Gretchen Chapman for providing invaluable suggestions on the project and for editing prior versions of this manuscript. Meng Li also thanks Rochel Gelman, Edward J Russo, and Danielle McCarthy for their insightful feedback on the dissertation, and Heidi Nicklaus for collecting data for Study 2. This work was supported by National Science Foundation Grants SES-1061726 and SES-1357170.

References

Agerström, J., & Björklund, F. (2009). Moral concerns are greater for temporally distant events and are moderated by value strength. *Social Cognition, 27*(2), 261–282. doi:10.1521/soco.2009.27.2.261.

Colby, H., DeWitt, J., & Chapman, G. B. (2015). Grouping Promotes Equality: The Effect of Recipient Grouping on Allocation of Limited Medical Resources. Psychological Science. doi: 10.1177/0956797615583978.

Cropper, M. L., Aydede, S. K., & Portney, P. R. (1994). Preferences for life saving programs: How the public discounts time and age. *Journal of Risk and Uncertainty, 8*(3), 243–265. doi:10.1007/BF01064044.

Declaration of Independence. (1776). *Declaration of independence by the representatives of the United States of America*. July 4, 1776.

Eyal, T., Liberman, N., & Trope, Y. (2008). Judging near and distant virtue and vice. *Journal of Experimental Social Psychology, 44*(4), 1204–1209. doi:http://dx.doi.org/10.1016/j.jesp.2008.03.012.

Goldfarb-Rumyantzev, A., Hurdle, J. F., Scandling, J., Wang, Z., Baird, B., Barenbaum, L., & Cheung, A. K. (2005). Duration of end-stage renal disease and kidney transplant outcome. *Nephrology Dialysis Transplantation, 20*(1), 167–175. doi:10.1093/ndt/gfh541.

Gong, H., & Medin, D. L. (2012). Construal levels and moral judgment: Some complications. *Judgment and Decision making, 7*(5), 628–638.

Goodwin, G. P., & Landy, J. F. (2014). Valuing different human lives. *Journal of Experimental Psychology: General, 143*(2), 778–803. doi:10.1037/a0032796.

Greene, J. D. (2001). An fMRI investigation of emotional engagement in moral judgment. *Science, 293*(5537), 2105–2108. doi:10.1126/science.1062872.

Hayes, A. F. (2013). Introduction to mediation, moderation, and conditional process analysis: A regressionbasedapproach. New York: Guilford Press.

Johannesson, M., & Johansson, P. O. (1997). Is the valuation of a QALY gained independent of age? Some empirical evidence. *Journal of Health Economics, 16*(5), 589–599. doi:10.1016/S0167-6296(96)00516-4.

Kahneman, D. (2003). A perspective on judgment and choice: Mapping bounded rationality. *American Psychologist, 58*(9), 697–720. doi:10.1037/0003-066x.58.9.697.

Kennedy, S. E., Mackie, F. E., Rosenberg, A. R., & McDonald, S. P. (2006). Waiting time and outcome of kidney transplantation in adolescents. *Transplantation, 82*(8), 1046–1050. doi:10.1097/01.tp.0000236030.00461.f4.

Lammers, J. (2012). Abstraction increases hypocrisy. *Journal of Experimental Social Psychology, 48*, (2), 475–480. doi:http://dx.doi.org/10.1016/j.jesp.2011.07.006.

Lewis, P. A., & Charny, M. (1989). Which of two individuals do you treat when only their ages are different and you can't treat both? *Journal of Medical Ethics, 15*(1), 28–34. doi:10.1136/jme.15.1.28.

Li, M., Vietri, J., Galvani, A. P., & Chapman, G. B. (2010). How do people value life? *Psychological Science, 21*(2), 163–167. doi:10.1177/0956797609357707.

Lipkus, I. M., Samsa, G., & Rimer, B. K. (2001). General performance on a numeracy scale among highly educated samples. *Medical Decision Making, 21*(1), 37–44. doi:10.1177/0272989x0102100105.

Meier-Kriesche, H.-U., & Kaplan, B. (2002). Waiting time on dialysis as the strongest modifiable risk factor for renal transplant outcomes: A paired donor kidney analysis 1. *Transplantation, 74*(10), 1377–1381. doi:10.1097/01.TP.0000034632.77029.91.

Meier-Kriesche, H.-U., Port, F. K., Ojo, A. O., Rudich, S. M., Hanson, J. A., Cibrik, D. M., Leichtman, A. B., Kaplan, B. (2000). Effect of waiting time on renal transplant outcome. *Kidney International, 58*(3), 1311–1317. doi: http://dx.doi.org/10.1046/j.1523-1755.2000.00287.x .

Norton, M. I., & Ariely, D. (2011). Building a better America—One wealth quintile at a time. *Perspectives on Psychological Science, 6*(1), 9–12. doi:10.1177/1745691610393524.

Organ Procurement and Transplantation Network. (2015). Retrieved March 6, 2015, from http://optn.transplant.hrsa.gov/governance/policies/

Persad, G., Wertheimer, A., & Emanuel, E. J. (2009). Principles for allocation of scarce medical interventions. *The Lancet, 373*(9661), 423–431. doi:10.1016/S0140-6736(09)60137-9.

Pliskin, J. S., Shepard, D. S., & Weinstein, M. C. (1980). Utility functions for life years and health status. *Operations Research, 28*(1), 206–224.

Ratcliffe, J. (2000). Public preferences for the allocation of donor liver grafts for transplantation. *Health Economics, 9*(2), 137–148. doi:10.1002/(sici)1099-1050(200003)9:2<137::aid-hec489>3.0.co;2-1.

Rawls, J. (1999). *A theory of justice*. Oxford: Oxford University Press.

Reyna, V. F., Nelson, W. L., Han, P. K., & Dieckmann, N. F. (2009). How numeracy influences risk comprehension and medical decision making. *Psychological Bulletin, 135*(6), 943–973. doi:10.1037/a0017327.

Rutecki, G. W., & Kilner, J. F. (1999). Dialysis as a resource allocation paradigm: Confronting tragic choices once again? *Seminars in Dialysis, 12*, 38–43.

Slovic, P. (1995). The construction of preference. *American Psychologist, 50*(5), 364–371. doi:10.1037/0003-066x.50.5.364.

Tetlock, P. E., Kristel, O. V., Elson, S. B., Green, M. C., & Lerner, J. S. (2000). The psychology of the unthinkable: Taboo trade-offs, forbidden base rates, and heretical counterfactuals. *Journal of Personality and Social Psychology, 78*(5), 853–870. doi:10.1037//0022-3514.78.5.853.

Tong, A., Howard, K., Jan, S., Cass, A., Rose, J., Chadban, S., … Craig, J. C. (2010). Community preferences for the allocation of solid organs for transplantation: A systematic review. *Transplantation, 89*(7), 796–805. doi:10.1097/TP.0b013e3181cf1ee1

Trope, Y., & Liberman, N. (2010). Construal-level theory of psychological distance. *Psychological Review, 117*(2), 440–463. doi:10.1037/a0018963.

Tsuchiya, A., Dolan, P., & Shaw, R. (2003). Measuring people's preferences regarding ageism in health: Some methodological issues and some fresh evidence. *Social Science & Medicine, 57*(4), 687–696. doi:10.1016/S0277-9536(02)00418-5.

Ubel, P. A., Baron, J., & Asch, D. A. (2001). Preference for equity as a framing effect. *Medical Decision Making, 21*(3), 180–189. doi:10.1177/0272989x0102100303.

Ubel, P. A., DeKay, M. L., Baron, J., & Asch, D. A. (1996). Cost effectiveness analysis in a setting of budget constraints: Is it equitable? *New England Journal of Medicine, 334*, 1174–1177. doi:10.1056/NEJM199605023341807.

Ubel, P. A., & Loewenstein, G. (1996). Distributing scarce livers: The moral reasoning of the general public. *Social Science & Medicine, 42*(7), 1049–1055. doi:10.1016/0277-9536(95)00216-2.

Vallacher, R. R., & Wegner, D. M. (1987). What do people think they're doing? Action identification and human behavior. *Psychological Review, 94*(1), 3–15. doi:10.1037/0033-295X.94.1.3.
Williams, A. (1997). Intergenerational equity: an exploration of the'fair innings' argument. Health Economics, 6(2), 117-132. doi: 10.1002/(SICI)1099-1050(199703)6:2 117::AID-HEC256>3.0.CO;2-B.
Zezelj, I. L., & Jokic, B. R. (2014). Replication of experiments evaluating impact of psychological distance on moral judgment. *Social Psychology, 45*(3), 223–231.

Chapter 6
Resource Allocation Decisions: When Do We Sacrifice Efficiency in the Name of Equity?

Tom Gordon-Hecker, Shoham Choshen-Hillel, Shaul Shalvi, and Yoella Bereby-Meyer

In 1975, Arthur M. Okun introduced the concept of equity–efficiency trade-offs. In his seminal book on the trade-off, he described it as "… our biggest socioeconomic tradeoff, and it plagues us in dozens of dimensions of social policy. We can't have our cake of market efficiency and share it equally" (Okun, 1975, p. 2). This idea does indeed seem to be a focal point of many economic and pseudo-economic decisions: Employers need to decide how to distribute an increase in the company's profits in a way that will be fair on one hand, but maximize the benefit for the company on the other hand; parents sometimes need to decide what to do with a single toy or candy if they have more than one child; politicians and policy makers need to decide on a taxation policy that transfers money from the rich to the less fortunate, while maintaining economic growth and the market's efficiency. Since Okun's seminal work, equity–efficiency trade-offs have been the subject of numerous studies. Social scientists from the fields of economics, psychology, public policy and management have studied from different perspectives the essential fact that society's strive for maximizing resources may, at times, increase the differences between people's payoffs.

Individuals must trade off equity and efficiency in a wide range of contexts as well—from constructing their views on public policy matters (Mitchell, Tetlock, Newman, & Lerner, 2003) to making trade-offs themselves in interpersonal

T. Gordon-Hecker (✉) • Y. Bereby-Meyer
Psychology Department, Ben-Gurion University of the Negev, Beer Sheva, Israel
e-mail: tomgo@post.bgu.ac.il; yoella@bgu.ac.il

S. Choshen-Hillel
Jerusalem School of Business Administration and the Federmann Center for the Study of Rationality, The Hebrew University of Jerusalem, Jerusalem, Israel
e-mail: shoham@huji.ac.il

S. Shalvi
Department of Economics, Center for Research in Experimental Economics and Political Decision Making (CREED), University of Amsterdam, Amsterdam, Netherlands
e-mail: s.shalvi@uva.nl

M. Li, D.P. Tracer (eds.), *Interdisciplinary Perspectives on Fairness, Equity, and Justice*, DOI 10.1007/978-3-319-58993-0_6

contexts (Messick, 1995; Shaw, 2013). Consider, for example, a parent who has twins—and only one ticket to a movie, to which all other tickets have been sold out. The parent can either give the ticket to one of the children, thereby creating inequity, or not give it to any of them—thus wasting the movie ticket but preserving equity. What would people do in such cases? And what factors influence their decision? In this chapter, we review recent research examining people's decisions in situations where preference for efficiency means deviating from equity, and the factors affecting such decisions. We start by reviewing some literature suggesting that people often reject inequity, regardless of efficiency considerations. We then review the literature for situations in which a conflict exists between equity and efficiency, and differentiate between situations where the allocator is monetarily affected by the allocation and situations where she is allocating the resource as a third party. We end by adding another refinement, differentiating between situations in which the allocation decision is made publicly and situations in which it is made privately.

On Equity

Equity is one of the most fundamental principles for resource allocation (Adams, 1965). According to equity theory, people pursue equitable situations in which the input/output ratio is constant for all members of society. That is, people prefer a state in which equal work results in equal pay (and unequal work results in unequal pay) and the greater the deviation from this state, the more they feel distressed (Walster, Berscheid, & Walster, 1973). Note that equity, equal pay for equal work, differs from mere equality, defined as equal pay regardless of the work invested (Mannix, Neale, & Northcraft, 1995). Although the two concepts often converge, this is not necessarily the case. For example, paying two equally deserving employees the same salary is both equitable and equal. Yet paying a person who puts in more time and effort a higher salary than his colleague who did not work as hard is equitable but not equal. Equity, more so than equality, is considered to be a fair allocation (Bar-Hillel & Yaari, 1993; Shaw & Olson, 2012).

Numerous studies show that people tend to display *inequity aversion*—they are averse to outcomes that deviate from equity, whether that inequity is advantageous or disadvantageous for them (Bolton & Ockenfels, 2000; Fehr & Schmidt, 1999; Loewenstein, Thompson, & Bazerman, 1989).

When allocating resources, people try a great deal to avoid allocations that deviate from equity, even when their own self-interest is pitted against equity. In the well-known dictator game, a participant receives a certain monetary endowment and needs to decide how to allocate this endowment between herself and another participant (Forsythe, Horowitz, Savin, & Sefton, 1994). The allocator receives no information regarding the relative contribution compared to his own, thus there is no reason for him to assume he deserves a greater payoff than the other participant does. Importantly, the decision is completely up to the allocator, and the other participant cannot reject it or retaliate in any way. Studies show that although there is no rational reason for the allocator to transfer any money to the other participant, allocators tend to transfer some money, thereby creating allocations that are more equitable than keeping all the money to themselves. A recent meta-analysis shows that on average, across many treatments and manipulations, people transfer 28.3% of the endowment to the other participant (Engel, 2011). Such decisions seem to be driven by concern with fairness, as they minimize the gap between the allocator and the recipient's final payoffs (at the allocator's own expense). Furthermore, it is difficult to explain this fair behavior by reputation considerations, since some of these findings were found in a double-blind design, where the experimenter cannot learn the allocator's decision, which did not reduce participants' transfers (Engel, 2011).

The willingness to forfeit some monetary payoff to maintain equity develops with age (Bereby-Meyer & Fiks, 2013; Fehr, Bernhard, & Rockenbach, 2008). Around the age of 6, children become more likely to throw away resources to maintain equity—even if these resources are their own (Shaw & Olson, 2012). Interestingly, older children (over the age of 6) are less likely to create inequity that is advantageous for them (i.e., they are willing to forfeit some of their own resources to maintain equity) and other unfair forms of inequity compared to their younger counterparts. However, they are actually more likely to create disadvantageous inequity, in which they receive less than their counterpart does, in order to promote other goals, such as maximizing efficiency (Shaw, Choshen-Hillel, & Caruso, 2016). Additionally, 8-year-old children tend to reject allocations that create inequity between themselves and another child, even if this means they will both get nothing (Blake & McAuliffe, 2011), and by the age of 9 they also feel good about equitable decisions (Kogut, 2012). When equitable allocation is not costly, children as young as 4 years old prefer equitable allocations over inequitable ones, even when the other recipient is a complete stranger (Moore, 2009).

The preference for equity seems to stem from basic, automatic mechanisms—people's attention is automatically drawn towards equal allocations (Halevy & Chou, 2014), and when put under cognitive load, participants are more willing to forfeit some of their own payoff in order to reduce inequity between themselves and another person (Schulz, Fischbacher, Thöni, & Utikal, 2014). As such a basic tendency, it comes as no surprise that the preference for equity is not rare. A meta-analysis suggests that approximately half of the population show prosocial preferences (Balliet, Parks, & Joireman, 2009), i.e., preferences for an allocation that maintains equity between the self and another person over allocations that are advantageous to the self but harm the other (Van Lange, 1999; Van Lange, De Bruin, Otten, & Joireman, 1997).

People exhibit inequity aversion even in situations where they themselves are not affected by the allocation. Sixteen-month-old toddlers seem to favor an agent that allocates resources equally among other actors over an agent who allocates them unequally (Geraci & Surian, 2011). The willingness to forgo resources in order to maintain equity develops around the age of 6–8 (Blake & McAuliffe, 2011; Shaw & Olson, 2012). Adults too tend to prefer equitable allocations among others (Engelmann & Strobel, 2004). People want to live in an equitable society (Norton & Ariely, 2011), and prefer that those who put the same amount of effort receive the same payoff (Cook & Hegtvedt, 1983). When they are responsible to allocating resources, people are also sensitive to the effort invested, and tend to reward more those who put more efforts, finding equity to be fairer than equality (Leventhal & Michaels, 1971). In health policy, for example, equity plays a major role in resource allocation of central budget to healthcare providers (Sheldon & Smith, 2000).

To summarize this section, we refer to the work of David Messick (1993), who describes the preference for equality as a "decision heuristic," making it the dominant option in many allocation dilemmas. Since the difference between equity and equality is based on recipients' contributions, when the contributions are the same, equality coincides with equity. Hence, one can conclude that when no recipient is more deserving than the other, people pursue equity automatically, and use it as a simple guideline in resource allocation dilemmas. This is true both when the allocator is affected by her decision and when she is simply asked to be the allocator of resources among other individuals.

Equity–Efficiency Conflict

Whereas most people generally prefer to promote equity in resource allocation, they may have to reconsider it, at times, when equity comes at the expense of efficiency. Here we use the term efficiency as surplus maximization (Engelmann & Strobel, 2004). A person who is motivated by efficiency considerations values the total monetary payoff for the group positively in his or her utility function. Take, for instance, taxation policy. Whereas a progressive taxation system might be a good way to reduce income inequality, it is often described as inefficient (Ballard, 1988; Browning & Johnson, 1984; Greenwald & Stiglitz, 1986). According to Okun (1975), a transfer of money from the rich to the poor through progressive taxation is done in a metaphorical "leaking bucket"—during the transfer, some money is inevitably lost. The question policy makers must face, then, is how much waste (if any) they are willing to accept in order to maintain equity. The answer to this question, according to Okun, "…cannot be right or wrong- any more than your favorite ice-cream flavor is right or wrong" (p. 92). How do individual decision makers approach equivalent dilemmas? Do they lean towards equity or efficiency? And what factors might affect their preference?

We start by differentiating between two types of situations in which such dilemmas might arise—one is a situation in which the allocator is monetarily affected by his decision, and the other in which he is not, i.e., he is a third party. Those two situations might differ vastly in the psychological mechanisms involved. Whereas in situations where the allocator is monetarily affected, considerations of self-interest, social comparison, and envy might come into play, those considerations are irrelevant when the allocator is not monetarily affected by his or her decision. Studies that examined such situations tried to tap into purer aspects of the decision regarding the equity–efficiency trade-off, by removing considerations of social comparison and own payoff maximization. Despite the fact that both lines of research often report similar results, we follow this distinction throughout the chapter, since they involve potentially different psychological mechanisms. When a person is a third party thinking about equity, she is mainly concerned about pure fairness. Yet when a person is involved in the allocation herself, she might be driven by other motivations, such as self-interest and social comparison.

Consider first people's equity–efficiency trade-offs, where the allocator is a part of the allocation (i.e., he or she is monetarily affected by the allocation). A common finding is that in such situations people tend to prefer income distributions that preserve equity, at the expense of efficiency. In other words, people prefer that each individual will receive the same outcome, even if this means shrinking the pie, and even if that shrinkage comes out of their own pocket. For example, participants were willing to pay out of their own pocket in order to restore equity by destroying resources that were unjustifiably held by others, and thus deviated from equity (Dawes, Fowler, Johnson, McElreath, & Smirnov, 2007). The same willingness to destroy one's own resources, in order to maintain equity, is observable in children as young as 6–8. When asked to react to a suggested allocation of goods between themselves and another child, 8-year-old children were willing to reject unfair allocations and not allocate any candies, even when the inequity was advantageous for them (i.e., they received more candies than the other child; Blake & McAuliffe, 2011; Shaw et al., 2016; Shaw & Olson, 2012).

Nevertheless, it has been shown that allocators, who are monetarily affected by their own decisions, are sometimes willing to deviate from equity in a bid for greater efficiency (Charness & Rabin, 2002; Engelmann & Strobel, 2004). Bar-Hillel and Yaari (1993) showed that when maintaining equity results in a vast waste of resources, people opt for inequity.

Furthermore, it seems that the preference for equity over efficiency and vice versa is sensitive to situational factors. Choshen-Hillel and Yaniv (2011, 2012) have suggested that the preference for equity over efficiency is affected by the allocator's degree of agency—the allocator's feeling of control over the resource allocation process. Participants in these studies were more likely to prefer an allocation that maximized total welfare, yet was inequitable, when they were agentic (could determine the payoff) compared to when they were not (could merely judge the payoff and could not affect it). Framing can also play an important role in constructing people's preferences, as people tend to have stronger reactions to inequity when they allocate burdens rather than gains (Griffith & Sell, 1988; Northcraft, Neale, Tenbrunsel, & Thomas, 1996).

A second line of research on the equity–efficiency conflict deals with situations in which the allocator is a third party, i.e., he or she is not one of the recipients. Such allocations are common in the context of policymaking, such as vaccination policies, budget allocation, and taxation policy. By and large, third-party allocators tend to prefer equity to efficiency just like those who are affected by the allocation do. When constructing an ideal hypothetical society, participants chose governmental plans that create a society where no one falls below the poverty line, even if it meant reducing the mean income of the entire population (Mitchell, Tetlock, Mellers, & Ordonez, 1993). Just like allocators who are a part of the allocation, third-party allocators are also susceptible to the effects of framing. For example, when vaccination policies are presented in terms of lives lost, people prefer vaccination policies that benefit younger people over older people, even when their expected years remained to live is held constant. Such preference reflects a "fair" allocation, as it reflects a desire to allow a younger person to live and experience life to the same extent his older counterpart had lived. However, when vaccination policies are presented in terms of lives saved, they prefer policies that prioritize people with more expected years to live (Li, Vietri, Galvani, & Chapman, 2010). This may be seen as a preference for efficiency. On that note, it is interesting to state that the American organ donations system has shifted from equity-driven considerations (i.e., giving priority to those who waited longer for a transplant) to efficiency-driven considerations (i.e., giving priority to those who have a higher probability for a successful transplant) (Elster, 1993).

Interestingly, the reference point plays a major role in the willingness to accept inequity. People were more tolerant towards inequity when it was the initial state, compared to when resources were distributed by the allocator inequitably between formerly equal recipients (Mitchell et al., 2003). Indeed, when asked to allocate a resource between two equally deserving recipients, children (Shaw & Olson, 2012), as well as adults (Choshen-Hillel, Shaw, & Caruso, 2015; Gordon-Hecker, Rosensaft-Eshel, Pittarello, Shalvi, & Bereby-Meyer, 2017; Shaw & Knobe, 2013), were willing to throw a resource (be it a chocolate bar, a monetary reward, or a rock concert ticket) in the trash rather than allocate it unequally. However, they did not wish to throw it away, when its allocation restored equity (Shaw & Olson, 2012).

A neuroimaging study has suggested that the tendency to prefer equity over efficiency in situations where they are at conflict is driven by the emotional system that encodes equity, overriding the rational system that encodes efficiency (Hsu, Anen, & Quartz, 2008). In this study, participants read a hypothetical scenario in which they were asked to reduce the amount of meals donated to children in an orphanage. They were asked to decide whether to take more meals, but from more children, so the children are treated more equally but more meals are taken away in total, or to take away less meals, but they will all be taken from one kid. Results showed that the putamen, an area associated with cognition, was correlated with efficiency, whereas the insula, which is associated with emotions, was correlated with equity, thus supporting the hypothesis that preference for equity stems from the emotional system. This is consistent with other brain studies, associating preference for equity with emotional areas such as the anterior insula (Sanfey, Rilling, Aronson, Nystrom, & Cohen, 2003; Zaki & Mitchell, 2013) and the amygdala (Gospic et al., 2011).

Although destroying resources to maintain equity may seem weird or even illogical, we have reviewed repeated evidence that people do indeed engage in such behavior. Why do people prefer to destroy resources rather than create inequity? Several lines of research propose theoretical accounts to explain this phenomenon. In the following section, we review the literature on the mechanisms underlying people's preference for equity over efficiency. We begin by examining situations in which the allocator's identity is known, and therefore considerations of self-image are expected to be taken into account. Next, we consider situations in which the allocator is anonymous, and therefore his or her decision should be affected mainly by internal psychological mechanisms.

Consider first the concept of self-image. In August 2008, Armin Heinrich released an iPhone application called "I am rich." The application does nothing but displaying a glowing red diamond on the screen, and comes with a price tag of $999.99. Why would anyone ever purchase such an application? The app's official description reads "The red icon on your iPhone or iPod Touch always reminds you (and others when you show it to them) that you were able to afford this." Clearly, people care about their public image and wish to maintain it to present themselves as good, compatible, or in other ways that can serve their interests (Baumeister, 1998; Goffman, 1959). Indeed, many people do so by signaling their wealth through purchasing luxurious products (Bagwell & Bernheim, 1996). However, people can maintain and improve their public image also by behaving in certain ways. It has been argued that people conform to social norms because behaving in a way that contradicts the social norm reflects an unusual, unappreciated disposition (Bernheim, 1994), and behaving according to social norms helps to maintain and form social relationships (Cialdini & Trost, 1998). One norm people conform to is the equal sharing—"50–50 norm." In one experiment, when participants played a dictator game, most of the participants split the endowment equally when it was certain that their decision would be implemented as is. However, if there was a chance that a different, unequal split will be enforced instead of their own split, participants tended to split the resources unequally (and in the same form of inequity as the forced split), arguably because the unfairness cannot be traced back to their decision. Hence, the researchers conclude that people tend to split resources equally not necessarily because they prefer equity, but because they want to *appear* fair (Andreoni & Bernheim, 2009).

Traditional research on inequity aversion implies that the reason people prefer equity over efficiency is that they find inequity inherently unfair. Since they care deeply about fairness, they try to preserve equity even if this means they must waste resources (Adams, 1965; Fehr & Schmidt, 1999). Choshen-Hillel et al. (2015), however, argued that the reason people waste in the name of equity is not that they worry about inequity per se, but that they worry about the partiality that inequitable allocations entail. According to the *partiality aversion* explanation, people waste resources to maintain equity mainly because they worry about the social signals associated with inequitable allocations, signals of unfair favoritism to one party or another. Indeed, people are unwilling to appear as if they favor one person over another, if both parties are equally deserving (Shaw, 2013). Consistent with this explanation, it has been shown that when inequitable allocations do not signal favoritism (such as when one places someone else in a better position than oneself), people actually favor efficiency over equity (Choshen-Hillel et al., 2015; Shaw et al., 2016). The partiality aversion account emphasizes the importance of public appearances. As mentioned by Shaw (2013), reputation considerations are the main factor that drives fair behavior, as "fairness functions as a way to signal impartiality to others, in order to avoid third-party condemnation" (p. 415). This, however, does not exclude the possibility that people also internalized the desire to act impartially.

Indeed, it has been found that participants display partiality aversion also in private, anonymous settings (Choshen-Hillel et al., 2015).

Although partiality aversion deals mainly with a desire to appear partial, Choshen-Hillel et al. (2015) also provided some evidence that people might prefer equity to efficiency under anonymous setting. Consider, for example, a contest in which contestants do not know each other, and do not know their ranks and relative performance either (because they are evaluated by an external referee). Further imagine that two contestants end up at the first place and are equally deserving of winning. Since only a single award was purchased, the contest organizer must decide whether to announce one of them as the winner, or announce no winner. Clearly, considerations of reputation should not play a role, since the contestants are not aware of the fact they ended up with similar rankings and no one would feel as if she was treated impartially if one person is crowned winner. Will, in such situations, people find no difficulty in violating equity and allocating the reward to one of the contestants? Empirical evidence to date is scarce to address these questions.

Work in related fields revealed that people wish to maintain a moral, honest and fair self-concept (Mazar, Amir, & Ariely, 2008), and therefore avoid major moral transgressions. Indeed, many studies have found that people do indeed lie, but they tend not to lie to the full extent, but to some extent that will allow them to secure a higher profit but still perceive themselves as moral beings (Fischbacher & Föllmi-Heusi, 2013; Shalvi, Dana, Handgraaf, & De Dreu, 2011). Accordingly, just as people internalize the desire to be somewhat honest, they also internalize the desire to be fair (Rustichini & Villeval, 2014) and avoid inequitable allocations even in private settings.

Indeed, when people are called upon to violate equity among others, they prefer to avoid making a decision altogether and prefer that someone else would make the decision, even if the recipients of the inequitable allocation will not know who made the decision. Beattie, Baron, Hershey, and Spranca (1994) have asked participants to imagine they were the trustee of their sister's estate and that her only valuable possession is an antique piano that can be given to one of her two children. The researchers show that participants wish to avoid choosing one of the two children, whether the recipients are aware of the identity of the decision maker or not. That is, people wish to refrain from deciding on how to implement inequity, even if it is not their own reputation at stakes.

People are also less worried about inequity when the allocator's sense of responsibility is reduced. For example, people are more likely to accept unfair offers in the Ultimatum Bargaining Game that are generated by a random device compared to a person (Blount, 1995). This is because the allocator has no intention to be unfair and is not responsible for the inequitable outcome (Lagnado & Channon, 2008). Similarly, when forced to allocate resources between themselves and an equally deserving other, people tend to prefer a random device to determine the allocation than deciding on the allocation themselves (Kimbrough, Sheremeta, & Shields, 2014; Shaw & Olson, 2014). Presumably, allocation of a reward to one of two equally deserving recipients, the allocator knows nothing about, is just as random as using a random device (preferring participant number 1734 over participant number 5672 is just as random as deciding that participant 1734 corresponds with "heads" in a coin flip). However, not using a random device also bears a sensation of personal responsibility—the allocator must personally decide if she prefers participant number 1734 or participant number 5672.

Recently, Gordon-Hecker and colleagues (2017) have shown that people are indeed inequity *responsibility* averse. That is, the reason why people are willing to destroy a resource is to avoid the personal responsibility of determining which of two equally deserving recipients should receive it, and not necessarily to avoid inequity in itself. The researchers have presented participants, in a strictly anonymous setting, with three decision alternatives. They could either allocate a resource to one of two equally deserving recipients, allocate it to the other recipient, or discard the resource altogether. The researchers found that many participants preferred to discard the resource rather than implement inequity. However, when allocators received the option of allocating the resource using a random device, discarding rates dropped drastically.

In one experiment, the researchers had participants serve as referees in a Trivia contest between two other participants. They graded the Trivia contest and were given a coupon for coffee and pastry and asked to give it to a recipient of their choice, or to discard it. Equity was manipulated, such that allocation of the reward could either result in inequity (i.e., the recipients did similarly well on the Trivia but only one of them got the reward) or in equity (i.e., participants performed differently on the contest and accordingly got the reward). The researchers found that participants were indeed inequity responsibility averse—when allocation resulted in equity, all participants allocated the reward to the more deserving recipient (the winner). However, when both recipients performed equally well, more than half of the participants preferred to discard the reward rather than choose which of the two recipients should receive it. Nonetheless, introducing a random envelope, that could have been used to allocate the reward randomly to one of the two, reduced discarding rates to zero. Since no information was given regarding the recipients other than their participant numbers, one can conclude that a decision between one of the two is just as random as a coin flip. Therefore, objectively, in both conditions the allocation was random, and none of them violated the principles of distributive justice (both recipients have an equal probability of getting the reward both when the allocation is decided upon randomly and when an anonymous allocator chooses one of the two without any information regarding their identity). However, personally implementing inequity bears a sensation of responsibility, and this, the authors claim, is what drives people to discard the reward altogether (Gordon-Hecker et al., 2017).

Conclusion

The world we live in is vastly inequitable, and most people believe equity is a value worth pursuing (Norton & Ariely, 2011). To complicate things further, equity at times comes at the expense of efficiency. In the current chapter, we reviewed studies that investigate people's approach to this conflict.

Throughout this chapter, we reviewed research that shows that people display inequity aversion and tend to resist allocations where one gets more than one's fair share. People refute inequity both when they are affected by their decisions and thus might be susceptible to effects of self-interest or envy, and when they are merely allocating between others, where only fairness considerations should be relevant for the decision. Next, we showed that when equity is pitted against efficiency, many people would still prefer wasteful, yet equitable allocation (even though, they might also sometimes opt for efficiency). We discussed important factors influencing the trade-off people make, mainly anonymity and framing. Lastly, we reviewed recent literature that elaborates on the concept of inequity and suggests that the role the allocator plays in implementing the inequity serves as a moderator for the preference for equity over efficiency. We suggest that what people see when deliberating between equity and efficiency is not the mere concept of equity, but rather other refinements of this concept, namely partiality and responsibility. We suggest that what people are averse to is not an inequity of outcomes, but rather the social signals associated with inequity. Furthermore, this aversion is internalized, and people try a great deal to avoid it even if the signals would never be observed by anyone other than themselves. Thus, when an allocation favors one person over another, people would be willing to go as far as destroying a resource in order to avoid the decision, be it a private or public decision. However, if that inequity can be created without favoring one person over the other, using procedures such as a random allocation or disadvantaging the self, then people are much more willing to accept such inequity.

The concepts of partiality and responsibility complement each other to provide a comprehensive framework that enables researchers to make clear predictions in different environmental settings (i.e., shared knowledge, anonymity). For example, whereas people wish to avoid both responsibility for implementing inequity and appearing partial, it seems as if what they are most concerned about is being responsible for partial allocations. Yet this prediction deserves further investigation.

Further experiments should test such predictions that will corroborate and extend the discussed concepts, in order to shed more light on the determinants underlying allocators' decisions. We believe that such experiments will help design environments that allow an optimal allocation of resources, with the goal of increasing both equity and efficiency in the world.

References

Adams, J. S. (1965). Inequity in social exchange. In L. Berkowitz (Ed.), *Advances in experimental social psychology* (Vol. 2, pp. 267–299). New York, NY: Academic Press.

Andreoni, J., & Bernheim, B. D. (2009). Social image and the 50–50 norm: A theoretical and experimental analysis of audience effects. *Econometrica, 77*(5), 1607–1636.

Bagwell, L. S., & Bernheim, B. D. (1996). Veblen effects in a theory of conspicuous consumption. *The American Economic Review, 86*(3), 349–373.

Ballard, C. L. (1988). The marginal efficiency cost of redistribution. *The American Economic Review, 78*(5), 1019–1033.
Balliet, D., Parks, C., & Joireman, J. (2009). Social value orientation and cooperation in social dilemmas: A meta-analysis. *Group Processes & Intergroup Relations, 12*(4), 533–547.
Bar-Hillel, M., & Yaari, M. (1993). Judgments of distributive justice. In B. A. Mellers & J. Baron (Eds.), *Psychological perspectives on justice: Theory and applications* (pp. 56–84). New York, NY: Cambridge University Press.
Baumeister, R. (1998). The self. In D. T. Gilbert, S. T. Fiske, & G. Lindzey (Eds.), *The handbook of social psychology* (Vol. 1, 4th ed., pp. 680–740). Boston, MA: McGraw-Hill.
Beattie, J., Baron, J., Hershey, J. C., & Spranca, M. D. (1994). Psychological determinants of decision attitude. *Journal of Behavioral Decision Making, 7*(2), 129–144.
Bereby-Meyer, Y., & Fiks, S. (2013). Changes in negative reciprocity as a function of age. *Journal of Behavioral Decision Making, 26*(4), 397–403.
Bernheim, B. D. (1994). A theory of conformity. *Journal of Political Economy, 102*(5), 841–877.
Blake, P. R., & McAuliffe, K. (2011). "I had so much it didn't seem fair": Eight-year-olds reject two forms of inequity. *Cognition, 120*(2), 215–224.
Blount, S. (1995). When social outcomes aren't fair: The effect of causal attributions on preferences. *Organizational Behavior and Human Decision Processes, 63*(2), 131–144.
Bolton, G. E., & Ockenfels, A. (2000). ERC: A theory of equity, reciprocity, and competition. *American Economic Review, 90*(1), 166–193.
Browning, E. K., & Johnson, W. R. (1984). The trade-off between equality and efficiency. *The Journal of Political Economy, 92*(2), 175–203.
Charness, G., & Rabin, M. (2002). Understanding social preferences with simple tests. *Quarterly Journal of Economics, 117*(3), 817–869.
Choshen-Hillel, S., Shaw, A., & Caruso, E. M. (2015). Waste management: How reducing partiality can promote efficient resource allocation. *Journal of Personality and Social Psychology, 109*(2), 210–231.
Choshen-Hillel, S., & Yaniv, I. (2011). Agency and the construction of social preference: Between inequality aversion and prosocial behavior. *Journal of Personality and Social Psychology, 101*(6), 1253–1261.
Choshen-Hillel, S., & Yaniv, I. (2012). Social preferences shaped by conflicting motives: When enhancing social welfare creates unfavorable comparisons for the self. *Judgment and Decision making, 7*(5), 618–627.
Cialdini, R. B., & Trost, M. R. (1998). Social influence: Social norms, conformity, and compliance. In D. T. Gilbert, S. T. Fiske, & G. Lindzey (Eds.), *The handbook of social psychology* (Vol. 2, 4th ed., pp. 151–192). Boston, MA: McGraw-Hill.
Cook, K. S., & Hegtvedt, K. A. (1983). Distributive justice, equity, and equality. *Annual Review of Sociology, 9*, 217–241.
Dawes, C. T., Fowler, J. H., Johnson, T., McElreath, R., & Smirnov, O. (2007). Egalitarian motives in humans. *Nature, 446*(7137), 794–796.
Elster, J. (1993). Justice and the allocation of scarce resources. In B. A. Mellers & J. Baron (Eds.), *Psychological perspectives on justice: Theory and applications* (pp. 56–84). New York, NY: Cambridge University Press.
Engel, C. (2011). Dictator games: A meta study. *Experimental Economics, 14*(4), 583–610.
Engelmann, D., & Strobel, M. (2004). Inequality aversion, efficiency, and maximin preferences in simple distribution experiments. *American Economic Review, 94*(4), 857–869.
Fehr, E., Bernhard, H., & Rockenbach, B. (2008). Egalitarianism in young children. *Nature, 454*(7208), 1079–1083.
Fehr, E., & Schmidt, K. M. (1999). A theory of fairness, competition, and cooperation. *Quarterly Journal of Economics, 114*(3), 817–868.
Fischbacher, U., & Föllmi-Heusi, F. (2013). Lies in disguise—An experimental study on cheating. *Journal of the European Economic Association, 11*(3), 525–547.

Forsythe, R., Horowitz, J. L., Savin, N. E., & Sefton, M. (1994). Fairness in simple bargaining experiments. *Games and Economic Behavior, 6*(3), 347–369.
Geraci, A., & Surian, L. (2011). The developmental roots of fairness: Infants' reactions to equal and unequal distributions of resources. *Developmental Science, 14*(5), 1012–1020.
Goffman, E. (1959). *The presentation of self in everyday life*. Garden City, NY: Double Day.
Gordon-Hecker, T., Rosensaft-Eshel, D., Pittarello, A., Shalvi, S., & Bereby-Meyer, Y. (2017). Not taking responsibility: Equity trumps efficiency in allocation decisions. *Journal of Experimental Psychology: General, 146*(6), 771–775.
Gospic, K., Mohlin, E., Fransson, P., Petrovic, P., Johannesson, M., & Ingvar, M. (2011). Limbic justice—Amygdala involvement in immediate rejection in the ultimatum game. *PLoS Biology, 9*(5), e1001054.
Greenwald, B. C., & Stiglitz, J. E. (1986). Externalities in economies with imperfect information and incomplete markets. *The Quarterly Journal of Economics, 101*(2), 229–264.
Griffith, W. I., & Sell, J. (1988). The effects of competition on allocators' preferences for contributive and retributive justice rules. *European Journal of Social Psychology, 18*(5), 443–455.
Halevy, N., & Chou, E. Y. (2014). How decisions happen: Focal points and blind spots in interdependent decision making. *Journal of Personality and Social Psychology, 106*(3), 398–417.
Hsu, M., Anen, C., & Quartz, S. R. (2008). The right and the good: Distributive justice and neural encoding of equity and efficiency. *Science, 320*(5879), 1092–1095.
Kimbrough, E. O., Sheremeta, R. M., & Shields, T. W. (2014). When parity promotes peace: Resolving conflict between asymmetric agents. *Journal of Economic Behavior & Organization, 99*, 96–108.
Kogut, T. (2012). Knowing what I should, doing what I want: From selfishness to inequity aversion in young children's sharing behavior. *Journal of Economic Psychology, 33*(1), 226–236.
Lagnado, D. A., & Channon, S. (2008). Judgments of cause and blame: The influence of intentionality and foreseeability. *Cognition, 108*(3), 754–770.
Leventhal, G. S., & Michaels, J. W. (1971). Locus of cause and equity motivation as determinants of reward allocation. *Journal of Personality and Social Psychology, 17*(3), 229–235.
Li, M., Vietri, J., Galvani, A. P., & Chapman, G. B. (2010). How do people value life? *Psychological Science, 21*(2), 163–167.
Loewenstein, G. F., Thompson, L., & Bazerman, M. H. (1989). Social utility and decision making in interpersonal contexts. *Journal of Personality and Social Psychology, 57*(3), 426–441.
Mannix, E. A., Neale, M. A., & Northcraft, G. B. (1995). Equity, equality, or need? The effects of organizational culture on the allocation of benefits and burdens. *Organizational Behavior and Human Decision Processes, 63*(3), 276–286.
Mazar, N., Amir, O., & Ariely, D. (2008). The dishonesty of honest people: A theory of self-concept maintenance. *Journal of Marketing Research, 45*(6), 633–644.
Messick, D. M. (1993). Equality as a decision heuristic. In B. A. Mellers & J. Baron (Eds.), *Psychological perspectives on justice: Theory and applications* (pp. 11–31). New York, NY: Cambridge University Press.
Messick, D. M. (1995). Equality, fairness, and social conflict. *Social Justice Research, 8*(2), 153–173.
Mitchell, G., Tetlock, P. E., Mellers, B. A., & Ordonez, L. D. (1993). Judgments of social justice: Compromises between equality and efficiency. *Journal of Personality and Social Psychology, 65*(4), 629–639.
Mitchell, G., Tetlock, P. E., Newman, D. G., & Lerner, J. S. (2003). Experiments behind the veil: Structural influences on judgments of social justice. *Political Psychology, 24*(3), 519–547.
Moore, C. (2009). Fairness in children's resource allocation depends on the recipient. *Psychological Science, 20*(8), 944–948.
Northcraft, G. B., Neale, M. A., Tenbrunsel, A., & Thomas, M. (1996). Benefits and burdens: Does it really matter what we allocate? *Social Justice Research, 9*(1), 27–45.
Norton, M. I., & Ariely, D. (2011). Building a better America—One wealth quintile at a time. *Perspectives on Psychological Science, 6*(1), 9–12.

Okun, A. M. (1975). *Equality and efficiency: The big tradeoff*. Washington, DC: Brookings Institution Press.
Rustichini, A., & Villeval, M. C. (2014). Moral hypocrisy, power and social preferences. *Journal of Economic Behavior & Organization, 107*, 10–24.
Sanfey, A. G., Rilling, J. K., Aronson, J. A., Nystrom, L. E., & Cohen, J. D. (2003). The neural basis of economic decision-making in the ultimatum game. *Science, 300*(5626), 1755–1758.
Schulz, J. F., Fischbacher, U., Thöni, C., & Utikal, V. (2014). Affect and fairness: Dictator games under cognitive load. *Journal of Economic Psychology, 41*, 77–87.
Shalvi, S., Dana, J., Handgraaf, M. J., & De Dreu, C. K. (2011). Justified ethicality: Observing desired counterfactuals modifies ethical perceptions and behavior. *Organizational Behavior and Human Decision Processes, 115*(2), 181–190.
Shaw, A. (2013). Beyond "to share or not to share": The impartiality account of fairness. *Current Directions in Psychological Science, 22*(5), 413–417.
Shaw, A., Choshen-Hillel, S., & Caruso, E. M. (2016). The development of partiality aversion: Understanding when (and why) people give others the bigger piece of the pie. *Psychological Science, 27*(10), 1352–1359.
Shaw, A., & Knobe, J. (2013). Not all mutualism is fair, and not all fairness is mutualistic. *Behavioral and Brain Sciences, 36*(1), 100–101.
Shaw, A., & Olson, K. R. (2012). Children discard a resource to avoid inequity. *Journal of Experimental Psychology: General, 141*(2), 382–395.
Shaw, A., & Olson, K. R. (2014). Fairness as an aversion to partiality: The development of procedural justice. *Journal of Experimental Child Psychology, 119*, 40–53.
Sheldon, T. A., & Smith, P. C. (2000). Equity in the allocation of health care resources. *Health Economics, 9*(7), 571–574.
Van Lange, P. A. (1999). The pursuit of joint outcomes and equality in outcomes: An integrative model of social value orientation. *Journal of Personality and Social Psychology, 77*(2), 337–349.
Van Lange, P. A., De Bruin, E., Otten, W., & Joireman, J. A. (1997). Development of prosocial, individualistic, and competitive orientations: Theory and preliminary evidence. *Journal of Personality and Social Psychology, 73*(4), 733–746.
Walster, E., Berscheid, E., & Walster, G. W. (1973). New directions in equity research. *Journal of Personality and Social Psychology, 25*(2), 151–176.
Zaki, J., & Mitchell, J. P. (2013). Intuitive prosociality. *Current Directions in Psychological Science, 22*(6), 466–470.

Chapter 7
The Logic and Location of Strong Reciprocity: Anthropological and Philosophical Considerations

Jordan Kiper and Richard Sosis

Introduction

Many behavioral economists and evolutionary anthropologists claim that a cornerstone of human cooperation is the willingness to pay the costs of helping cooperators or punishing cheaters, which is known as *strong reciprocity* (e.g., Bowles, Boyd, Matthew, & Richerson, 2012; Boyd & Richerson, 2009; Diekmann, Jann, Przepiorka, & Wehrl, 2014; Gintis, Henrich, Bowles, Boyd, & Fehr, 2008; Gintis & Fehr, 2012). Yet critics have put forth several reasons purporting to challenge the very idea of strong reciprocity (e.g., Burnham & Johnson, 2005; Guala, 2012; Hagen & Hammerstein, 2006; Price, 2008; Yamagishi et al., 2012). In this chapter, we examine some of these criticisms and related challenges through anthropological and philosophical lenses, and provide a few ethnographic examples of wartime altruism to illustrate the difficulties of isolating strong reciprocity in the real world.

Semantic issues should be acknowledged here at the outset, including the fact that the term *strong reciprocity* is not a straightforward one. Hearing the words *strong* and *reciprocity* together, one would assume that what was being discussed was the robust exchange of something for mutual benefit—but that is not entirely the case. The term *strong reciprocity* designates one of two things that both entail a cost for an agent: rewarding cooperators when it would be more advantageous to exploit them or punishing defectors when it would be more advantageous to ignore them (Gintis, 2000a, p. 177). In either case, the key is that an agent pays a high price for enforcing reciprocity among others, but does so without any personal benefit for himself or herself, which defies traditional models of self-interested maximization in economics and biology (Gintis et al., 2008, p. 243). Evolutionary theory has thus crept into the picture to answer the question as to *why* anyone would behave in such a manner.

J. Kiper (✉) • R. Sosis
Department of Anthropology, University of Connecticut, Storrs, CT, USA
e-mail: jordan.kiper@uconn.edu; richard.sosis@uconn.edu

M. Li, D.P. Tracer (eds.), *Interdisciplinary Perspectives on Fairness, Equity, and Justice*, DOI 10.1007/978-3-319-58993-0_7

There is nevertheless an equally important issue that has come to vex those who defend strong reciprocity. Does the behavior even exist outside of laboratory experiments? Metaphysics aside, the question is empirically motivated, insofar as evidence for strong reciprocity comes almost entirely from cross-cultural studies of economic games. Moreover, field research has centered on the costs and benefits of individual third-party punishments, which are rare and notoriously difficult to measure. So three questions persist: whether strong reciprocity is an artifact of economic games, whether it occurs in the real world, and, if so, why did it evolve?

A general consensus among critics and defenders is that these queries cannot be fully answered (or dismissed) without more data and, most importantly, a unified evolutionary theory of justice (see Debove, Baumard, & Andre, 2016). The result is that strong reciprocity remains an active and dynamic area of research in economics, psychology, and anthropology. Our aim here is to advance this line of research by approaching strong reciprocity from two different perspectives and thereby making two specific contributions. First, we take a philosophical stance and outline the logical argument for strong reciprocity in detail, drawing attention to its most questionable premises. Second, we take an anthropological approach and address what we see as the most critical issue facing strong reciprocity, which is that there is little evidence for strongly reciprocal behavior in the real world, outside of economic games. We conclude that (1) despite some weak premises, the foundational argument for strong reciprocity is logically sound, and (2) while it is very unlikely that strong reciprocity is an artifact entirely limited to experimental settings, it is difficult to detect the behavior in nonexperimental contexts. Lastly, we suggest that while the impulses of strong reciprocity can motivate justice and fairness, one of the reasons that strong reciprocity is difficult to detect in real-world contexts is that cultural forces influence and often limit the manifestation of strong reciprocity impulses.

Strong Reciprocity

Ever since Herbert Gintis' publication "Strong Reciprocity and Human Sociality" (2000a), economists and evolutionary biologists have broadly classified reciprocity as either weak or strong. *Weak reciprocity* is tit-for-tat behavior that benefits, or is at least optimal, for reciprocating agents, while *strong reciprocity* is cooperative behavior that is suboptimal for the practicing agent (Guala, 2012, p. 1). Broadly speaking, weak reciprocity operates efficiently in societal contexts or cultures where there are visible credentials for agents, such as image-scoring or reputational score keeping, which concerns someone's perceived quality. Strong reciprocity, on the other hand, is expected to occur in societal contexts where the previously mentioned credentials are absent, as in large societies where there is an immense variance in the likelihood of iterated cooperation. What makes strong reciprocity so remarkable is that it is a selfless policing behavior insofar as an agent freely rewards or punishes others at a personal cost.

Cooperation and Justice

Besides diverging from rational choice theory, strong reciprocity touches upon two major topics in the behavioral and brain sciences. The first is *cooperation*, which here means any process by which individuals or groups coordinate their actions for mutual benefit (Axelrod, 1984, p. 6). This consists of kin selection (Hamilton, 1964) and altruistic behavior such as direct, indirect, or network reciprocity (see Alexander, 1987; Nowak & Sigmund, 1998; Trivers, 1971); adaptive behaviors such as costly signaling or self-imposed handicaps (Sosis, 2006; Zahavi, 1975); and coaptations of language, communication, and social cognition for coordinating group efforts (e.g., Moll & Tomasello, 2007). The second topic is *justice*, which is understood widely enough to include the human proclivity for fairness when exchanging resources, enjoying privileges, and enforcing punishments (Rawls, 1971, pp. 8–9). Fairness consists of comparing one's efforts and subsequent rewards with those of others as well as caring about equity (e.g., Brauer & Hanus, 2012). Because doing so allows one to detect cheaters or persons whose rewards are greater than their efforts, justice goes hand in hand with fairness such that justice itself is thought of as fairness (see Rawls, 1971).

Of course, justice and fairness also share a close relationship with cooperation. Without fairness and reciprocity, the mutual trust between individuals is severed and the coordinated efforts of groups collapse, resulting in overall lost benefits and decreased fitness compared to cooperative groups (Axelrod & Hamilton, 1984). This in turn raises the question about the proximate mechanisms that bring about justice. Under this topic have come numerous anthropological accounts about various reciprocal behaviors that maintain social bonds (e.g., Mauss, 1990/1950; Sahlins, 1972) and psychological descriptions of communicative strategies that influence social exchanges (e.g., Cialdini, 2006). But only over the last decade have neuroscientists shown that justice is rooted in what is best described as *moral emotion*. Whenever we help someone in need, our reward centers are activated, including the subgenual region, which is associated with oxytocin and social attachment. The result is that when we help, we often experience a "warm glow"—a feeling of pleasure in doing good—that constitutes an emotional basis for engaging in moral acts, thus accounting for many costly behaviors (e.g., Andreoni, 1990). Similarly, when witnessing unfairness, we experience negative emotions and action patterns generated by neural substructures such as the anterior insula (Hsu, Anen, & Quartz, 2008; Kaltwasser, Hildebrandt, Wilhelm, & Sommer, 2016; Knoch et al., 2008; Tabibnia, Satpute, & Lieberman, 2008). This discovery identifies a cognitive mechanism for justice and with it a rather unexpected result. Rather than responding only when we alone experience injustice, our moral emotions are triggered whenever we see anyone experiencing an injustice, including strangers (e.g., Mendez, 2009; see also Sanfey, Rilling, Aaronson, Nystom, & Cohen, 2003).

It is here that strong reciprocity enters the picture. In lab experiments where individuals witness one participant cheating another, there is heightened activity in the anterior insula. Yet in experiments where individuals can actually punish the cheater, they also experience activity in the caudate nucleus, a brain region dedicated to learning, reward, and pleasure (de Quervain et al., 2004; Luo et al., 2006; Pascual, Rodrigues, & Gallardo-Pujol, 2013). Similar brain regions are activated whenever individuals see a participant cooperating with others and seek to reward them for doing so (Li & Yamagishi, 2014; Watanabe et al., 2014). Remarkably, individuals in many laboratory experiments will go out of their way—even giving up their own resources—to punish cheaters and reward cooperators (e.g., Engel, 2011; Fehr & Fischbacher, 2004; Fehr & Gachter, 2002). These data have led researchers to label such behavior as *strong reciprocity* and to speculate about its ultimate cause.

Laboratory Experiments

Most of the evidence for strong reciprocity comes from experiments involving economic games such as the dictator, ultimatum, and public goods game (see Fehr & Gachter, 2001, 2002; Fehr & Fischbacher, 2004; Fischbacher, Gachter, & Fehr, 2001). In each of these games, participants are given money and rules for playing out a game simultaneously and anonymously with other players in a lab, usually over a computer interface. Because participants can increase their earnings, it is expected that players will adopt a rational strategy in which they pursue ordered preferences to maximize self-interest, which is presumed to be money earned during the game itself. Under most circumstances, however, participants typically do not maximize their earnings but rather the perceived equity among players.

As a brief sketch, consider the nature of the ultimatum game, which involves the interplay of anonymous and unseen participants. At the onset of play, participant P receives an amount of money to offer participant S, who is usually located in another room. If S accepts P's offer, P keeps the remainder, but if S rejects the offer, both P and S get nothing (Henrich, Boyd et al., 2005). Because the game allows its participants to behave selfishly, it is expected that P will offer as little money as possible to S. Likewise, S is expected to accept whatever P offers, since any offer gives S more than he or she possesses. But participants tend to split their resources (Fehr & Fischbacher, 2003). This is unexpected in light of the neoclassical economic view known as *Homo economicus* or "human the self-interested." In other words, the game is one-shot and the participants remain anonymous, so there is no immediate or long-term reward for P to benefit S or vice versa—and yet most participants forsake self-maximization to benefit others.

The behavior not only challenges paradigmatic views in neoclassical economics but also traditional evolutionary theories of cooperation. Because strong reciprocity takes place between unrelated individuals and does not contribute to inclusive fitness, it cannot be explained by kin selection theory. Since it occurs in economic experiments that involve one-shot interactions in which participants cannot later reciprocate, it cannot be explained by the theory of reciprocal altruism either. Similarly, because participants are anonymous and thus cannot earn a reputation, it cannot be explained as a form of indirect reciprocity. Finally, it is unlikely that strong reciprocity is a costly signal or handicap indicating the participant's type-quality because there is no subsequent interaction between participants (see Fehr, Fischbacher, & Gachter, 2002, p. 10).

Field Experiments

Such anomalousness raises the question of whether strong reciprocity occurs outside the laboratory. For those who defend strong reciprocity, there are several reasons for believing that it does. First, humans are often willing to aid strangers when an audience is absent and reciprocity is unlikely—a point we shall return to later when discussing persons disrupted by warfare (Gintis et al., 2008, p. 251). Second, humans exercise costly social-norms and conform to social expectations even when they are alone and unobserved or among complete strangers (Bowles & Gintis, 2002, p. 125). Third, the connection between strongly reciprocal behavior and moral emotions for fairness suggests that prosociality and notions of justice are indeed motivated by strong reciprocity (Gintis, Bowles, Boyd, & Fehr, 2003, p. 154).

Critics of strong reciprocity nonetheless find these examples unconvincing. The problem is that it is often difficult to determine whether a behavior is an instance of strong reciprocity or another evolved form of cooperation. For instance, aiding strangers, conforming to social norms, and entertaining moral notions of justice can be just as easily rationalized by inclusive fitness (West, Mouden, & Gardner, 2011, p. 252). In light of such criticisms, ethnographic field experiments involving variations of the previously mentioned games have been carried out in non-western countries (e.g., Fehr & Leibbrandt, 2011; Rustagi, Engel, & Kosfeld, 2010). While these cross-cultural experiments reveal that every sampled culture thus far exemplifies some degree of strongly reciprocal behavior, they also show that the behavior varies according to the participant's cultural understanding of reciprocity and economic interactions.

For example, in Papua New Guinea, participants in the ultimatum game reject any offer greater than 50% (see Tracer, 2003). The reason for this variation is that relative to other cultures, the people of Papua New Guinea give modest gifts (i.e., equivalent to a 10% offer in economic games) to signal affection between kin and allies, but large gifts (i.e., roughly equivalent to or greater than a 50% offer) to ingratiate recipients. Ingratiation in Papua New Guinea is known to engender long-term servitude between partners, which is in the direction of a receiver serving the allocator, as it reflects the traditional mode of economic exchange and tribal politics. Accepting large gifts is thus avoided, even in experiments involving economic games. This is not the case for westerners or anyone else steeped in a market economy, where splitting shares (i.e., equivalent to a 50% offer in economic games) is a sign of mutualism, which facilitates economic partnerships in market interactions (Henrich & Boyd, 2001).

As a result, the defenders of strong reciprocity are correct when they observe that experiments involving economic games cross-culturally elicit strongly reciprocal behavior. Yet the cultural variation in strong reciprocity raises questions about its ontogeny and enculturation. These include questions about the inculcation of reciprocal norms during childhood (Feldman, 2015), the internalization of one's cultural norms regarding economic exchange (e.g., Guiso, Sapienza, & Zingales, 2009), and whether the behavior is simply an artifact of economic games (Guala, 2012; Yamagishi et al., 2012).

The Evolution of Cooperation

Despite its alleged limitation to economic games, strong reciprocity is said to be central to the evolution of human cooperation (e.g., Bowles et al., 2012; Gintis & Fehr, 2012). This may seem counterintuitive if one reflects on the principle of self-interest in traditional economics or evolutionary biology. In both cases, it is presumed to be in the best interest of agents to be self-maximizing—in fact, doing so generally leads to Nash equilibria (i.e., where agents gain nothing by unilaterally changing their behavior if they know the strategies of other agents). Economically speaking, this means increasing one's own profits and, in biological terms, maximizing one's inclusive fitness (e.g., Bowles & Gintis, 2002). Hence, an adaptive strategy for self-interested agents is weak reciprocity: to cooperate directly or indirectly with relatives or known reciprocators and to avoid cheaters.

However, this picture of human cooperation is incomplete if one reflects on what is required for weak reciprocity to function among groups. Such a group would need to have a history of interaction and the potential for future interactions; be relatively small or at least not excessively large and anonymous; and freely circulate reputational information about individuals among the group (Guala, 2012). Of course, these conditions do not always hold in human communities such as state-level societies where an individual regularly interacts with strangers. Likewise, it is not unusual for persons to act selflessly toward strangers or to give anonymously, and to do so without expecting direct or indirect reciprocity, but rather, as many philanthropists say, "because it is the right thing to do." Strong reciprocity is said to fill these gaps: it occurs outside the conditions of weak reciprocity and accounts for ostensibly selfless behavior (see Fehr et al., 2002). Moreover, having strong reciprocators in a group is potentially adaptive insofar as they support cooperation by rewarding cooperators, and, most importantly, enforce cooperation by engaging in the costly punishment of cheaters (e.g., Bowles & Gintis, 2004; Boyd, Gintis, Bowles, & Richerson, 2003; Gintis, 2000a).

These claims have generated controversy. First, it is not clear whether enforcing cooperation by punishing cheaters (*negative strong reciprocity*) occurs as much in the real world as selflessly supporting cooperators (*positive strong reciprocity*). Second, it is difficult to see how strong reciprocity would be adaptive when strong reciprocators are likely to incur diminished gains compared to weak reciprocators (Guala, 2012). In what follows, we address the issue of diminished gains and return to negative versus positive reciprocity.

Group Selection Theory

The problem of diminished gains is obviated by group selection theory or the idea that nature can select at the level of groups (e.g., Sober & Wilson, 1998; Wilson & Sober, 1994). Albeit a somewhat complex topic, which often gets muddled or glossed over by critics of strong reciprocity (see Pisor & Fessler, 2012), group selection theory can be understood as follows. If groups conform to different behaviors, then differences minimize within those groups but maximize between them. When faced with threats, such variability allows some groups to be more successful than others and thereby be more adaptive (Leland & Brown, 2002, p. 64). Of course, this is not to say that members within cooperative groups are in any way equal or that group selection benefits every individual, since what most likely contributes to group selection is a shift in prosocial sentiments that favor central or powerful group members (e.g., Baldassarri, 2013). Hence, it is most likely that group selection is akin to reframing perceived equity, such that cooperative groups outcompete less cooperative ones.

Championing this view, evolutionists interested in strong reciprocity have argued that strongly reciprocal behavior is costly for individuals but adaptive for groups (e.g., Boyd, Gintis, & Bowles, 2010; Boyd et al., 2003; Gintis, 2000b). Specifically, it would be especially adaptive when populations become large and anonymous or when the *shadow of the future* (i.e., anticipation of future reciprocal interactions between individuals) is cut short by culturally disruptive phenomena such as natural disasters or warfare. In these circumstances, strong reciprocators would enforce group cooperation while purely weak reciprocators would not (Fehr & Fischbacher, 2003, p. 790). Over time groups with strong reciprocators would fare better than those with only weak reciprocators, eventually allowing the former to outcompete, overtake, or absorb the latter (see Fehr et al., 2002; Henrich & Boyd, 2001). Because these circumstances characterize most cultures since the Neolithic, they entail that strong reciprocity would have been an adaptive behavior and that group selection would serve as the mechanism for stabilizing it across human populations (Gintis et al., 2008, p. 241).

But isn't this argument in conflict with traditional evolutionary biology? Similar to defenders of strong reciprocity today, V.C. Wynne-Edwards (1962, 1964) once argued that organisms cooperate for the welfare of their species, to which George Williams (1966) famously replied that cooperation is just like any other behavior: it is fully explicable at the level of genes and a fortiori the fitness of the individual. For most of the twentieth century, developments in evolutionary biology were on Williams's side (e.g., Dawkins, 2006/1976). It was widely believed that because genes are the heritable element behind selected phenotypes, the individual is in fact the level at which natural selection occurs. Hence, there was no need to resort to the group level when accounting for naturally selected behavior.

Nonetheless, evolutionists toward the end of the twentieth century and early twenty-first century began recognizing two things. First, terms such as *inclusive fitness*, *kin selection*, and *group selection* were not mutually exclusive terms or competitive explanations of adaptiveness, as they had so often been characterized. Instead, they were different ways of discussing the same thing, namely, the manner in which nature works at multiple levels of phenomena when selecting adaptive traits (see Nowak, Tarnita, & Wilson, 2010). Second, and related to the prior observation, groups could indeed stand as adaptive units (Wilson & Sober, 1994). Lastly, strong reciprocity is observed in nature among bacteria and other organisms (Inglis, West, & Buckling, 2014).

To illustrate, consider a classic thought experiment by John Maynard Smith (1964), which was ironically designed with the intent to counter group selection but actually highlights its logic. If we imagine two haystacks sitting side by side and containing mice, and if those mice gathered resources from the environment just outside their haystacks but mated only with mice from within their own haystack, then they would experience two levels of selection. One would exist between individuals within their own haystack (*individual selection*) and the other between the two populations (*group selection*). For example, if one population gathered more resources than the other, the more resourceful haystack would have a competitive advantage over the other, such as surviving a harsh winter, leaving more offspring, and thus increasing their fitness. Over time nature would favor the alleles of mice from the more resourceful haystack.

Another way of saying this is that there is multilevel selection. Genes are nested within cells, which are nested within organisms, who are themselves nested within groups. The survival of any trait is the effect of nature selecting at the levels of groups all the way down to genes and genetic drift (Grafen, 1985). Therefore, whenever a group trait is selected, so too are underlying genes within individuals of the group (Wilson & Sober, 1994).

Gene-Culture Coevolution

Defenders of strong reciprocity have gone one step further. According to *dual-inheritance theory* or *gene-culture coevolution*, genes engender humans capable of culture, and culture is effectively the construction of a niche that in turn creates pressures selecting for certain genes (Gintis et al., 2008, p. 247). In other words, while nature can act on groups and therein select for individual traits, human groups create culture and culture can engender additional selective pressures on individuals within the group. This dynamic is especially significant for humans such that it is responsible for numerous species characteristics. For instance, the social advent of herding brought about selective pressures that favored human genes that extended the ability to digest lactose beyond early childhood, which endowed groups with preferences for milk and this in turn compelled them to transform their natural environment to facilitate that preference (Leland & Brown, 2002). Numerous other examples could be given, including the advent of writing and cultural transformations due to technology and science (Cochran & Harpending, 2009). The point is that the human genome allows individuals to transform their natural environment so as to facilitate social arrangements. Moreover, these arrangements create a niche that constrains and promotes aspects of the human genome, thus selecting for patterns of cognition, affection, and behavior.

It is theorized that strong reciprocity emerged from a process of gene-culture coevolution. According to Gintis (2011), what got the whole process going was the selection for phenotypic plasticity in dynamically changing ancestral environments. With phenotypic plasticity came the capacity to learn and thus the epigenetic transmission of information otherwise known as culture. Having the capacity for learning and communicating cultural innovations to subsequent generations, early human communities developed norms supporting weak reciprocity (p. 881). This would explain the selective pressures for an accompanying set of prosocial traits that appear to have emerged in early human communities such as moral indignation, guilt, and empathy (Sterelny, 2011). Such traits are rooted in nonhuman primates, including old-world monkeys, who also experience empathy and moral emotions (Dugatkin, 1999). These in turn would have generated moral values and the internalization of prosocial norms to induce community members into conforming to social duties (Gintis, 2011, p. 881). With the advent of cultural technologies for internalizing social norms, such as religion, culture would have put additional selective pressures on neural structures for prosociality. As numerous ethnographic studies show (e.g., Cushing, 1998; Grusec & Kuczynski, 1997; Nisbett & Cohen, 1996), a distinguishing feature of internalizing norms is that individuals are taught—sometimes with great intensity as with rites of passage—to behave prosocially even when community members are not observing them. With such technologies neural structures for internalizing and practicing social norms would have then been privileged in human evolution (Gintis, 2011, p. 881).

The tendency for strong reciprocity would thus emerge from neural structures dedicated to weak reciprocity and prosociality such as the superior temporal sulcus (Moll et al., 2005), interior insula (e.g., Hsu et al., 2008), and caudate nucleus (e.g., Pascual et al., 2013). However, these could then be co-opted to respond to more wide-ranging forms of altruism, such as expressing more indignation to injustices outside of one's kin or affines, by selective pressures at the group level. Indeed, it is possible that strong reciprocity is related to human niche specialization, such that it emerged out of social conflict as an alternative social option, which resulted in less conflict and reduced social problems (Bergmuller & Taboorsky, 2010). The argument here is a familiar one for any group selected trait. When early human communities acquired strong reciprocators, they cooperated more than communities with only weak reciprocators, which brought about selective pressures that favored alleles for the neural substrates underlying strong reciprocity (Gintis, 2003, p. 407). The selection of these genetic factors most likely "ratcheted" the behavior, increasing strong reciprocity and allowing groups of strong reciprocators to outcompete less cooperative groups or even drive them into extinction. This scenario likely began early in human evolution but was enhanced with the appearance of settled communities around 10,000 years ago (e.g., Boyd & Richerson, 2009).

The Logic of Strong Reciprocity

We are now in a position to appreciate the overall logic of strong reciprocity as a scientific idea and thereby see exactly where critics take aim. Here is a thumbnail sketch of the argument for strong reciprocity that is based on its chief premises (P1–10) as discussed in several articles (Bowles et al., 2012; Bowles & Gintis, 2002; Boyd et al., 2010; Boyd et al., 2003; Fehr & Fischbacher, 2003; Fischbacher, Gachter, & Fehr, 2001; Fehr & Henrich, 2003; Fehr & Rockenbach, 2003; Schneider & Fehr, 2010; Gintis, 2000a, 2000b, 2011; Gintis et al., 2003; Gintis & Fehr, 2012; Gintis et al., 2008; Henrich et al., 2006).

P1	Strong reciprocity appears to be a type of altruistic behavior.
2	Altruistic behaviors are attributable to some predisposition to cooperate with others.
3	The predisposition to cooperate with others reduces to self-interest.
4	Strong reciprocity must reduce to self-interest (from 1, 3).
5	But laboratory and field experiments indicate that strong reciprocity is not motivated by self-interest.
6	Some altruistic behaviors do not reduce to self-interest (from 2, 5).
7	It is possible that strong reciprocity results from group selection.
8	Strong reciprocity can sustain cooperation in the face of group threats.
9	If strong reciprocity can sustain groups, then it is adaptive when groups face famine, war, or dispersal—all of which were prevalent during human evolution.
10	Strong reciprocity is possibly adaptive (from 8, 9).

This can be spelled out a bit further as follows.

Based on behavioral economic experiments, (1) strong reciprocity is a distinct type of altruistic behavior insofar as it is detrimental to the agent performing it but beneficial to another. For instance, “rejections in the ultimatum game can be viewed as altruistic acts because most people view the equal split as the fair outcome” (Fehr & Fischbacher, 2003, p. 786). (2) Altruistic behaviors are cooperative behaviors insofar as they are conducive to reciprocity. However, (3) when an organism cooperates with others, it does so in virtue of some naturally selected predisposition such that (4) any predisposition for cooperation must derive from the organism’s self-interest for maximizing resources or inclusive fitness (e.g., Gintis et al., 2008; Henrich et al., 2004). At least that much seems clear with regard to neoclassical economic theory and traditional evolutionary biology. (5) But “humans often cooperate in ‘one-shot’ interactions” and “in these situations there is little chance of direct or indirect reciprocation, so self-interest-based explanations of cooperation are unconvincing” (Bowles & Gintis, 2002, p. 125). (6) Because kin selection theory, reciprocal altruism, indirect reciprocity, and costly signaling cannot account for strong reciprocity, it does not reduce to traditional theories of self-interest (e.g., Fehr et al., 2002, p. 10). (7) If strong reciprocity sustains group cooperation, then it is selected at the group level. (8) Recent theoretical models of gene-culture coevolution show that strong reciprocity is capable of generating within-group cooperation where weak reciprocity would not, and thus giving such groups an advantage over others (e.g., Fehr & Fischbacher, 2003, p. 790). (9) Throughout human evolution, groups faced extreme threats of famine, war, and dispersal. Groups with strong reciprocators would have survived these threats where purely weak reciprocators would not because strong reciprocity reinforces cooperation (see Fehr, Fischbacher, & Gachter, 2001; Fehr & Henrich, 2003; Henrich & Boyd, 2001). Therefore, data on strong reciprocity and gene-culture coevolution suggest that strong reciprocity is an adaptive behavior, which was unrecognized in science until experiments revealed its importance (e.g., Gintis, 2011).

Criticisms and Potential Challenges

Taking stock of the above argument, it is clear to us that the basic logic is valid. The main question then is whether it is also sound. In this section, we highlight three criticisms that draw into question some of the premises behind the argument for strong reciprocity and thereby point to issues that require further empirical and theoretical investigation.

Evidence in "the Wild"

The perennial challenge put forth by critics takes aim at the first premise and its underlying assumption that experimental data sufficiently demonstrate that strong reciprocity is a behavior in the real world. Critics argue that the ethnographic data for strong reciprocity, which allegedly demonstrate the behavior "in the wild," are simply cross-cultural economic experiments that replicate the very conditions in which the behavior was originally identified (e.g., Price, 2008; Trivers, 2006). Responding to this criticism, defenders of strong reciprocity have cited several ethnographic studies purporting to describe altruistic punishment and thus various examples of negative strong reciprocity (e.g., Henrich et al., 2004; Marlowe et al., 2008). However, critics point out that these studies can be interpreted in numerous ways and that even the original ethnographers who recorded them are unsure as to whether the punishments they observed constitute strong reciprocity. In short, costly punishment observed in ethnographic settings is usually described as collective retribution or coalitional punishment, designed as such to offset the costs of punishing free riders and, thus, obviating the risk of negative strong reciprocity (e.g., Boehm, 2012).

Furthermore, because punishments observed in ethnographic settings are almost always balanced reciprocity between individuals or collective third-party punishment, it is difficult to confidently identify such behaviors as strong reciprocity. The gap between ethnographic and experimental evidence has led many critics to claim that strong reciprocity is an artifact of economic games (see Guala, 2012; Hsu et al., 2008). We consider this criticism to be the central problem to strong reciprocity and one we shall address throughout the rest of this chapter.

For now, we wish to stress that several researchers of strong reciprocity have responded that critics adopt an understanding of experimental data that is too narrow, and that a wider interpretation is not only valid but also more fruitful (Bowles et al., 2012; Gintis & Fehr, 2012; Henrich & Chudek, 2012). A "narrow" interpretation of strong reciprocity is that behavior in economic games is invaluable for shedding light on the proximate psychological motives and enculturated reactions to violations of social norms. Beyond that, any claim that strong reciprocity is an evolved behavior imports more than what is warranted by the data. A "wide" interpretation is that experiments involving economic games simplify the conditions of cooperation in the real world and isolate the costs of strong reciprocity that are difficult to measure in ethnographic settings (see Guala, 2012, p. 5). Moreover, these experiments are internally valid insofar as they correctly identify the proximate mechanisms of strong reciprocity and are externally valid insofar as they help rationalize strong reciprocity in the real world (e.g., Bowles et al., 2012). Although the latter claim is contested, it is worth stressing that the external validity of any experiment is conjectural and that the conjectures made by defenders of strong reciprocity are well grounded.

Several experimenters have shown, for instance, that strongly reciprocal behavior in laboratory settings significantly correlates with behavior observed in various field experiments (e.g., Henrich, Heine, & Norenzayan, 2010). These experiments reveal the bare costs that persons are willing to pay in order to sustain cooperation, and this helps shed light on the ways in which cultures use proclivities for justice and cooperation to collectively control for freeriding while minimizing retaliatory costs against strongly reciprocal individuals. Experiments may also reveal strategies for human cooperation that are expressed differently in the real world. Consider the example of ostracism. In economic experiments, punishment is rendered by direct ostracism or ending all cooperation with a defector, which is costly to the punisher. However, this is rarely observed in ethnographic settings, most likely because it is easier for humans simply to avoid defectors, which is costly but not as drastic as laboratory behavior. Finally, group selection theory provides a theoretical framework to explain the ultimate cause of the behavior and to rationalize the ubiquity of strong reciprocity in various cross-cultural field experiments as well as neurological studies of injustice and cooperation (see Pisor & Fessler, 2012).

Type Distinction and Adaptiveness

Nonetheless, the issue of lacking concrete evidence for strong reciprocity outside of laboratory experiments provides the grounds for additional criticisms. One is that without further real-world evidence, it is still possible to question what strong reciprocity is exactly (Price, 2008). The argument is that the nature of economic experiments is purposefully restricting—for example, limiting participants to an anonymous interaction that is often one-shot, which is done, of course, to isolate variables of interest. However, doing so challenges external validity in the case of strong reciprocity, because the behavior was identified within experimental settings and it has been difficult to document outside of such settings. As a result, strong reciprocity could be the basic impulse for reciprocity as it gets expressed in unusual settings such as the ultimatum game (Trivers, 2006, p. 965).

Another criticism centers on the premise that strong reciprocity is adaptive. Critics note that the argument for strong reciprocity pivots between experimental evidence and real-world behavior (Burnham & Johnson, 2005). Specifically, defenders use real-world behaviors, such as weak reciprocity, to make sense of strong reciprocity in experimental settings. They argue that the behavior is a distinct one, because, in economic settings, it cannot be reduced to kin selection, direct reciprocity, indirect reciprocity, or costly signaling (Fehr et al., 2002, p. 10). Using this mode of reasoning, critics argue that if strong reciprocity is adaptive, then its adaptiveness must also apply to experimental settings. After all, defenders argue strongly that strong reciprocity is adaptive because of its group-level benefits. But in the context of economic games, strong reciprocity is conferred to unknown persons and not to the agent's group. Hence, the behavior is not adaptive (Burnham & Johnson, 2005, p. 122).

As a defense, it should be stressed that this argument is somewhat of a modal mischaracterization, that is, an inaccurate portrayal of the purported truth conditions of premises seven and ten from above. For defenders of strong reciprocity, the behavior is not necessarily adaptive in particular economic games but rather possibly adaptive outside of games at the group level, which is a reasonable proposition given the consistent emergence of the behavior in experimental settings, despite the difficulty of detecting it in the real world (see Fehr & Fischbacher, 2003; Fehr & Henrich, 2003; Henrich & Boyd, 2001). Nevertheless, critics also argue that even if we assume strong reciprocity is adaptive for groups, the infrastructures of economic games do not apply to real-world settings. For instance, one-shot anonymous interactions between individuals from different groups in the real world would still be acting in such a way that the behavior would not benefit any group (Burnham & Johnson, 2005, p. 122).

Even though this criticism could be dismissed for confusing the modal propositions comprising the argument of strong reciprocity, it highlights a peculiarity about strong reciprocity that once again arises from experimental evidence and its application to the real world. Defenders of strong reciprocity argue that the behavior observed in economic games can be applied to real-world behavior (e.g., Fehr et al., 2002; Gintis, 2011; Gintis et al., 2003; Gintis et al., 2008). But if we juxtapose this method of reasoning with other behavioral experiments, a problem becomes clear. In most experiments, analyses move from real-world observations to isolated motives in experiments and, with newfound data, back to real-world behaviors:

($M1$) Observe behavioral pattern in the real world → Discover motives in economic experiments → Make sense of real-world behavior

Strong reciprocity is therefore an unusual mode of scientific inquiry, because it begins with experimental observations rather than real-world behavioral patterns but proceeds to speculate about possible real-world behaviors:

(*M*2) Observe behavioral pattern in economic experiment → Discover motives in experiment → Make sense of behavior in experiment

What can be concluded definitively from this mode of reasoning is only that people have strongly reciprocal motives in economic games.

Of course, identifying such motives could underscore a real-world behavior or it might just reveal an artifact of economic games. Alternatively, we advocate a middle ground. While experimental evidence for strong reciprocity clearly identifies an impulse for justice in humans, the impulse does not get expressed as strongly in the real world as it does in economic games. A way forward, then, is to investigate the cultural mechanisms that promote or inhibit the impulse in real-world settings.

Wartime Altruism

One real-world setting in which strong reciprocity is said to be identifiable is among disrupted communities, such as those affected by a natural disaster or warfare, where altruists sustain group cooperation (e.g., Gintis et al., 2008; Mathew & Boyd, 2011). Granting this observation, we provide a few ethnographic examples of wartime altruism, considering whether they are tantamount to strong reciprocity. Wartime altruism is of course a prosocial behavior, and like any other prosocial behavior it involves specific temporal discounting, that is, a regressed time horizon in which greater value is given to the "now" (see Doyle, 2013). In times of war, human beings discount time, often acting in ways that bring immediate reward, for better or worse. Persons in war are known to undertake incredibly unjust and immoral actions against conspecifics, but war also brings out incredible acts of justice and altruism among some individuals. The question is: do such prosocial actions in war constitute strong reciprocity?

Costly Punishment in War

Speaking directly to the role of punishment in promoting cooperation, Mathew and Boyd (2011) examined third-party punishment among the Turkana, an egalitarian, nomadic pastoral society in East Africa. As a group engaging in wartime raids, the Turkana faced significant risks whenever warriors deserted a raiding party. To discourage desertions, the Turkana imposed community-wide sanctions in the form of corporal punishments and fines, which is altruistic since it is a cost that individuals across the group are willing to accept in order to secure justice and cooperation. By taking on such costs, individuals paid a high price alongside others in their community to ensure that freeriders were punished. Based on a sample of 88 raids, Mathew and Boyd (2011) found that collective third-party punishment significantly lowered desertions and contributed to higher levels of cooperation. As they argue, this example shows that altruistic punishment is significant for small-scale societies but also that negative strong reciprocity could have evolved at the group level in traditional human societies. Granted, the Turkana punish cheaters as a group, which offsets the costs of punishment; though it is done as a group, which differs from economic games, it appears to be compelled by the same moral emotions and with the same consequence of group-level benefits.

Notwithstanding these results, it is difficult to say with certainty that wartime punishment for the Turkana is negative strong reciprocity. After all, even though it is costly, Turkana punishment in war is actually a form of community-wide third-party punishment, which can be more easily rationalized as a costly signal of trustworthiness among community members (Jordan, Hoffman, Bloom, & Rand, 2016). Furthermore, it seems to be an exception to an emerging pattern: when ethnographers of traditional societies (bands, tribes, chiefdoms) detect costly punishment, it is usually second-party punishment, where one is cheated and thereafter avenges oneself; and when third-party punishment does occur, it tends to be collective, thus distributing the costs and risks of doing so (see Lee, 2013/1984, p. 118). Where non-collective third-party punishment is most evident is among persons in state-level societies—but, again, in cross-cultural experiments (e.g., Marlowe et al., 2008). Hence, the Turkana case once again exemplifies the problem of type distinction, and as one of the allegedly best instances of negative strong reciprocity outside of economic games, it is unconvincing.

Costly Cooperation in War

Examples of costly cooperation are more frequent in times of war (e.g., Gintis, 2000a), and they suggest the importance of direct or indirect group-level benefits when communities are disrupted by collective violence. To consider whether these constitute strong reciprocity, we draw from two separate sets of interview data of survivors and ex-fighters of the Yugoslav Wars. The first comes from post-conflict interviews collected by political activist and physician Svetlana Broz (2002), while the second comes from semi-structured interviews collected during 18 months of fieldwork (2015–2016) in the Balkans by Jordan Kiper. What these interviews suggest is that altruistic impulses for what seems to be strong reciprocity are remarkably common in war, as observed by defenders of strong reciprocity (e.g., Gachter & Herrmann, 2009). However, when acted upon, these instances of altruism either fit the descriptions of other evolutionary cooperative behaviors or do not present clear benefits to the reciprocator's group.

When the Yugoslav Wars ended in Bosnia, Broz (2002) began compiling wartime narratives ($n = 90$), with the intent of recording a political history of the wars as told by survivors and ex-fighters (xv–xvi). Besides recording accounts of war crimes, Broz was surprised to find that many interviewees reported being helped by altruists during the war, often by family, friends, or neighbors—but in some cases by strangers. When Kiper conducted similar interviews with survivors and ex-fighters of the Yugoslav Wars in Croatia, Serbia, and Bosnia Herzegovina (*n* =174), he was also surprised by the frequency in which interviewees reported being helped by an altruistic stranger. Combining both sets of interviews (*n* =264), 31 testimonies were about being in a situation of need and receiving help from an unknown person with whom the recipient could not reciprocate. Of these cases, 17 involved being helped by a member of one's ethnoreligious group, but with each of these cases, the altruist was in the company of others and therefore his or her behavior is more accurately characterized as indirect reciprocity or a costly signal to observers. In the remaining 14 cases, the altruist was a stranger from the "other side" of the conflict and, most importantly, put himself or herself at risk by helping, and therefore acted alone and did so in relative secrecy.

Based on these 14 cases, 6 involved a fighter from the other side. These included a fighter protecting someone from being beaten, tortured, or killed (*n* = 2) and helping someone escape from an occupied territory or warzone (*n* = 4). Of the eight cases where a noncombatant helped, interviewees reported being refugees at the time and receiving resources as they fled (*n* = 5), being given rides to escape warzones or pass through enemy checkpoints (n = 2), and being hidden from combatants (*n* = 1). We can only speculate as to why persons undertook such costs to help someone who would have been considered their enemy at the time. Perhaps they recognized a family member in the person of need (Broz, 2002), could not stand to see an injustice (p. 371), or simply felt it was the right thing to do (Kiper, unpublished interview data).

Still, the critical question is how this behavior benefits the strong reciprocator's group. One could argue that instead of benefiting their group directly, persons who help outsiders, especially in war, convey the humanity of their own group. Doing so could turn an enemy and thus potential combatant into a sympathetic noncombatant. This sentiment is summarized well by a former Chetnik who was left for dead by his fellow Serbian soldiers after a battle, and then discovered by a Muslim. To the man's surprise, the Muslim did not kill him but rather treated his wounds and took him to a nearby hospital, which, perhaps because the Muslim vouched for the man, accepted him without any questions. Because of the war, the man never found his benefactor and went back to his home once he had healed—but this time as a pacifist. As he reported: "After all I've experience I know there is no force on this earth and no idea that could force me to pick up a gun again" (Broz, 2002, p. 333). Despite this possibility, costly cooperation between would-be enemies in war does not appear to be strong reciprocity. Instead, it is simply another form of general reciprocity, since the group identities of involved parties are known, and the recipient essentially reciprocates with the altruist by forsaking violence against the latter's group.

The Impossibility of Detection

Our brief analysis of wartime altruism is meant to shed light on what we take to be the fundamental problem of strong reciprocity: even in cases where one would expect to find it, strong reciprocity is difficult to detect with any certainty. As we discussed earlier, this is a problem of type distinction. Any alleged ethnographic instance of strongly reciprocal behavior will blur the lines with other forms of evolved cooperation, which can usually explain the behavior in question with greater clarity and simplicity than strong reciprocity theory. Once again, this problem is rooted in the mode by which strong reciprocity was discovered, that is, as an anomalous behavior within economic games and thereafter sought in the real world, instead of the reverse, which tends to be the common route of investigating a behavior. Likewise, detecting strong reciprocity where we would expect one-shot encounters, such as war, famine, or any other natural disaster, involves real-world problems that often complicate traditional economic theories. For instance, classical economic models assume that humans discount time in a rather consistent way. However, wartime altruism shows that time discounting varies for humans in real-world settings. Detecting the extent of temporal discounting is nevertheless difficult in contexts of war, as people may see their temporal horizon differently, even from moment to moment, depending on their circumstances. Taken together, defenders of strong reciprocity may have to face up to the problem that because the real world cannot match the experimental conditions in which strong reciprocity was discovered, the behavior may be impossible to detect with certainty outside of experimental settings.

Final Thoughts

Our brief discussion of wartime altruism is not intended to assert that strong reciprocity does not exist. Experimental evidence on strong reciprocity suggests that humans indeed have a remarkable inclination for fairness, while cultural group selection provides a sufficient means by which such an inclination would have been selected. Granted that successfully repeated experiments isolate real phenomena and produce materially realized effects (Radder, 2003), experiments on strong reciprocity isolate something real and consequential. What remains partially unanswered, we argue, is the exact nature of strong reciprocity as a phenomenon isolated in experiments, and how that phenomenon changes from the contexts of economic games to the real world. It may no longer be warranted to assume that strong reciprocity in experiments gets expressed as such in the real world, given the lack of concrete ethnographic examples thereof.

We suggest, then, that a narrow interpretation of strong reciprocity may be the best way to move forward. That is to say, researchers should no longer presume that experiments reveal a behavior that one can expect to find in the real world but rather they isolate a basic psychological or emotional impulse. This impulse underlies the basic human proclivity for fairness and thus justice, which centers on others following or violating social norms, and was probably selected at the group level, just as theorists of strong reciprocity claim. However, much like other naturally selected psychological impulses, the underpinnings of strong reciprocity must be shaped by culture. Consequentially, a potentially rewarding direction for future research is to examine the phenomenology of strong reciprocity and investigate how cultures suppress, cultivate, and manipulate strong reciprocity as a psychological or emotional proclivity to achieve justice. The experimental settings in which strong reciprocity has emerged do not appear to capture the constraints of human social organization, despite the enormous diversity in which humans structure their societies. Strong reciprocity research, therefore, that takes considerations of cultural influences seriously offers a promising approach for understanding the evolution of strong reciprocity and its role in facilitating justice and fairness.

References

Alexander, R. (1987). *The biology of moral systems*. New York, NY: Aldine de Gruyter.

Andreoni, J. (1990). Impure altruism and donations to public goods: A theory of warm-glow giving. *The Economic Journal, 100*(401), 464–477.

Axelrod, R. (1984). *The evolution of cooperation*. New York, NY: Basic Books.

Axelrod, R., & Hamilton, W. D. (1984). The evolution of cooperation. *Science, 211*, 1390–1396.

Baldassarri, D. (2013). Prosocial behavior: Evidence from lab-in-the-field experiments. *PLoS One, 8*(3), e58750. https://www.ncbi.nlm.nih.gov/pmc/articles/PMC3608652/.

Bergmuller, R., & Taboorsky, M. (2010). Animal personality due to social niche specialization. *Trends in Ecology and Evolution, 25*(9), 504–511.

Boehm, C. (2012). *Moral Origins: The Evolution of Virtue, Altruism, and Shame*. New York: Basic Books.

Bowles, S., Boyd, R., Matthew, S., & Richerson, P. J. (2012). The punishment that sustains cooperation is often coordinated and costly. *Behavioral and Brain Sciences, 35*(1), 20–21.

Bowles, S., & Gintis, H. (2002). Homo reciprocans. *Nature, 415*, 125–128.

Bowles, S., & Gintis, H. (2004). The evolution of strong reciprocity: Cooperation in heterogenous populations. *Theoretical Population Biology, 65*(1), 17–28.

Boyd, R., Gintis, H., & Bowles, S. (2010). Coordinated punishment of defectors sustains cooperation and can proliferate when rare. *Science, 328*(5978), 617–620.

Boyd, R., Gintis, H., Bowles, S., & Richerson, P. (2003). The evolution of altruistic punishment. *PNAS, 100*(6), 3531–3535.

Boyd, R., & Richerson, P. J. (2009). Culture and the evolution of human cooperation. *Philosophical Transactions of the Royal Society of London B: Biological Sciences, 364*(1533), 3281–3288.

Burnham, T., & Johnson, D. (2005). The biological and evolutionary logic of human cooperation. *Analyse & Kritik, 27*, 113–135.

Brauer, J., & Hanus, D. (2012). Fairness in non-human primates? *Social Justice Research, 25*(3), 256. http://scholarworks.gsu.edu/cgi/viewcontent.cgi?article=1046&context=psych_facpub.

Broz, S. (2002). *Good people in an evil time: Portraits of complicity and resistance in the Bosnian war*. New York, NY: Other Press.

Cialdini, R. (2006). *Influence: The Psychology of Persuasion*. New York, NY: Harper Business.

Cochran, G., & Harpending, H. (2009). *The 10,000 year explosion: How civilization accelerated human evolution*. New York, NY: Basic Books.

Cushing, P. J. (1998). Competing the cycle of transformation: Lessons form the rites of passage model. *Pathways: The Ontario Journal of Experimental Education, 9*(5), 7–12.
Dawkins, R. (2006). *The selfish gene*. Oxford: Oxford University Press. (Original work published in 1976).
de Quervain, D. J., Fischbacher, U., Treyer, V., Schellhammer, M., Schnyder, U., & Buck, A. (2004). The neural basis of altruistic punishment. *Science, 305*, 1254–1258.
Debove, S., Baumard, N., & Andre, J. B. (2016). On the evolutionary origins of equity. *BioRxiv*. http://dx.doi.org/10.1101/052290.
Diekmann, A., Jann, B., Przepiorka, W., & Wehrl, S. (2014). Reputation and the evolution of cooperation in anonymous online markets. *American Sociological Review, 79*(1), 65–85.
Doyle, J. (2013). Survey of time preference, delay discounting models. *Judgment and Decision making, 8*(2), 116–135.
Dugatkin, L. A. (1999). *Cheating monkeys and citizen bees*. New York, NY: Simon & Shuster.
Engel, C. (2011). Dictator games: A meta study. *Experimental Economics, 14*(4), 583–610.
Fehr, E., Fischbacher, U., & Gachter, S. (2002). Strong reciprocity, human cooperation, and the enforcement of social norms. *Human Nature, 13*(1), 1–25.
Fehr, E., & Gachter, S. (2001). Cooperation and punishment in public goods experiments. *American Economic Review, 90*(4), 980.
Fischbacher, U., Gachter, S., & Fehr, E. (2001). Are people conditionally cooperative? Evidence from a public goods experiment. *Economic Letters, 71*(3), 397–404.
Fehr, E., & Gachter, S. (2002). Altruistic punishment in humans. *Nature, 415*, 6868.
Fehr, E., & Fischbacher, U. (2003). The nature of human altruism. *Nature, 425*, 785–791.
Fehr, E., & Rockenbach, B. (2003). Detrimental effects of sanctions on human altruism. *Nature, 422*, 137–140.
Fehr, E., & Henrich, J. (2003). Is strong reciprocity a maladaptation? On the evolutionary foundations of human altruism. In P. Hammerstein (Ed.), *Genetic and Cultural Evolution of Cooperation* (pp. 55–82). Cambridge, MA: MIT Press.
Fehr, E., & Fischbacher, U. (2004). The nature of human altruism. *Nature, 425*, 785–791.
Fehr, E., & Leibbrandt, A. (2011). A field study on cooperativeness and impatience in the tragedy of the commons. *Journal of Public Economics, 95*(10), 1144.
Feldman, R. (2015). Mutual influences between child emotion regulation and parent-child reciprocity support development across the first 10 years of life: Implications for developmental psychopathology. *Development and Psychopathology, 27*(1), 1007–1023.
Fischbacher, U., Gachter, S., & Fehr, E. (2001). Are people conditionally cooperative? Evidence from a public goods experiment. *Economics Letters, 71*(3), 397–404.
Gachter, S., & Herrmann, B. (2009). Reciprocity, culture, and human cooperation: Previous insights and a new cross-cultural experiment. *Philosophical Transactions of the Royal Society Biological Sciences, 364*, 791–806.
Gintis, H. (2000a). Strong reciprocity and human sociality. *Journal of Theoretical Biology, 206*, 169–179.
Gintis, H. (2000b). Group selection and human prosociality. *Journal of Consciousness Studies, 7*(1), 215–219.
Gintis, H. (2003). The hitchhiker's guide to altruism: Genes, culture, and the internalization of norms. *Journal of Theoretical Biology, 220*(4), 407–418.
Gintis, H. (2011). Gene-culture coevolution and the nature of human sociality. *Philosophical Transactions of the Royal Society Biological Sciences, 366*, 878–888.
Gintis, H., Bowles, S., Boyd, R., & Fehr, E. (2003). Explaining altruistic behavior in humans. *Evolution and Human Behavior, 24*, 153–172.
Gintis, H., & Fehr, E. (2012). The social structure of cooperation and punishment. *Behavioral and Brain Sciences, 35*(1), 28–29.
Gintis, H., Henrich, J., Bowles, S., Boyd, R., & Fehr, E. (2008). Strong reciprocity and the roots of morality. *Social Justice Research, 21*(2), 241–253.
Grafen, A. (1985). A geometric view of relatedness. *Oxford Survey of Evolutionary Biology, 2*, 28–89.

Grusec, J. E., & Kuczynski, L. (1997). *Parenting and Children's internationalization of values: A handbook of contemporary theory*. New York, NY: John Wiley & Sons.
Guala, F. (2012). Reciprocity: Weak or strong? What punishment experiments do (and do not) demonstrate. *Behavioral and Brain Sciences, 35*(1), 1–59.
Guiso, L., Sapienza, P., & Zingales, L. (2009). *The Quarterly Journal of Economics, 124*(3), 1095–1131.
Hagen, E., & Hammerstein, P. (2006). Game theory and human evolution: A critique of some recent interpretations of experimental games. *Theoretical Population Biology, 69*, 339–348.
Hamilton, W. D. (1964). The genetical evolution of social behavior I & II. *Journal of Theoretical Biology, 7*(1), 1–52.
Henrich, J., & Boyd, R. (2001). Why people punish defectors: Weak conformist transmission can stabilize costly enforcement of norms in cooperative dilemmas. *Journal of Theoretical Biology, 208*, 79–89.
Henrich, J., & Chudek, M. (2012). Understanding the research program. *Behavioral and Brain Sciences, 35*(1), 29–30.
Henrich, J., Boyd, R., Bowles, S., Camerer, C., Fehr, E., & Gintis, H. (2004). *Foundations of Human Sociality: Economic Experiments and Ethnographic Evidence from Fifteen Small-Scale Societies*. New York: Oxford University Press.
Henrich, J., Heine, S. J., & Norenzayan, A. (2010). The weirdest people in the world? *Behavioral and Brain Sciences, 33*, 61–83.
Henrich, J., Boyd, R., Camerer, C., Fehr, E., Gintis, H., McElreath, R., Alvard, M., Barr, A., Ensminger, J., Henrich, N.S., Hill, K., Gil-White, F., Gurven, M., Marlowe, F.W., Patton, J.Q., & Tracer, D. (2005). 'Economic man' in cross-cultural perspective: Behavioral experiments in 15 small-scale societies. *Behavioral and Brain Sciences, 28*(6), 795–815.
Henrich, J., McElreath, R., Barr, A., Ensminger, J., Barrett, C., Bolyanatz, A., … Zilker, J. (2006). Costly punishment across human socieites. *Science, 312*, 1767–1770.
Hsu, M., Anen, C., & Quartz, S. R. (2008). The right and the good: Distributive justice and neural encoding of equity and efficiency. *Science, 320*, 1092–1095.
Inglis, F., West, S., & Buckling, A. (2014). An experimental study of strong reciprocity in bacteria. *Biological Letters, 10*, 20131069.
Jordan, J., Hoffman, M., Bloom, P., & Rand, D. (2016). Third-party punishment as a costly signal of trustworthiness. *Nature, 530*, 473–476.
Kaltwasser, L., Hildebrandt, A., Wilhelm, O., & Sommer, W. (2016). Behavioral and neuronal determinants of negative reciprocity in the ultimatum game. *Social Cognition and Affective Neuroscience, 11*(11), 1608–1617.
Knoch, D., Nitsche, M. A., Fischbacher, U., Eisenegger, C., Pascual-Leone, A., & Fehr, E. (2008). Studying the neurobiology of social interaction with transcranial direct current stimulation—The example of punishing unfairness. *Cerebral Cortex, 18*, 1987–1990.
Li, Y., & Yamagishi, T. (2014). A test of the strong reciprocity model: A relationship between cooperation and punishment. *Shinrigaku Kenkyu, 85*(1), 100–105.
Lee, R. (2013). *The Dobe Ju/'hoansi*. Belmont, CA: Wadsworth. (Original work published 1984).
Leland, K. N., & Brown, G. R. (2002). *Sense and nonsense: Evolutionary perspectives on human behavior*. Oxford: Oxford University Press.
Luo, Q., Nakic, M., Wheatley, T., Ritchell, R., Martin, A., & Blair, R. J. (2006). The neural basis of implicit moral attitude—An IAT study using event-related fMRI. *NeuroImage, 30*, 1449–1457.
Marlowe, F. W., Berbesque, C., Barr, A., Barrett, C., Bolyanatz, A., Camilo, J., … Tracer, D. (2008). More 'altruistic' punishment in larger societies. *Proceedings of the Royal Society Biological Sciences, 275*, 587–592.
Mathew, S., & Boyd, R. (2011). Punishment sustains large-scale cooperation in prestate warfare. *Proceedings of the National Academy of Sciences of the United States of America, 108*(28), 11375–11380.
Mauss, M. (1990). *The gift: The form and reason for exchange in archaic societies*. New York, NY: W.W. Norton & Company. (Original work published in 1950).

Maynard Smith, J. (1964). Group selection and kin selection. *Nature, 201*, 1144–1147.
Mendez, M. F. (2009). The neurobiology of moral behavior: Review and neuropsychiatric implications. *CNS Spectrums, 14*(11), 608–620.
Moll, J., Zahn, R., de Oliveira-Souza, R., Krueger, F., & Grafman, J. (2005). The neural basis of human moral cognition. *Nature Reviews Neuroscience, 6*, 799–809.
Moll, H., & Tomasello, M. (2007). Cooperation and human cognition: The Vygotskian intelligence hypothesis. *Philosophical Transactions of the Royal Society Biological Sciences, 362*(1480), 639–648.
Nisbett, R. E., & Cohen, D. (1996). *Culture of honor: The psychology of violence in the south.* Boulder, CO: Westview Press.
Nowak, M., & Sigmund, K. (1998). Evolution of indirect reciprocity. *Nature, 393*, 573–577.
Nowak, M., Tarnita, C. E., & Wilson, E. O. (2010). The evolution of eusociality. *Nature, 466*(7310), 1057–1062.
Pascual, L., Rodrigues, P., & Gallardo-Pujol, D. (2013). How does morality work in the brain? A functional structural perspective of moral behavior. *Frontiers in Integrative Neuroscience, 7*(65), 1–8.
Pisor, A. C., & Fessler, D. M. (2012). Importing social preferences across contexts and the pitfall of over-generalization across theories. *Behavioral and Brain Sciences, 35*(1), 34–35.
Price, M. E. (2008). The resurrection of group selection as a theory of human cooperation. *Social Justice Research, 21*, 228–240.
Radder, H. (2003). *The philosophy of scientific experimentation.* Pittsburgh, PA: University of Pittsburgh Press.
Rawls, J. (1971). *A theory of justice*. Cambridge, MA: Harvard University Press.
Rustagi, D., Engel, S., & Kosfeld, M. (2010). Conditional cooperation and costly monitoring explain success in forest commons management. *Science, 330*(6006), 961–965.
Sahlins, M. (1972). *Stone Age Economics*. Chicago, IL: Aldine-Atherton.
Sanfey, A. G., Rilling, J. K., Aaronson, J. A., Nystom, L. E., & Cohen, J. D. (2003). The neural basis of economic decision-making in the ultimatum game. *Science, 300*, 1755–1758.
Schneider, F., & Fehr, E. (2010). Eyes are watching but nobody cares: The irrelevance of eye cues for strong reciprocity. *Proceedings of the Royal Society of London: B-Biological Sciences, 277*, 1315–1323.
Sober, E., & Wilson, D. S. (1998). *Unto others: The evolution and psychology of unselfish behavior*. Cambridge, MA: Harvard University Press.
Sosis, R. (2006). Religious behaviors, badges, and bans: Signaling theory and the evolution of religion. In P. McNamara (Ed.), *Where god and science meet: How brain and evolutionary studies Alter our understanding of religion* (pp. 61–68). Westport, CT: Praeger.
Sterelny, K. (2011). From hominins to humans: How *sapiens* became behaviourally modern. *Philosophical Transaction of the Royal Society:B-Biological Sciences*, 366(1566), 809–822.
Tabibnia, G., Satpute, A. B., & Lieberman, M. D. (2008). The sunny side of fairness: Preference for fairness activates reward circuitry (and disregarding unfairness actives self-control circuitry). *Psychological Science, 19*, 339–347.
Tracer, D. (2003). Selfishness and fairness in economic and evolutionary perspective: An experimental economic study in Papua New Guinea. *Current Anthropology, 44*(3), 432–443.
Trivers, R. (1971). The evolution of reciprocal altruism. *The Quarterly Review of Biology, 46*(1), 35–57.
Trivers, R. (2006). Reciprocal altruism: 30 years later. In P. M. Kappeler & C. P. van Shaik (Eds.), *Cooperation in primates and humans* (pp. 67–84). New York, NY: Springer-Verlag Berlin.
Watanabe, T., Takezawa, M., Nakawake, Y., Kunimatsu, A., Yamasure, H., Nakamura, M., ... Masuda, N. (2014). Two distinct neural mechanisms underlying indirect reciprocity. *Proceedings of the National Academy of Sciences of the United States of America, 111*(11), 3990–3995.
West, S. A., Mouden, C. E., & Gardner, A. (2011). Sixteen misconceptions about the evolution of cooperation in humans. *Evolution and Human Behavior, 32*, 231–262.

Williams, G. (1966). *Adaptation and Natural Selection*. Princteon, NJ: Princeton University Press.

Wilson, D. S., & Sober, E. (1994). Reintroducing group selection to the human behavioral sciences. *Behavioral and Brain Sciences, 17*(4), 585–654.

Wynne-Edwards, V. C. (1962). *Animal dispersion in relation to social behavior*. Edinburgh: Oliver & Boyd.

Wynne-Edwards, V. C. (1964). Group selection and kin selection: Reply to Maynard Smith. *Nature, 201*, 1147.

Yamagishi, T., Horita, Y., Mifune, N., Hashimoto, H., Li, Y., Shinada, M., ... Simunovic, D. (2012). Rejection of unfair offers in the ultimatum game is no evidence of strong reciprocity. *Proceedings of the National academy of Sciences of the United States of America, 109*(50), 20364.

Zahavi, A. (1975). Mate selection—A selection for a handicap. *Journal of Theoretical Biology, 53*, 205–214.

Chapter 8
Fairness in Cultural Context

Carolyn K. Lesorogol

Introduction

A considerable body of research in experimental economics and evolutionary anthropology focuses on the role of social norms in understanding the basis for human cooperation (Henrich et al. 2010, 2006; Krupka & Weber, 2013). This work begins with the puzzle of why humans cooperate at all—how they overcome the individual urge to free-ride on the contributions of others in the process of producing social goods (Olson, 1965). Or why we generally find a high degree of social order in society rather than the proverbial "war of all against all" that we might expect from individuals with a high capacity for autonomous action (Wrong, 1994). The frequent result in experimental games showing that players do not adhere to what "*Homo economicus*" is expected to do (i.e., play to maximize individual gains) but rather exhibit other-regarding behavior, even when selfish behavior could not be detected or punished, challenges assumptions in economics about rational behavior. Although anthropologists may not be surprised that players do not behave according to canonical economic assumptions, the idea that "culture" explains their behavior is also not entirely satisfying, and requires further explanation.

If people are not playing according to their narrow self-interest, then perhaps they are playing according to internalized social norms that encourage or even compel them to behave in other-regarding ways. The idea here is that people do not leave their social norms at the door when they are put in an experimental situation that is abstracted from everyday experience, where they are playing anonymously, where their choices in games are not known by others, and where there can be no retaliation

C.K. Lesorogol (✉)
George Warren Brown School of Social Work, Washington University in St. Louis, St. Louis, MO, USA

Department of Anthropology, Washington University in St. Louis, St. Louis, MO, USA
e-mail: clesorogol@wustl.edu

M. Li, D.P. Tracer (eds.), *Interdisciplinary Perspectives on Fairness, Equity, and Justice*, DOI 10.1007/978-3-319-58993-0_8

for culturally inappropriate behavior. Even in such a context, people may still make choices guided by norms, morals, or beliefs that suggest that they should act in ways that may benefit others in addition to themselves. The power of such internalized norms and their ability to influence behavior in situations that purposely remove social pressure or sanction suggest an important mechanism for social cooperation. If people cooperate when there is no external social pressure to do so, then they are even more likely to cooperate when social pressure is present (Ensminger, 2000; Ostrom, 2014). Understanding how internalized norms or beliefs operate then becomes quite central to solving the puzzle of cooperation, or pro-social behavior more generally.

One of the most frequently cited social norms that appears to guide choices in experimental games is fairness. The Dictator Game (DG) is a widely used experimental game. Two anonymous players are given a stake of money and one player is told to divide the stake between herself and the other player. The second player receives whatever the first player allocates, and the first player keeps the remainder. The results of the DG are often interpreted as a measure of the fairness or altruism of the first player. A purely self-interested player would keep the entire stake, since there is no negative consequence to doing so—the game is anonymous, so no one will know Player 1's identity, and the second player has no opportunity to retaliate against Player 1. Results in the DG vary cross-culturally. Samples of US university students show modal offers at zero (the economically rational choice) and 50% (the equal division of the stake, considered a fair offer) (Camerer, 2003). Cross-cultural samples show a much wider range of offers, but relatively few offers of zero and some offers exceeding 50% (Henrich et al., 2010, 2006). Results in other experimental games show similar tendencies toward behavior that diverges from pure self-interest and indicates a propensity for trust and cooperation, even in anonymous one-off interactions.

Much of the interest in experimental games and their implications for understanding pro-social behavior emanate from scholars seeking universal explanations for human behavior, often trying to explain the evolution of pro-social behaviors in human societies (Boyd & Richerson, 2009; Gintis, Henrich, Bowles, Boyd, & Fehr, 2008; Krasnow, Delton, Cosmides, & Tooby, 2016). This is one reason that games are designed in abstract ways that allow cross-cultural comparison and assist in making more generalizable explanations. Ironically, however, the operations of social norms, so critical to understanding pro-sociality, is itself a product of specific social and cultural contexts. Although there may be a few moral norms that approach universality (e.g., against murder), most norms vary across cultures. Thus, for anthropologists, it may be more interesting and relevant to understand the operation of specific social norms in context rather than the general observation that people behave in pro-social ways. Furthermore, a deeper understanding of the nuances of how norms influence behavior may only be feasibly studied within a cultural context. This does not discount the value of cross-cultural comparison or the search for generalizable explanations, but rather suggests that both of these pursuits can be enriched by paying attention to cultural context. Indeed, the large cross-cultural project that has spurred much consideration of these questions clearly valued both the particularity of culturally contextualized understandings as well as seeking general explanations through cross-cultural comparison (Ensminger & Henrich, 2014).

In this chapter, I discuss a series of experiments conducted among the Samburu, a group of livestock herders in northern Kenya. My aim is twofold. First, I will discuss how focusing on a particular cultural context is helpful in clarifying how fairness norms operate and interpreting the results in experimental games. Second, I will reflect on some of the implications of a consideration of cultural context for experimental work.

Games in Samburu County, Kenya

The Samburu are a livestock herding society living primarily in Samburu County in northern Kenya (see Map 8.1). Samburu County is located about 450 km north of the capital, Nairobi, and is a semiarid region of 20,000 km^2 with a population of roughly 200,000. Most Samburu people rely on their herds of cattle, sheep and goats, and, in drier areas, some camels for subsistence and cash needs. Livestock are herded on land that has been managed communally in this region for over a century. During the colonial period, the British regime assumed ownership of all land in the region, declaring it Crown Land. Samburu herders had access to land for herding, although the colonial government did interfere with herding through establishment of grazing schemes that dictated the numbers of livestock allowed in certain regions during particular times. The grazing schemes were abandoned following Kenya's independence in 1963, and the land was deemed Trust Land, held in trust by the local, county government, on behalf of the residents. In the 1970s, the Kenya government initiated a land adjudication program in the region that resulted in some parts of the county becoming "group ranches" in which groups of resident households were given joint title to an area of land. In some cases, individuals were granted private title to land. Group ranches have essentially remained communally managed with minimal enforcement of borders or membership. Privatized land is more restricted, although in most cases other herders continue to access private areas upon negotiation, particularly during dry seasons and droughts (Lesorogol & Boone, 2016).

Although livestock remain the foundation of livelihood for most households, Samburu are increasingly engaging in other activities, such as wage labor, small-scale commodity trade, livestock trade, and, in some areas, crop cultivation, to supplement household income and meet needs (Lesorogol, 2008b). This diversification demonstrates that Samburu people are increasingly integrated into markets, even though they live in a relatively remote, rural part of Kenya.

Levels of formal education remain relatively low compared to other parts of the country, but more Samburu children are attending school than ever before. Our survey results indicated that 61% of girls and 67% of boys had some formal education, but few (3% and 5%, respectively) continued to secondary school (Lesorogol, Chowa, & Ansong, 2011). Although Samburu people are increasingly integrated

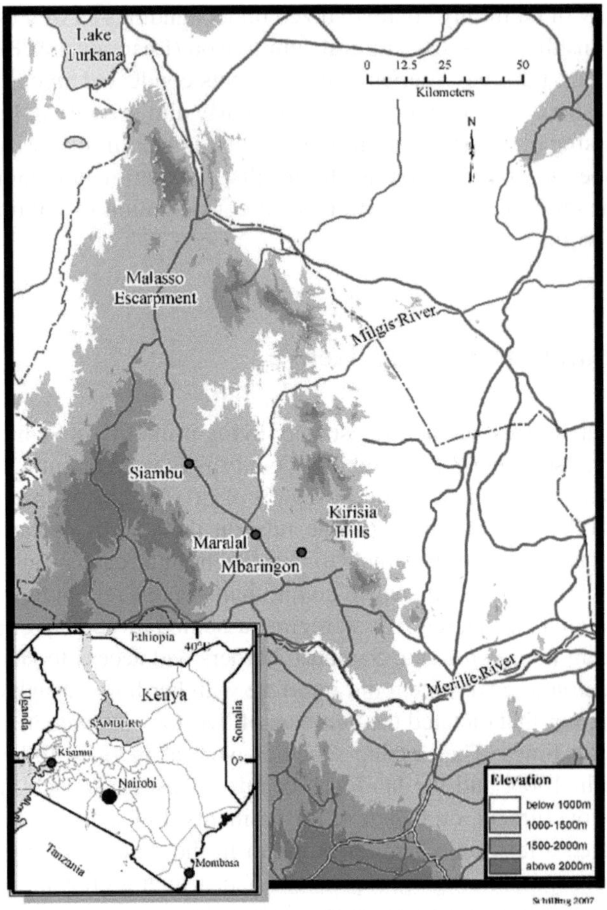

Map 8.1 Samburu County in Kenya

into the market economy and formal education, they retain many of their cultural traditions, carry out large-scale cooperative rituals as well as day-to-day sharing in many domains, continue to live in extended family groups, and primarily practice mobile pastoralism with strong reliance on livestock.

Dictator Games and Concepts of Fairness

The experiments discussed here were conducted in 2001 and 2003 as part of two separate research projects. Full details of those projects, methods, and results can be found in Lesorogol (2005, 2007, 2008a, 2014). Here, I want to focus on the ways in which an understanding of the Samburu cultural context informed the interpretation of the experimental results. The first set of experiments was conducted in 2001 in two

Samburu communities, Mbaringon and Siambu. The larger research project was a study of privatization of pastoral commons that had occurred in the late 1980s. As a result of the Kenya government-led land adjudication process, one community—Siambu—had privatized its formerly communal land into equally sized parcels for each registered household in the community. Mbaringon continued with common land management although it became a "group ranch." I was interested to understand if and how privatization of land in Siambu had changed social and economic relations in the community. I had conducted interviews and observations in both communities and there were some indications that people in Siambu held views that seemed more individualistic and less cooperative than was standard for Samburu people. For example, even people who had originally opposed privatization of land in Siambu were, by the time I interviewed them in 2000 (about a decade after privatizing), very much in favor of private land holdings. The reason that they gave was that individual land ownership gave them more freedom to decide how to use their land, because they did not have to abide by community restrictions or elders' decisions about land use. This seemed like a significant departure from pastoralist values of shared land management. It was difficult to generalize about the degree to which people in Siambu actually behaved in more individualistic (or selfish) ways, however. Using economic experiments seemed like a good way to try to systematically measure behavior and to make comparisons across communities. Therefore, I implemented a series of experimental games to compare Siambu and Mbaringon residents, including the Dictator Game (DG).

As noted above, the DG is considered a good measure of other-regarding, altruistic, or fair-minded behavior. I conducted the DG using a stake of 100 Kenya shillings, about a day's casual labor wages at the time. Players were recruited from a random sample of households in each community that had been participating in the research project. The samples were comparable in terms of demographic characteristics. Players remained anonymous and Player 1 had the choice of allocating any amount of the stake to Player 2 in 10 shilling increments. Figure 8.1 shows the distribution of offers made by Player 1s in Siambu and Mbaringon. There were few offers of zero, some offers of 50%, and modal offers of 20% (Mbaringon) and 30% (Siambu). The distributions of offers in the two communities were similar and the Mann–Whitney nonparametric test did not reveal a significant difference between them. From this, I could conclude that Siambu residents did not appear to be any more selfish (at least, in the game) than those in Mbaringon, contrary to what my ethnographic research had suggested. What I found more interesting, however, was the modal offer at 20–30%. Why 20–30%?

US samples had modes at 0% and 50%, which made sense from a perspective of pure self-interest (0%) versus an equal split of the stake (50%), the seemingly fairest offer. Why didn't the Samburu have the same modes? Also, during the game, some players had explained that they were giving Player 2 twenty shillings because they thought that was fair. Others indicated that a 50–50 split was fair. In discussions with some elders about the game, some of them agreed, saying that Player 1 needed to consider the needs of his family and that giving 20% to Player 2 was appropriate.

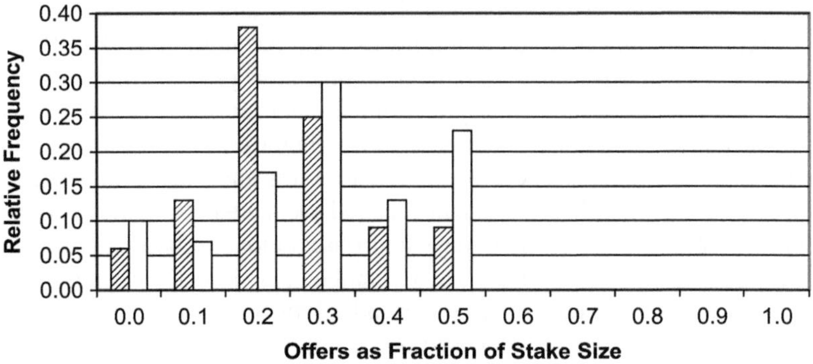

Fig. 8.1 Distribution of offers in the dictator game, originally published in Lesorogol (2005) Hatched bars, Mbaringon ($N = 32$); white bars, Siambu ($N = 30$)

I decided to investigate the question of fairness a bit further. I conducted a series of interviews with residents of both communities and posed real-world scenarios that resembled the abstract scenario of the DG, such as dividing an amount of sugar or meat. Two interesting aspects emerged from the interviews. First, allocations depended on ownership of the resource. Second, allocations of 20–25% were standard in some common sharing situations. For example, women often receive requests for sugar (Samburu people love to drink heavily sweetened tea). When asked how much sugar she would give, if she had a kilogram of sugar (a very common amount for women to keep on hand), the answer was usually "a glass," which is about 200 g, or 20% of a kilogram. Similarly, when people slaughter a goat or sheep, there are established rules for how to share meat. When asked how much meat they would give to someone who arrived when they were slaughtering a goat, virtually everyone responded that they would give them one hind leg of the goat, about 20–25%. There is even a saying to this effect, "moru e laiguetani"—the hind leg for the (uninvited) guest. In these real-world scenarios, ownership of the "stake"—sugar or the goat—is clear: it belongs to the owner (i.e., Player 1). In that case, giving out 20–25% is considered fair and, in the case of meat, expected. According to the directions for the DG, however, the stake is allocated to both players, implying joint ownership. What happens when ownership is joint? A third scenario that I inquired about was what would happen if two friends came upon a dead gazelle in the forest; how would they share it? In that case, a 50–50 split was the frequent answer. The reasoning was that finding a dead gazelle together in the forest meant that both people had an equal right to share the meat, since no one could claim ownership. Thus, the normative solution would be to split the meat equally. In the DG, the directions stipulate that the stake is initially allocated to both players, but then Player 1 is given authority to divide the stake any way she chooses. Thus, it is possible for players in the DG to construe ownership as joint, following the initial allocation of the stake, or as Player 1 having more ownership rights, because she is given the right to divide the stake. Since both interpretations of the game instructions are reasonable, the interviews suggest that choices made in the abstract DG may have hinged on how players interpreted ownership of the stake. It also seemed clear that when people make choices in the abstract game, they may be referencing social norms, but it is unclear which norms are being cued by the game scenario. The spread of offers may reflect the fact that multiple norms are being cued.

To further test these ideas, I designed a DG that closely resembled the goat slaughtering example and conducted this contextualized version, and another abstract version, in a third Samburu community, Ngurunit, where I had not played any games or done the interviews about fairness. One group of players in Ngurunit played the abstract DG and another group played the contextualized DG. The results (shown in Fig. 8.2) showed a clear (and statistically significant using the Mann–Whitney test) difference between offers in the abstract game and those in the contextualized game (Table 8.1).

In the contextualized game, players were told that they were slaughtering a goat and that the anatomy of the goat was represented by the ten 10 shilling coins that were on the table in front of them. We further explained that while they were slaughtering the goat, someone came by their settlement (the "uninvited guest" scenario discussed above). They were asked how much meat they would give to the person, and to represent that amount by choosing how many coins out of the ten to give, representing the meat they would give to the "guest." Almost all players explained that they would give the hind leg to the guest and decided that was equal to 20 or 30 shillings out of the 100. Even the few players who did not do so explained their allocation with reference to this or a similar norm. For example, one player said he would give the head of the goat (which is also culturally appropriate) and another said the goat was too small, so she couldn't afford to give the guest the leg. She knew what the norm was but made a conscious decision not to follow it. In contrast, the group of players who played the abstract game did not spontaneously explain their reasoning, and the spread of offers was much wider, but with a mode at 30%, similar to the earlier experiments. The contextualized game offers evidence that when faced with an unambiguous situation that cues a culturally salient norm, most people adhered to it. Not everyone did, though, which illustrates the idea that although norms are guides for behavior, they are not ironclad. However, even people who diverged from the norm understood that one existed and felt compelled to explain their rationale for not abiding by it. Player decisions in the contextualized game were clearly driven by the distributive situation, slaughtering a goat, and not whether the goat was real or represented by coins.

These examples show that understanding the cultural context aids in interpreting experimental results. It also cautions us that abstract games may not always cue what we believe they are cueing—or at least, that these designs are subject to multiple interpretations (conscious or not) among players. At the same time, the experiments raised questions about how Samburu people conceptualize fairness leading to an interesting investigation of that phenomenon.

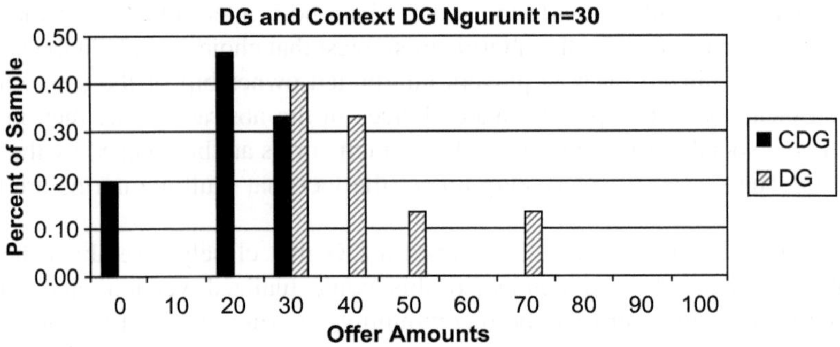

Fig. 8.2 Offers in DG and contextualized DG (CDG), originally published in Lesorogol (2007)

Table 8.1 Offers in the uncontextualized and contextualized games, originally published in Lesorogol (2007)

Offer	Median	Mean	Mode
Uncontextualized (*n* = 15)	40	41.3	30
Contextualized (*n* = 15)	20	19.3	20

"Strong Reciprocity," Punishment and Property Rights

As noted above, pro-social behavior in human societies appears to depend on the existence and functioning of social norms that encourage such behavior. In the DG just discussed, contextualizing the game to a common sharing situation where ownership and sharing norms were clear and known to all prompted behavior that was expected in such a situation. Although there was some variation in behavior, overall the players understood the operative norm and followed it, even in a situation where there was no obvious chance of being punished for violating the norm. This kind of behavior indicates that people have internalized the norm and it is their own sense of doing the "right" thing that enforces the pro-social behavior. If they did not follow the norm, they might feel an internal sense of guilt. This is sometimes called "first-party punishment" because the "punishment" for not following the rule is carried out by the individual him/herself. The smooth functioning of society certainly relies on a heavy dose of first-party punishment, as individuals regulate their own behavior and, as a result, social interaction is much more predictable and smoother. Imagine a world in which no one regulated their own normative behavior.

Although first-party enforcement of social norms is probably the most dominant, it is not the only form of enforcement of norms and rules, which we may collectively term social institutions (North, 1990; Ostrom, 1990). In many cases, other actors do the enforcement. When someone violates a norm, the person directly impacted (wronged) may react negatively, letting the person know that this was a violation of the rules. This is termed "second-party punishment" or enforcement. In other cases, an uninvolved third party (think police, courts, arbitration, etc.) may pass judgment on the violation; this constitutes "third-party punishment." Recently, scholars have proposed that punishment behavior, and specifically costly punishment—where the punisher pays a price to exact punishment on another—is fundamental to the evolution of pro-social behaviors in human populations (Fehr & Fischbacher, 2003; Fehr, Fischbacher, & Gächter, 2002; Gintis, 2000; Gintis et al., 2008). The reasoning behind this idea of "strong reciprocity" is that without external enforcement of social norms, people are less likely to continue to exhibit pro-social behavior. Fehr et al. (2002) define strong reciprocity as follows:

> A person is a strong reciprocator if she is willing to sacrifice resources (a) to be kind to those who are being kind (strong positive reciprocity) and (b) to punish those who are being unkind (strong negative reciprocity). The essential feature of strong reciprocity is a willingness to sacrifice resources for rewarding fair and punishing unfair behavior *even if this is costly and provides neither present nor future material rewards for the reciprocator.* (p. 3; emphasis in original)

They differentiate "strong reciprocity" from other evolutionary theories of cooperation such as kin selection and reciprocal altruism that, they argue, rely on the self-interest of actors, even if that is over the long term (Gintis, 2000). Fehr and Fischbacher (2004, p. 77) go further, arguing that second-party punishment will tend to be much stronger than third-party punishment in experimental games, and presumably also in real life. The logic is that a harm done directly to a second party incurs a higher cost for the second party, thus stimulating a direct, negative response. On the other hand, the third party to the interaction is not directly harmed by the unfairness meted out to the second party; so, even though they may punish the player who behaved antisocially, the punishment is likely to be less than that of a second party who is directly wronged. In their experiments, they find that players are much more likely to punish violations of norms that affect them directly (second-party enforcement) than those to which they are merely witness (third-party enforcement).

Against the backdrop of these emerging theories, I conducted two games with Samburu players that involved second-party punishment (the Strategy Method Ultimatum Game—SMUG) and third-party punishment (the Third Party Punishment Game—TPPG). Both of these games resemble the DG, except that in the SMUG, Player 2 has the option to reject an offer from Player 1. If she does so, then both Player 1 and Player 2 get nothing. If she does not, then each player receives whatever Player 1 had allocated. The ability to reject offers provides Player 2 the opportunity to punish Player 1's behavior, but at the cost of not receiving whatever Player 1 may have allocated. In the strategy method version of this game, Player 2 specifies which offers he will accept or reject for each of the 10 possible offers (0–100 in 10 shilling increments) before knowing what Player 1 had offered. Then, if Player 1 had allocated an amount that Player 2 had said she would accept, both players receive those amounts, but if it is an offer that Player 2 said she would reject, both players receive nothing. In the TPPG, Player 1 and Player 2 play the DG, as explained above. Then, a third player, who is endowed with a stake (in this case, 50% of the DG stake, thus, 50 Kenya shillings), is informed of Player 1's offer and has the choice to accept Player 1's offer or to punish Player 1 by paying part of his stake in order to deduct money from Player 1, at a 1–3 ratio (e.g., pay 10 shillings to have 30 shillings reduced from Player 1s take home amount). Like the SMUG, the TPPG was played using the strategy method so Player 3 indicated which offers she would punish prior to knowing Player 1s actual offer.

In contrast to Fehr and Fischbacher's experimental results, the Samburu results showed that Player 2s in the SMUG were much less likely to punish low offers compared to Player 3s in the TPPG. Figure 8.3 shows the results. The bars in Fig. 8.3 represent the frequency with which Player 2 (SMUG) and Player 3 (TPPG) punished offers in the game. For example, Player 2s rejected offers of zero 32% of the time, while Player 3s rejected them 93% of the time. Player 2s were even less likely to punish offers of 10 (10%) or 20 (10%) compared to Player 3s who punished offers of 10 sixty-percent of the time and offers of 20 forty-percent of the time. What accounted for the difference in punishment behavior in these games?

We tested for effects of individual demographic variables on punishment behavior in both games. Interestingly, the only individual level variable that correlated with punishment was age; older players were more likely to punish low offers in each game (Lesorogol, 2014, pp. 371–2). The significance of age could be interpreted in a number of ways. First, older individuals may be more likely to adhere to and sustain cultural norms by enforcing those norms through punishment behavior. Particularly in contexts when social change is occurring rapidly, it may be older members of the community who serve as a kind of reservoir of culture and knowledge and that this is manifested in their likelihood to punish divergence from normative behavior. Second, Samburu communities have a dispute resolution system that relies on elder men arbitrating and ruling on disputes. A very common punishment is to charge the offending party a fine, say, for stealing cattle. Thus, older players may be more likely to see their role in the game as a participant in the council of elders, especially in the TPPG that most resembles a situation of dispute resolution calling for third-party punishment. Both of these interpretations help explain the tendency for older players to punish low offers at higher rates than younger players. There are other possible explanations for the effects of age on punishment behavior, but these two are consistent with Samburu cultural traditions that place much authority in the hands of elders to maintain order and punish offenders (Spencer, 1965).

The other question, with reference to the theory of "strong reciprocity," is why there was a higher rate of punishment in the TPPG compared to the SMUG, when other experiments had found the opposite. One possible explanation regards how Player 2 interpreted ownership of the stake in the SMUG. In the instructions for the SMUG, it is specified that the stake is allocated to BOTH players. This implies that both players have equal rights to the stake. According to the earlier ethnographic work on sharing norms (discussed above), equal ownership would imply that the stake should be equally shared between Player 1 and Player 2. In that case, we would expect Player 2 to reject offers below 50% at a high rate. Yet, this did not happen. Even though the instructions specify equal ownership, Player 1 is given the right to divide the stake. In this sense, Player 1 could construe the stake as belonging

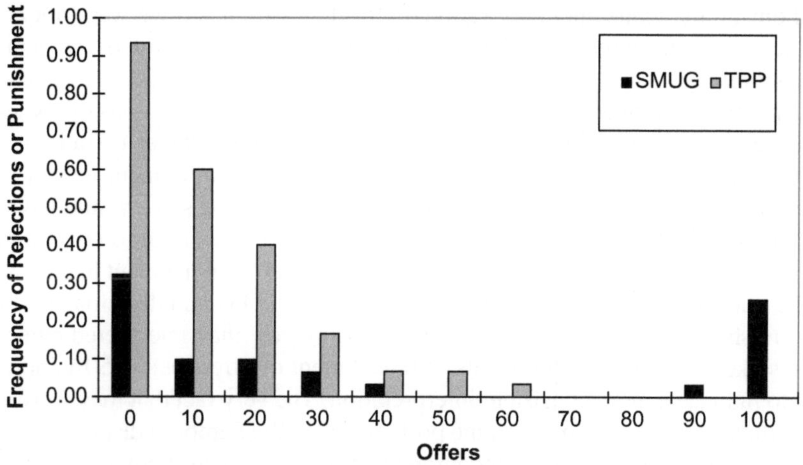

Fig. 8.3 Rejections in SMUG and TPPG, originally published in Lesorogol (2014)

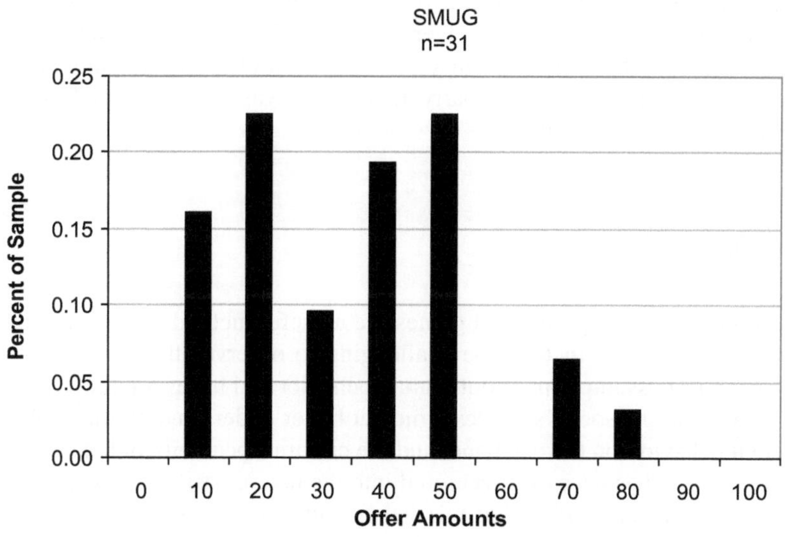

Fig. 8.4 Offers in the SMUG, originally published in Lesorogol (2014).

only (or, mostly) to herself. In that case, an offer below 50% would be considered fair. In fact, the offers in the SMUG show a pattern that is consistent with some players seeing themselves as equal owners with Player 2 and others as full owners of the stake (Fig. 8.4).

Although there is a wide distribution of offers, there are modes at 20% and 50%. Thus, it is possible that some players construed equal ownership of the stake and allocated 50% to Player 2, while others saw themselves as owning the stake and allocated a fair 20% to Player 2. We don't know for sure because players were not vocal during the game about the rationale for their offers and we were not able to conduct postgame interviews due to conducting subsequent rounds of games in this community.

As in the DG, Player 2s may also have had multiple interpretations of ownership of the stake. Those who felt that ownership was shared with Player 1 would be more likely to reject offers below 50%, as violations of their entitlement to half of the stake. In contrast, those who considered Player 1 to own the stake would have considered the offer from Player 1 to be a gift, and it is very unusual to reject a gift in Samburu culture. This would help explain the low level of punishment in the SMUG.

The question of ownership is also relevant to the TPPG and decisions by Player 3 to punish Player 1 may have been influenced by how they interpreted ownership of the stake. The much higher levels of punishment of offers below 50%, however, seem to indicate a more consistent interpretation. The very fact that they were asked to adjudicate on the offer in the game probably cued the Samburu dispute resolution practice, and it may also have encouraged people to punish more since they may have felt that was their role. Again, postgame interviews were not conducted since more games were being played in this community, so we don't know for sure the motivations of players. The SMUG and TPPG results seem to confirm the notion of "strong reciprocity" in that players were willing to incur a cost to punish behavior that deviated from the norm, even in a one-shot situation with anonymity. However, unlike some experiments, second-party punishment was actually much less frequent than third-party punishment.

Conclusion

For anthropologists, experimental games are a useful method for generating many instances of behaviors that can be challenging to observe ethnographically. They enable us to test assumptions about human behavior and have stimulated a growing body of work in the social sciences aimed at better understanding the evolution of pro-social behavior, on the one hand, and the cultural specificity of behavior, on the other. Recent studies have even ventured into the neural basis for pro-social behaviors, finding that generosity or fair-minded play in games, and punishment behavior, activates reward centers in the brain (Buckholtz & Marois, 2012; Fehr & Camerer, 2007). These findings may provide additional support for the coevolution of social behavior and human biology. All of this work suggests that social norms matter, and that other-regarding, cooperative, or fairness norms matter quite a bit. For humans living in large, unrelated social groups, this is very fortunate as it makes the challenge of maintaining social order (however imperfectly) much easier. We still don't fully understand why and how pro-social norms emerge, change and are sustained over time in actual human societies. Anthropologists have contributed to explanations for pro-social norm emergence that focus on evolutionary fitness and processes of cultural transmission of successful strategies (Boyd & Richerson, 2009; Salali, Juda, & Henrich, 2015) as well as institutional theories that demonstrate the utility of cooperation and trust for life in large-scale, market-oriented societies (Ensminger & Henrich, 2014).

The studies discussed here are more particular and use experiments to advance understanding of the nature of concepts like fairness and cooperation in a specific cultural context, that of the Samburu. Their contribution is twofold. On the one hand, games provide a means to compare behavior across groups, within a society, more systematically than many ethnographic approaches allow. Thus, they help to triangulate findings from observations and interviews. In this case, the hypothesis that privatizing land in Siambu was leading to more individualistic (selfish, unfair) behavior was not supported by the game results. On the other hand, the games can also be used to explore the nature and operation of norms related to fairness and sharing. Investigation of these concepts, in the Samburu context, was spurred by game results that seemed ambiguous. The contextualized DG provided strong support for the idea that people do bring their norms into the game situation, and if the game is tailored closely to a well-known norm, they will play accordingly. Local norms and institutions may also influence how people interpret the game situation, including aspects of ownership of the stake and modes of punishment. A fuller understanding of local norms and beliefs aids in interpreting experimental results, but experiments can also be designed to expand our understanding of local contexts.

References

Boyd, R., & Richerson, P. J. (2009). Culture and the evolution of human cooperation. *Philosophical Transactions of the Royal Society of London. Series B, Biological Sciences, 364*(1533), 3281–3288. doi:10.1098/rstb.2009.0134.

Buckholtz, J. W., & Marois, R. (2012). The roots of modern justice: Cognitive and neural foundations of social norms and their enforcement. *Nature Neuroscience, 15*(5), 655–661.

Camerer, C. (2003). *Behavioral game theory: Experiments in strategic interaction*. Princeton, NJ: Princeton University Press.

Ensminger, J. (2000). Experimental economics in the bush: Why institutions matter. In C. Menard (Ed.), *Institutions, contracts and organizations* (pp. 158–171). Northampton, MA: Edward Elgar.

Ensminger, J., & Henrich, J. (2014). *Experimenting with social norms: Fairness and punishment in cross-cultural perspective*. New York, NY: Russell Sage Foundation.

Fehr, E., & Camerer, C. F. (2007). Social neuroeconomics: The neural circuitry of social preferences. *Trends in Cognitive Sciences, 11*(10), 419–427.

Fehr, E., & Fischbacher, U. (2003). The nature of human altruism. *Nature, 425*(6960), 785–791.

Fehr, E., & Fischbacher, U. (2004). Third-party punishment and social norms. *Evolution and Human Behavior, 25*(2), 63–87.

Fehr, E., Fischbacher, U., & Gächter, S. (2002). Strong reciprocity, human cooperation, and the Enforcement of Social Norms. *Human Nature, 13*(1), 1–25.

Gintis, H. (2000). Strong reciprocity and human sociality. *Journal of Theoretical Biology, 206*(2), 169–179.

Gintis, H., Henrich, J., Bowles, S., Boyd, R., & Fehr, E. (2008). Strong reciprocity and the roots of human morality. *Social Justice Research, 21*(2), 241–253.

Henrich, J., Ensminger, J., McElreath, R., Barr, A., Barrett, C., Bolyanatz, A., … Ziker, J. (2010). Markets, religion, community size, and the evolution of fairness and punishment. *Science (New York, N.Y.), 327*(5972), 1480–1484. doi:10.1126/science.1182238.

Henrich, J., McElreath, R., Barr, A., Ensminger, J., Barrett, C., Bolyanatz, A., … Ziker, J. (2006). Costly punishment across human societies. *Science, 312*, 1767–1770.

Krasnow, M. M., Delton, A. W., Cosmides, L., & Tooby, J. (2016). Looking under the hood of third-party punishment reveals design for personal benefit. *Psychological Science, 27*(3), 405–418. doi:10.1177/0956797615624469.

Krupka, E., & Weber, R. (2013). Identifying social norms using coordination games: Why does dictator game sharing vary? *Journal of the European Economic Association, 11*(3), 495–524.

Lesorogol, C. K. (2005). Experiments and ethnography: Combining methods for better understanding of behavior and change 1. *Current Anthropology, 46*(1), 129–136.

Lesorogol, C. K. (2007). Bringing norms in. *Current Anthropology, 48*(6), 920–926.

Lesorogol, C. K. (2008a). Land privatization and pastoralist well-being in Kenya. *Development and Change, 39*(2), 309–331.

Lesorogol, C. K. (2008b). *Contesting the commons: Privatizing pastoral lands in Kenya*. Ann Arbor, MI: University of Michigan Press.

Lesorogol, C. K. (2014). Gifts or entitlements: The influence of property rights and institutions for third-party sanctioning on behavior in three experimental economic games. In J. Ensminger & J. Henrich (Eds.), *Experimenting with social norms: Fairness and punishment in cross-cultural perspective* (pp. 357–375). New York, NY: Russell Sage.

Lesorogol, C. K., & Boone, R. B. (2016). Which way forward? Using simulation models and ethnography to understand changing livelihoods among Kenyan pastoralists in a "new commons". *International Journal of the Commons, 10*(2). doi:10.18352/ijc.656.

Lesorogol, C. K., Chowa, G., & Ansong, D. (2011). Livestock inheritance and education: Attitudes and decision making among Samburu pastoralists. *Nomadic Peoples, 15*(2), 82–103.

North, D. (1990). *Institutions, Institutional Change and Economic Performance*. New York, NY: Cambridge University Press.

Olson, M. (1965). *The logic of collective action: Public goods and the theory of groups*. Cambridge, MA: Harvard University Press.

Ostrom, E. (1990). *Governing the commons: The evolution of institutions for collective action (political economy of institutions and decisions)*. Cambridge: Cambridge University Press.

Ostrom, E. (2014). Collective action and the evolution of social norms. *Journal of Natural Resources Policy Research, 6*(4), 235–252.

Salali, G. D., Juda, M., & Henrich, J. (2015). Transmission and development of costly punishment in children. *Evolution and Human Behavior, 36*(2), 86–94.

Spencer, P. (1965). *The Samburu: A study of gerontocracy in a nomadic tribe*. Berkeley, CA: University of California Press.

Wrong, D. (1994). *Problem of order*. New York, NY: Simon and Schuster.

Chapter 9
Justice Preferences: An Experimental Economic Study in Papua New Guinea

David P. Tracer

Introduction

Both evolutionary and canonical economic theories predict that humans should behave as selfish maximizers of material gains (Cremaschi, 1998; Dawkins, 1989; Hamilton, 1964; Robson, 2001; Smith, 1776). There is abundant evidence, however, that humans behave much more cooperatively than is predicted by either of these theories (Fehr & Fischbacher, 2003; Henrich et al., 2005; Tracer, 2003). From cooperative hunting to contributing to charitable causes to helping stranded motorists, humans in all societies, industrialized and small-scale alike, frequently engage in acts that benefit other unrelated individuals, often at a nontrivial cost to themselves. Recent attempts to explain the prevalence of cooperative behavior have appealed to the role of punishment in stabilizing pro-sociality (Boyd, Gintis, Bowles, & Richerson, 2003; Fehr & Fischbacher, 2004; Fehr & Gächter, 2002). In particular, if individuals have preferences that lead them to punish noncooperators, even at a cost to themselves, then it may drive otherwise selfishly predisposed individuals to cooperate. This explanation is alternately known as the theory of "altruistic" or "costly" punishment. Experiments conducted across a wide range of human societies in which one party divides a sum of money between himself and an anonymous second party but can be punished either by that second party or by an unaffected third party, albeit at a cost, have yielded results that seem to support the theory of altruistic punishment (Henrich et al., 2006; Tracer, Mueller, & Morse, 2014). Second and third parties engage frequently in costly punishment, especially when first parties contribute much less than the average investment.

Punishment, however, is only one form of "justice" in which humans engage. Apart from punishing violators of social norms, a form known as "retributive

D.P. Tracer (✉)
Departments of Health & Behavioral Sciences and Anthropology,
University of Colorado Denver, Denver, CO, USA
e-mail: david.tracer@ucdenver.edu

M. Li, D.P. Tracer (eds.), *Interdisciplinary Perspectives on Fairness, Equity, and Justice*, DOI 10.1007/978-3-319-58993-0_9

justice," humans may instead prefer to compensate victims. Victim compensation is one component of "restorative justice" which focuses on the needs of victims (as well as offenders and communities) rather than simply being punitive. Moreover, some forms of restorative justice involve components of both sanctioning of transgressors and compensation of victims, such as when an agreed upon fine is imposed upon a transgressor that is then used to compensate a victim (Zehr & Towes, 2004).

Previous experiments positing to show that punishment is what sustains cooperation in humans have by and large restricted subjects to only acting retributively or taking no action at all. A potential problem with this experimental design, however, is that if subjects have a preference for taking any action in contrast to remaining inert in an experiment, then it may appear as if subjects have a preference for altruistic punishment. This is akin to a "demand effect" (Zizzo, 2010). Subjects may feel that taking some action in an experiment is what is expected of them by the experimenter, particularly when they are receiving a fee to participate and/or additional payoffs. Additionally, as Bardsley (2008:122) notes "evaluations of options depend on the composition of the choice set" and if punishment is the only active choice, this may exaggerate its importance. To remediate these potential effects, a novel experiment was constructed in which subjects have the option to engage in no action at all or a suite of actions that includes both retributive and restorative justice actions. This experiment is among the first to illuminate human preferences for retributive versus restorative justice using experimental methods. In addition, it also aims to advance theories about the maintenance of human cooperation: if a nontrivial proportion of people prefers to compensate the victims of unfair actions over punishment of those who acted unfairly, it may bring into question whether cooperation in humans is maintained purely by altruistic punishment as many researchers have posited.

Methods

Justice preferences in humans were examined by conducting a novel experiment involving trios of individuals and real monetary stakes in three rural villages of Papua New Guinea. A total of 46 trios of subjects voluntarily participated in the experiment. In each trio, one person was designated the "contributor," a second the "recipient," and a third the "enforcer," however, to the participants, the three were referred to simply as "person one," "person two," and "person three" so as to minimize any expectations of how participants should act. The identities of the members of each trio were kept anonymous to one another and were known only by the experimenter. In addition, recipients and enforcers were randomly assigned to contributors to further make it more difficult for the players to figure out with whom they were playing. The contributor and recipient were allotted a joint endowment of 10 monetary units (MU) equal to about 1 day's unskilled wage in the area; however, it should be noted that since few of the subjects regularly engaged in wage labor, this is a relatively large stake. The contributor then got to divide the endowment in private between himself and the recipient. The contributor could give the recipient any amount from 0 MU up to the full 10 MU in 1 MU increments. After all 46 contributors made their decisions, and each of the 46 enforcers was randomly paired with a contributor. Each enforcer was given an endowment of 5 MU and, after hearing the contributor's decision, was given the opportunity to take one of four potential actions corresponding to a retributive justice treatment, a restorative justice treatment, a combination treatment, or no action at all. The potential actions were: pay 1 of his MUs to remove 3 MUs from the contributor (retributive/punishment), pay one of his MUs to add 3 MUs to the recipient (restorative/compensation), pay two of his MUs to both remove 3 MUs from the contributor and add 3 MUs to the recipient (combination), or keep all of his 5 MUs and do nothing. It should be noted that, in essence, both the restorative and combination treatments are compensatory to victims; however, in the "pure" restorative treatment, the compensation can be construed as coming from an external institution such as a local or government agency, whereas in the combination treatment, the compensation comes directly from the individual that inflicted the perceived wrong upon the victim. Following the enforcers' actions, the members of the trios were individually and randomly called back into a secluded research area to receive their payoffs.

The initial allocation of MUs in the experiment was set up such that, if contributors divided the allocation equally with recipients and enforcers took no action, each member of the trio would leave with exactly 5 MUs. If individuals are purely selfish maximizers of material gains, as predicted by evolutionary and economic theories, then contributors are expected to contribute 0% to recipients and enforcers should never pay any of their MUs to punish contributors or compensate recipients. If altruistic punishment is what stabilizes cooperation in humans despite their otherwise selfish tendencies, then enforcers might be willing to pay to exact retributive justice upon contributors when they make unbalanced offers, but they are never expected to pay 1 MU to engage in restorative justice to compensate victims, let alone pay 2 MU of their own endowment to engage in the combination retributive/restorative justice option.

Results: Justice Preferences

Mean contributions did not differ significantly among the three Papua New Guinea villages (one-way ANOVA with Scheffe post hoc comparisons among all groups, $p = 0.817$); consequently, experimental results and analyses are reported for all villages combined. The sample was 50.4% male and 49.6% female. Table 9.1 lists additional descriptive statistics for the sample of 138 participants. The sample ranged in age from 18 to 80 years with a mean of 33.1 years (s.d. = 13.3); most participants were unmarried or had one wife though several were in polygynous unions, and the average number of children in families of the participants was just over 3. Participants averaged 3.65 years of education with males completing 5.2 years on average and females completing 2.2 years (two-tailed t-test, $p < 0.0001$).

Table 9.1 Descriptive statistics for the participants (n = 138)

Variable	Min	Max	Mean	s.d.
Age (years)	18	80	33.1	13.3
Wives (#)	0	2	0.81	0.48
Children (#)	0	12	3.27	2.48
Education (years)	0	10	3.65	3.37
Gardens (#)	0	11	4.63	2.19
Cash crop income (Kina/mo.)	0	1500	129.50	240.73
Other work (y/n)[a]	0	1	0.12	0.32

[a]0 = no, 1 = yes

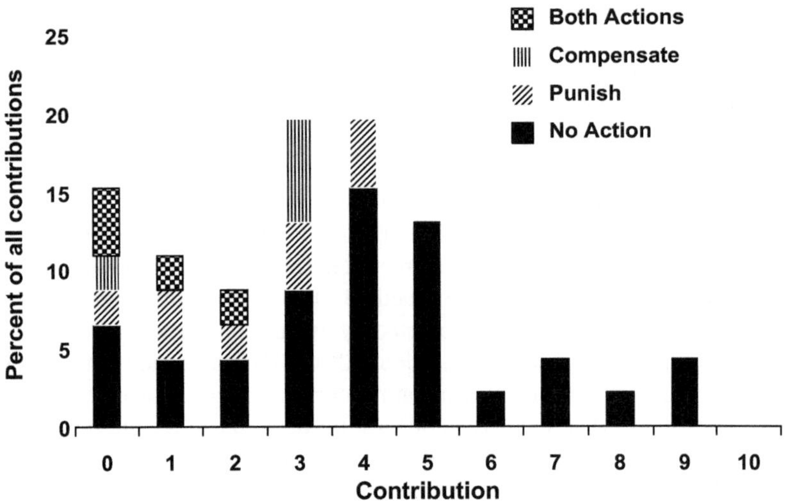

Fig. 9.1 Distribution of contributions to recipients made by contributors (n = 46) and actions taken by enforcers (n = 46) as a proportion of those contributions. Contributors could allocate any proportion of the 10 MU stake in 1 MU increments to recipients. Enforcers were allocated 5 MU and could spend: 1 MU to remove 3 MU from the contributor (retributive justice), 1 MU to add 3 MU to the recipient (restorative justice), 2 MU to do both, or keep the 5 MU and do neither

Most participants were subsistence horticulturalists; however, many garnered some income from planting and selling cash crops such as cocoa and vanilla. Very few individuals worked for any other source of wage income.

Figure 9.1 shows the distribution of contributions made by contributors (n = 46). Contributors gave between 0 and 9 MU to recipients; however, the frequency of contributions above 5 MU is relatively low and no offers of 10 MU occurred. The modal contributions are equal at 3 and 4 MU and together comprise 39.2% of all contributions made. Overall, the mean contribution is 3.3 MU (s.d. = 2.375).

A series of regressions between the demographic and socioeconomic variables listed in Table 9.1 and contribution amounts showed only annual cash cropping income to be significantly inversely correlated with contribution amounts, those with more income tended to contribute less (least squares regression analysis, $\beta = -0.377$, $p = 0.01$).

Table 9.2 Enforcers' actions by proposers' offers

Offer	n_{offer}	n_{action}	% action per n_{offer}	% of total action
0	7	4	57.1	25.0
1	5	3	60.0	18.8
2	4	2	50.0	12.5
3	9	5	55.6	31.2
4	9	2	22.2	12.5
5	6	0	0	0
6	1	0	0	0
7	2	0	0	0
8	1	0	0	0
9	2	0	0	0
10	0	0	0	0
Total	46	16		100.0

There is a significant inverse correlation between contribution amounts and whether enforcers paid to take any action (Pearson correlation, $r^2 = -0.44$, $p = 0.002$). Table 9.2 shows the percentage of time that enforcers took action by contributors' offers. For contributions of 5 MU and higher (fair as well as more than fair offers), enforcers never paid to engage in retributive justice, restorative justice, or both actions. For contributions of 4 MU and lower, enforcers were often willing to pay to exact some form of justice. Enforcers paid to take action at least 50% of the time for contributions of 0–3 MU; they also paid to take some action 22.2% of the time for contributions of 4 MU.

Figure 9.1 also displays the distribution of actions taken by enforcers as a proportion of the amounts given by contributors. Over the distribution of all offers, enforcers paid to take retributive, restorative, or both actions in 16 out of 46 cases or 34.7% of the time. Of the 16 cases in which enforcers took action, they paid to engage in a retributive (punishment) treatment 37.5% of the time, in a restorative (compensation) treatment 37.5% of the time, and were willing to pay double to do both 25.0% of the time.

Although the sample is small, the experiment revealed interesting sex differences in the frequency of actions taken by enforcers. In a series of regression analyses of enforcer actions with demographic variables, only sex consistently showed a significant relationship (least squares regression analysis with sex dummy, male = 0 female = 1, $\beta = -0.351$, $p = 0.028$). Figure 9.2 shows the percentage of actions taken by the enforcers stratified by sex. When enforcers elect to take action, there is a propensity for males to pay to engage in punishment of contributors; males punish low contributions 15.2% of the time while females do so only 7.7% of the time. By contrast, females show a disposition toward compensation of victims, whether that compensation comes from an outside source (the restorative treatment costing 1 MU) or particularly, when it comes from the contributor (the combined retributive/restorative treatment costing 2 MU). When both forms of compensation are combined, men compensate recipients 15.1% of the time while females compensate recipients a remarkable 38.5% of the time.

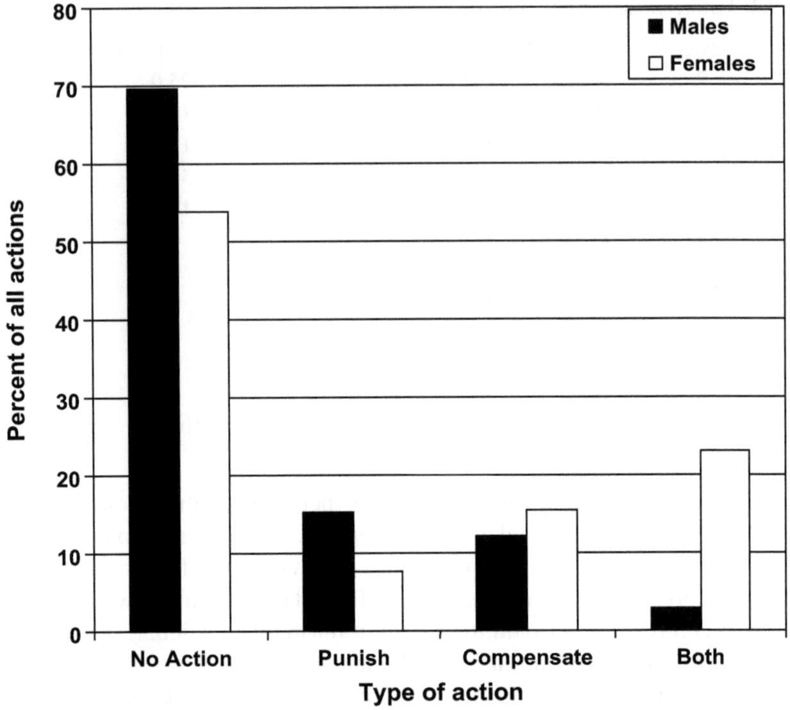

Fig. 9.2 Types of actions taken by enforcers ($n = 46$), stratified by sex and expressed as a percent of all actions taken by members of their own sex. Each sexes' total equals 100%. When they choose to pay to exact justice, men display a propensity to engage in retributive actions whereas women choose compensation or the combined treatment more frequently

Discussion: Punishment, Compensation, and the "Fairer" Sex

The results of this novel justice experiment in Papua New Guinea add to the mounting evidence that humans have a profound taste for fairness and cooperation (Bowles & Gintis, 2002; Fehr & Gächter, 2002; Gintis, Bowles, Boyd, & Fehr 2003; Tracer, 2003). The Papua New Guinean subjects who participated in this study, despite having a modal annual combined income from cash cropping and wage labor of only 100 kina (roughly US$30), nevertheless contributed on average 33% of their stakes, and showed a willingness to pay to take remediative action in situations they perceived as unfair. Had the action in which enforcers could engage been limited to punishment only, as have other researchers (Fehr & Fischbacher, 2004; Henrich et al., 2006), it might have appeared as though costly punishment was the only form of justice that enforcers were willing to exact upon unfair contributors. By allowing enforcers to sanction contributors, compensate recipients, do both, or take no action, however, we have illustrated that the altruistic nature of humans and their taste for justice are vastly more complex than previously illustrated. Overall, enforcers were willing to pay 1/5 of their allocation of 5 MUs to compensate recipients as frequently as they did to punish contributors. This demonstrates that cooperation may not be maintained solely by altruistic punishment and that explanatory models of human pro-sociality need take account of humans' more general taste for "altruistic justice," both in its retributive and restorative forms. It is also concordant with recent studies showing that actions such as reputation and image scoring are more efficient at promoting cooperation than is punishment (Grimalda, Pondorfer, & Tracer, 2016) and that punishment under some circumstances may be harmful to cooperation (Hauser, Nowak, & Rand 2014; Powers, Taylor, & Bryson 2012).

As early as 1871, Charles Darwin ascribed to women a propensity to exhibit "greater tenderness and less selfishness" than men (Darwin, 1871). In two prior "dictator experiments" in which subjects received a pool of MU and could elect to share none or any proportion of it with an anonymous second party, women contributed significantly more, and in one case, twice as much, on average, as men (Andreoni & Vesterlund, 2001; Eckel & Grossman, 1998). Similarly in a "trust game" where subjects could allocate any proportion of a pool of MU with an anonymous second party who, after having their allocation tripled, can then reciprocate and share some back, it was found that women were more likely to reciprocate than were men (Croson & Buchan, 1999). These findings, taken in tandem with evidence from sociology and political science, including, for example, that women's voting preferences are driven more by social welfare issues than are men, are consistent with the conclusion that women may be more socially oriented while men are more individually oriented (Gidengil, 1995; Welch & Hibbing, 1992). The present results add novel corroborative evidence to this conclusion. While men show a propensity to pay to punish individuals perceived as unfair, women tend more often to strive for compensating victims by either adding MUs to the pool of the recipient or effecting a transfer of MUs from the contributor to the recipient. It is important to note as well that while all of the previous studies cited were carried out exclusively among samples of university students, the current study is the first to show sex differences in justice preferences in a more naturalistic setting. Other researchers are encouraged to replicate this study among larger samples of "natural" populations (i.e., outside of university settings) in other regions of the world in order to further test for the robustness of these sex-specific differences.

The results of this study have significant implications for understanding the evolution of sociality in humans and, in particular, sexual dimorphism in the human behavioral repertoire. A number of studies conducted in diverse foraging societies have now demonstrated that men often share a lower proportion of their foraged resources with their own families than do women (Bird, 1999). Researchers working both in human societies and with our closest living primate relatives, chimpanzees, have advanced the hypothesis that in contrast to female foraging, male's hunting may be at least as much about gaining prestige and signaling desirability as a mate as it is about acquiring nutritional resources (Hawkes, 1990; Smith, Bird, & Bird, 2003; Stanford, 1996). In this regard, men's behavioral repertoires may favor greater egocentricity and, perhaps, social competitiveness than those of women. These sexually dimorphic propensities are evinced for the first time experimentally in the present study.

Acknowledgements I gratefully acknowledge the support of the MacArthur Foundation Network on Economic Environments and the Evolution of Individual Preferences and Social Norms and the University of Colorado Center for Faculty Development. I thank M. Li, C. Lesorogol, F. Marlowe, B. Ruffle, and O. Azar for their helpful suggestions as well as the Au participants and my field assistant, Rachel Foreman, who helped to carry out the experiment.

References

Andreoni, J., & Vesterlund, L. (2001). Which is the fair sex? Gender differences in altruism. *The Quarterly Journal of Economics, 116*, 293–312.

Bardsley, N. (2008). Dictator game giving: Altruism or artefact? *Experimental Economics, 11*, 122–133.

Bird, R. (1999). Cooperation and conflict: The behavioral ecology of the sexual division of labor. *Evolutionary Anthropology, 8*, 65–75.

Bowles, S., & Gintis, H. (2002). Homo reciprocans. *Nature, 415*, 125–128.

Boyd, R., Gintis, H., Bowles, S., & Richerson, P. J. (2003). The evolution of altruistic punishment. *Proceedings of the National Academy of Sciences of the United States of America, 100*, 3531–3535.

Cremaschi, S. (1998). Homo oeconomicus. In H. D. Kurz & N. Salvadori (Eds.), *The Elgar companion to classical economics* (pp. 377–381). Northampton, MA: Edward Elgar.

Croson, R., & Buchan, N. (1999). Gender and culture: International experimental evidence from trust games. *American Economic Review, 89*, 386–391.

Darwin, C. (1871). *The descent of man and selection in relation to sex*. New York, NY: Penguin Classics.

Dawkins, R. (1989). *The selfish gene* (New ed.). New York, NY: Oxford University Press.

Eckel, C. C., & Grossman, P. J. (1998). Are women less selfish than men?: Evidence from dictator experiments. *The Economic Journal, 108*, 726–735.

Fehr, E., & Fischbacher, U. (2003). The nature of human altruism. *Nature, 425*, 785–791.

Fehr, E., & Fischbacher, U. (2004). Third party punishment and social norms. *Evolution and Human Behavior, 25*, 63–87.

Fehr, E., & Gächter, S. (2002). Altruistic punishment in humans. *Nature, 415*, 137–140.

Gidengil, E. (1995). Economic man-social woman?: The case of the gender gap in support for the Canada-United States free trade agreement. *Comparative Political Studies, 28*, 384–408.

Gintis, H., Bowles, S., Boyd, R., & Fehr, E. (2003). Explaining altruistic behavior in humans. *Evolution and Human Behavior, 24*, 153–172.

Grimalda, G., Pondorfer, A., & Tracer, D. P. (2016). Social image concerns promote cooperation more than altruistic punishment. *Nature Communications, 7*, 12288. doi:10.1038/ncomms12288.

Hamilton, W. D. (1964). The genetical evolution of social behavior I and II. *Journal of Theoretical Biology, 7*, 1–52.

Hauser, O. P., Nowak, M. A., & Rand, D. G. (2014). Punishment does not promote cooperation under exploration dynamics when anti-social punishment is possible. *Journal of Theoretical Biology, 360*, 163–171.

Hawkes, K. (1990). Why do men hunt? Some benefits for risky strategies. In E. Cashdan (Ed.), *Risk and uncertainty in tribal and peasant economies* (pp. 145–166). Westview Press: Boulder, CO.

Henrich, J., Boyd, R., Bowles, S., Camerer, C., Fehr, E., Gintis, H., … Tracer, D. (2005) "Economic man" in cross-cultural perspective: Behavioral experiments in 15 small-scale societies. *Behavioral and Brain Sciences 28*, 795–815.

Henrich, J., McElreath, R., Barr, A., Ensminger, J., Barrett, C, Bolyanatz, A., … Ziker, J. (2006) Costly punishment across human societies. *Science 312*, 1767–1770.

Powers, S. T., Taylor, D. J., & Bryson, J. J. (2012). Punishment can promote defection in group-structured populations. *Journal of Theoretical Biology, 311*, 107–116.

Robson, A. J. (2001). The biological basis of economic behavior. *Journal of Economic Literature, 39*, 11–33.

Smith, A. (1776). *The wealth of nations*. London: Strahan and Cadell.

Smith, E. A., Bird, R. B., & Bird, D. W. (2003). The benefits of costly signaling: Meriam turtle hunters. *Behavioral Ecology, 14*, 116–126.

Stanford, C. (1996). The hunting ecology of wild chimpanzees: Implications for the evolutionary ecology of Pliocene hominids. *American Anthropologist, 98*, 96–113.

Tracer, D. P. (2003). Selfishness and fairness in economic and evolutionary perspective: An experimental economic study in Papua New Guinea. *Current Anthropology, 44*, 432–438.

Tracer, D. P., Mueller, I., & Morse, J. (2014). Cruel to be kind: Effects of sanctions and enforcers on generosity in Papua New Guinea. In J. Ensminger & J. Henrich (Eds.), *Experimenting with social norms: Fairness and punishment in cross-cultural perspective* (pp. 177–196). New York, NY: Sage Foundation.

Welch, S., & Hibbing, J. (1992). Financial conditions, gender, and voting in American national elections. *The Journal of Politics, 54*, 197–213.

Zehr, H., & Towes, B. (2004). *Critical issues in restorative justice*. Monsey, NY: Criminal Justice Press.

Zizzo, D. J. (2010). Experimenter demand effects in economic experiments. *Experimental Economics, 13*, 75–98.

Chapter 10
Framing Charitable Solicitations in a Behavioral Experiment: Cues Derived from Evolutionary Theory of Cooperation and Economic Anthropology

Shane A. Scaggs, Karen S. Fulk, Delaney Glass, and John P. Ziker

Social goods generated through philanthropy are essential for the redistribution of resources (Andreoni & Scholz, 1998), and they provide a strategic means to resolve some civic social dilemmas (Brown & Ferris, 2007). The overwhelming need to fund social goods has fostered considerable interest in identifying factors that increase philanthropic giving. Cross-sectional surveys have indicated that most charitable donations are generated when the donor encounters a *solicitation* (Bekkers, 2005; Bryant, Slaughter, Kang, & Tax, 2003). Bekkers and Wiepking (2011) determined that solicitation is the core mechanism motivating charitable giving, while other investigations have identified individual characteristics which effect donor behavior (Brown & Ferris, 2007; Radley & Kennedy, 1995; Tonin & Vlassopoulos, 2014; Wang & Graddy, 2008). While some research has focused on the preconditions necessary to achieve a donation, the specific nuances that underlie the social ties between potential donor and solicitor and the precise nature of interactions that successfully result in a donation remain unclear.

Theoretical perspectives from evolutionary game theory and anthropological cross-cultural data provide insight into the benefits individuals obtain by forming and maintaining qualitatively different types of cooperative relationships. A series of pathways, such as kin biased altruism, direct reciprocity, indirect reciprocity, and signaling, are theorized to explain the costs and benefits of cooperation under various conditions, and between alternative social partners (Bshary & Bergmüller, 2008; Bshary & Bronstein, 2004, 2011; Dugatkin, 1999; Lehmann & Keller, 2006;

S.A. Scaggs
Department of Anthropology, Oregon State University, Corvallis, OR, USA
e-mail: scaggss@oregonstate.edu

K.S. Fulk • D. Glass • J.P. Ziker (✉)
Department of Anthropology, Boise State University, Boise, ID, USA
e-mail: karenfulk@u.boisestate.edu; delaneyjglass@gmail.com; jziker@boisestate.edu

M. Li, D.P. Tracer (eds.), *Interdisciplinary Perspectives on Fairness, Equity, and Justice*, DOI 10.1007/978-3-319-58993-0_10

Nowak & Sigmund, 1998, 2005). These beneficial outcomes are viewed as phenotypic responses to selection pressures that have occurred throughout the evolutionary history of animal cooperation. These mechanisms are also fundamentally important for understanding human altruism. Ethnographic data provide scholars a cross-cultural, comparative vantage point for determining which mechanisms favor cooperative behaviors and institutions among humans within particular sociocultural environments. Analyses of giving traditions within small-scale societies underscore the roles kin-bias, reciprocity, and signaling have in ecological contexts akin to those of our deepest human ancestors.

This chapter explores the impact social cues have on solicitations for charitable gifts within a public goods game. The social cues investigated are based on patterns relevant to evolutionary theory and to cross-cultural ethnographic data. Our objectives for this study were to understand if, and to what degree, socially cued solicitations produce predictably variable donation amounts. The literatures on the evolution of cooperative social behavior and ethnographies of giving provided theoretical context for developing our cued responses. In reviewing the philanthropic literature, we sought explanations for the efficacy of alternative methods of solicitation. Following Sulek's (2010, p. 204) definition of philanthropic giving as "an objective act such as giving money, time, or effort, to a charitable cause or public purpose," we developed a set of independent and control variables to use in analysis alongside our cued solicitation responses.

In this chapter we summarize the literature foundational to the design of our study, and its social significance. We also discuss the implementation, execution, and the results of our pilot experiments. In conclusion, we highlight the socio-behavioral relevance of our study to charitable organizations and researchers alike. This includes addressing the limitations of our study, and the need for further research to explore the relevant interactions between donors and solicitors, notably those social cues which promote or impede donation efforts.

Charity and Philanthropy in Evolutionary Theory and Economic Anthropology

Charitable Behavior and Philanthropic Solicitation

Individuals independently motivated to engage in charitable behavior are referred to as *pure altruists* (Allouch, 2013; Andreoni, 1989, 1990; Simpson & Willer, 2008; Tonin & Vlassopoulos, 2014). A personal concern for the well-being of others characterizes pure altruists (Tonin & Vlassopoulos, 2014). The most prevalent justification for such benevolence is the *warm glow hypothesis* (Allouch, 2013; Andreoni, 1989, 1990; Bischoff & Kauskopf, 2015). This view posits that donor's feelings of satisfaction and joy prompt independent, anonymous donations. Evidence from social neuroscience supports this view. Engaging in interpersonal charitable behavior is associated with increased activity in the fronto-mesolimbic reward system of the brain (Moll et al., 2006). Donating is specifically linked to the subgenual region, notable for its role in social attachment. However, despite the potentiality of this biological mechanism to prompt charitable actions, the warm glow hypothesis and its neurological counterpart do not sufficiently explain variability in giving behavior, nor why so few individuals engage in charitable activities without interpersonal stimuli (Radley & Kennedy, 1995).

In contrast to the pure altruists, most people only make donations subsequent to some form of direct *solicitation*. Cross-sectional surveys have demonstrated that most donations (more than 85%) were made in response to a solicitation (Bekkers, 2005; Bryant et al., 2003). However, in their review of motivations for philanthropic behavior, Bekkers and Wiepking (2011) suggested solicitation was only one of two prerequisites for charitable giving—the second was donor *awareness of need*. From this perspective, the function of a solicitation is, in part, to make potential donors aware of the opportunity to contribute. This view is supported by other scholars who contend that solicitation is just one component of the *source* of a donation (Sargeant & Woodliffe, 2007).

It is also evident that the method of solicitation impacts the success of fundraising efforts. Personal solicitations and door-to-door fundraising produce larger and more frequent donations than impersonal letters or mass requests (Naeem & Zaman, 2016; Yörük, 2012). When donors acknowledge even the slightest interpersonal familiarity, solicitations efforts tend to be more successful, and donations increase (Macaulay, 1975; Sargeant & Woodliffe, 2007). These favorable outcomes may be the by-product of the stronger social ties that result from supporting the solicitor's cause (Bekkers & Wiepking, 2011). For example, Meer (2011) reported that among alumni donors, the size of charitable gifts usually increased when a donor was solicited by a previous roommate, or when the two shared sororal or fraternal affiliations. Additional support was obtained by evaluating historic charitable records. Using donor survey data from the 1990s, Yörük (2012) determined that respondents ranked being solicited by a *close associate* or having *previously volunteered* for the organization as the most important reasons for donating.

The sensitivity of donor response to shared affiliations and specific social relationship cues are consistent with the perspective that publicly generated goods are embedded in social networks and structures (Simpson & Willer, 2005; Wang & Graddy, 2008). A solicitor in such a network is characterized by a greater degree of betweenness, a measure of network centrality (Freeman, 1977). In this way, the solicitor, acting as a representative of a charitable organization, functions as an intermediary between the donor and the beneficiary, directly connecting the other two parties. Social capital theory suggests that the solidarity of relationships throughout these networks promotes reciprocal exchange (Putnam, 1995; Radley & Kennedy, 1995). Since charities rely on affective sentiments, such as trust, to form and maintain enduring relationships with prospective donors (Sargeant & Lee, 2004), a solicitor surely acts as a trust-broker when soliciting new or additional contributions.

Evolutionary Pathways to Cooperation

We derived the social cues for this experiment by considering the dominant hypotheses in game theory models of cooperation (Bowles & Gintis, 2011; Dawkins, 1976; Dugatkin, 1999; Henrich, 2009). Such models, when applied to individual decision-making in social dilemmas, assume that fitness-maximizing behaviors evoke large benefit–cost ratios (i.e., low cost investments that bring about greater return benefits). Costs include investments of time or capital into a common pool, whereas benefits accrue via increased access to resources, broadened social networks, or improved reputations. Social dilemmas are situations where individuals profit from selfishness while other members of the group support the public good. The group outcome (i.e., the average payoff) is best when everyone contributes and is worse when everyone defects from the public good.

An individual solicited to make a charitable donation is faced with a one-shot, one-sided investment decision, as modeled in social dilemmas. An individual in these scenarios should defect, other things equal, as his or her payoff is always highest by not donating anything. Such behavior enables the defector to receive a portion of others' contributions to the collective fund, while inputting nothing. The outcome is referred to as *free riding*, and the challenge free riders create for provisioning of public goods is the free-rider problem (Hardin, 1977). Overcoming this collective action problem is a challenge to organizations funded via charitable donations. Understanding the effects, if any, of social cues on solicitation responses is of high interest to charities and other organizations supporting the public good. There are several possibilities we investigate.

Kin selection (inclusive fitness) has a deep history in literature on the evolution of cooperation (Dawkins, 1976; Hamilton, 1964a, 1964b) and in explanatory mathematical models of helping behavior (Lehmann & Keller, 2006). In such models, altruistic behavior evolves if the costs of the altruistic investments are less than the benefits to the actor via indirect fitness of kin, or if actors can identify linkages between altruistic investments and traits that allow for directed investment in others that share the same allele(s) (i.e., the green beard effect) (Dawkins, 1976). Following this logic, we hypothesized that supporting the fundraising efforts of a family member affords indirect fitness benefits—especially if the goods generated support the family's interests. To investigate kinship as a motivating force, we used the cue *close family member* in our experiment and discussed the benefit as supporting family interests.

One of the more widely hypothesized mechanisms for the evolution of cooperation is *reciprocal altruism* (Trivers, 1971) or *direct reciprocity* (DR) (Bshary & Bronstein, 2011). The underlying principle of DR entails rewarding cooperative partners and avoiding investments in individuals who are defectors. We hypothesized that a positive response to a solicitation by a friend strengthens trust and increases the probability of reciprocated support in the future. Within our experiment we used the cue *close friend* to represent reciprocal altruism and referenced reciprocal support in the future to explain the potential benefit of responding to the friend's solicitation on behalf of the charitable organization.

Bshary and Bergmüller (2008) distinguished two forms of indirect reciprocity (IR). The first is based on experiences of having received help, while the second is based on image scoring—an index of an individual's past cooperative behaviors toward third parties. When based on the experience of help received from third parties, IR entails an upstream prosocial act that carries no anticipation of future direct benefits or expectation of counter gifts (Bshary & Bronstein, 2004, 2011; Sahlins, 1972). Mathematical models suggest that this form of IR may persist when small group size (Pfeiffer, Rutte, Killingback, Taborsky, & Bonhoeffer, 2005) or increased proximity between agents occurs (Nowak & Roch, 2007), thereby increasing the probability of encountering a cooperative conspecific. If these conditions are not met, cooperation may still evolve if actors assort themselves into subgroups nonrandomly, resulting in a higher probability of cooperating with another cooperator (Fletcher & Doebeli, 2009; Rankin & Taborsky, 2009).

When IR occurs via image scoring, cooperative states can emerge if individual actors are capable of discriminating between cooperative and noncooperative partners by recalling information about past behaviors (i.e., reputation) (Panchanathan & Boyd, 2004). Individuals invest only in partners that have sufficiently helped others in the past and the act of helping increases an individual's image score (Bshary & Bergmüller, 2008).

When a potential donor is solicited by an individual with whom he or she is less well-acquainted, the only information available is gained from the initial cues derived at first contact (Naeem & Zaman, 2016), or from drawing on prior knowledge about the charitable cause represented (Bekkers & Wiepking, 2011). Awareness of a charitable organization's reputation is a category of information that can condition a cooperative or defective donation response. We hypothesized that when there is no prior knowledge of the cause at hand, a prospective donor may rely on prior experience to condition a prosocial response. In addition, if representing a nonprofit organization is any cue to the cooperative reputation of the solicitor, we expected a donation in this context to fall under the mechanism of indirect reciprocity via image scoring (Alexander, 1987; Nowak & Sigmund, 1998, 2005). Following the logic of IR, we designated the benefits of donating in terms of improving community well-being and used the cue *local nonprofit member* in our experimental protocol.

Some solicitors hold a position of prestige that makes him or her more well-known to potential donors. Often individuals that are considered prestigious, such as celebrities or politicians, solicit donations on behalf of charitable organizations. In return, donors are praised and recognized with memorials, dedications, galas, and other public honors. In this context, a desire may motivate donor behavior to signal quality using costly, but generous, contributions. The donor may benefit from increased status, an expanded social network, or improved access to additional resources by engaging in *costly signaling* (CS) (Chapais, 2015; Zahavi, 1975; Zahavi & Zahavi, 1997). Bshary and Bergmüller (2008) refer to this strategy as indirect positive pseudo-reciprocity. Costly signals purportedly provide information about a person's phenotypic quality or cooperative tendencies, as evidenced in behavioral studies of risk taking, hunting, and religion (Bliege Bird, Smith, & Bird,

2001). Following the logic of costly signaling, we designated the benefits of donating in terms of being publicly recognized with the celebrity and used the cue *local celebrity* as the solicitor in our experimental protocol.

Ethnographic Examples of Sharing

The contributions of ethnographers to the understanding of cross-cultural similarities and discrepancies in prosocial behavior also have helped us define our cues for this experiment. Extant hunter-gatherers provide a comparative lens into the human condition that cannot be gained by analyzing WEIRD (Western, Educated, Industrialized, Rich, Democratic) societies (Henrich, Heine, & Norenzayan, 2010). By investigating traditional livelihoods, we obtained a sense of the adaptiveness social behaviors provide within ecological contexts similar to those of our hominid ancestors. Through this line of evidence, we gained some insight into the origin of philanthropic institutions.

In his seminal work, *The Gift: Forms and Functions of Exchange in Archaic Societies*, Marcel Mauss (1969) offered ethnographic examples of gift economies prevalent in traditional societies. The aim of such conventions is to establish future exchanges or reinforce existing cooperation between households or communities. For example, solicitory gifts among the Trobriand Islanders signified appreciation and cordiality and "must be reciprocated" (Mauss, 1969, p. 39). Mauss expanded this concept of indebtedness by remarking that the Trobrianders' *sagali* food distributions were used as rewards for work or rituals performed (p. 94), rather than for buffering insecurity—a habit found more commonly in hunter-gatherer societies. Marshall Sahlins (1972, p. 213) discussed charity in his comparative work *Stone Age Economics* stating that "helping people in distress creates very intense solidarity." Sahlins formalized the most charitable form of helping behavior with the term *generalized reciprocity* because it contains no expectation of return benefits. While Sahlins argued that generalized reciprocity should occur mostly between kin, these benefits coincide with expectations of indirect reciprocity as well.

Exchange institutions, such as those described by Mauss and Sahlins, exist across small-scale societies in numerous ecological contexts and are investigated by considering evolutionary hypotheses of cooperation—the most common being kin selection, reciprocal altruism, and costly signaling (Gurven, 2004). For example, the Tsimane of Amazonian Bolivia live in economically independent familial households and most gifts are exchanged between close kin (Gurven & Winking, 2008). Similarly, in the Taimyr region of northern Siberia, indigenous hunter-fisher-trappers distribute food resources in a *sustained one-way flow,* most often directed toward spouses, offspring, and friends (Ziker, 2002; Ziker & Schnegg, 2005). Additionally, reciprocal exchanges were found to intensify between the most productive households and most skilled hunters (Ziker, Rasmussen, & Nolin, 2016).

The nomadic Hadza of Tanzania give valuable items to kin, friends, and friends of friends based on the positive assortment of high contributors through the mechanism of IR (Henrich, 2012). Much is written about the contentious nature of Hadza sharing contending that hunters share food, not to reduce risk or provisions families, but to enhance reputation with neighbors (Hawkes, O'Connell, & Blurton Jones, 2001). However, more recent studies of the Hadza demonstrate food sharing satisfies the goal of kin provisioning (Wood & Marlowe, 2013). In contrast, among the Ache of neotropical Paraguay, better hunters typically give away more hunted game than they receive on any given day. While not following a strict tit-for-tat logic, such behavior likely functions to buffer against future risk, as these hunters receive more (on average) during hard times, or when sick or injured (Gurven, Allen-Arave, Hill, & Hurtado, 2000). Reciprocal exchange, following the expectations of direct reciprocity, provides a risk buffering function and is widely documented among hunter-gatherers. In the Kalahari Desert of Botswana, the egalitarian! Kung hunter-gatherers distribute nonfood items within camps and across vast distances according to a semiformal system of mutual assistance, known as *hxaro* (Wiessner, 2002). The benefits of *hxaro* have been thought of in terms of a regional insurance policy based on delayed reciprocity (Wiessner, 2002). This brief review illustrates that several mechanisms favoring sharing behavior may be operating simultaneously among the Hadza and other hunter-gatherer populations.

In India, the philanthropic behavior of the Uttar Pradesh is described as an investment in the community economy that functions to "reduce disparities between villagers" (Lapoint & Joshi, 1985–1986, p. 43). The authors also suggest that benefits returned to the donor arrive "in the form of public esteem" (p. 43). Among the Chang-hua in China, charitable donations tend to originate from the urban-elite in the community, as they have accumulated a surplus of resources that allow them to make costly investments (Meskill, 1979). However, this also represents a philanthropic tendency to redistribute goods to benefit the greater good.

Focusing only on the individual donor in these ethnographic contexts, three themes emerge. First, givers that preferentially direct assistance to kin, friends, or close associates do so to promote solidarity and future exchange. Long-term reciprocity between cooperative partners may confer inclusive fitness benefits and buffer against future risk or misfortune. Secondly, givers who prefer to donate to public institutions may be motivated by prestige. An individual is better able to achieve this aim when he or she is among the most prosperous or skilled members of the community (Lapoint & Joshi, 1985–1986; Henrich, 2012; Meskill, 1979; Ziker et al., 2016). Lastly, whether through kin, friends, prestigious individuals, or representatives, the pooled goods generated through long-term reciprocity typically function to reduce resource inequality.

Design considerations for our study were predicated on the existing theoretical and empirical research. We implemented social cues to reflect key concepts and the costs/benefits of charitable actions as modeled in kin selection, reciprocal altruism, indirect reciprocity, and costly signaling. In addition, the ethnographic literature supported the use of a public goods game (Ledyard, 1997) as a vehicle to examine the effects of these cues and made it an ideal approach to evaluate the interactions social cues impart on charitable behaviors.

Methods

This study investigated whether solicitations that are framed with evolutionarily significant relationship cues have varying effects on charitable giving. We hypothesized framing effects would reveal cognitive biases and personal expectations held by study participants (Gerkey, 2013). To test this, we conducted two experimental economic games—a public goods game (PGG) and an allocation decision game (ADG) developed as a modified PGG. We utilized a self-report questionnaire to collect potential explanatory variables for the observed economic behavior.

Public Goods Games

Behavioral economics has a rich history of use for investigating social dilemmas. The public goods game is suited for modeling common pool resources (Ledyard, 1997). PGGs have also been utilized to investigate privately funded resource pools such as those accumulated through charitable giving (Andreoni & Scholz, 1998; Becker, 1974; Bekkers & Wiepking, 2011). The Public Goods Game (PGG), also known as the *n*-person prisoner's dilemma (Bowles & Gintis, 2011), uses a formal payout structure to set the optimal strategy for an individual in conflict with the optimal strategy for the group. The participant is endowed with an amount of currency x_i and asked to decide an amount d_i of this endowment to contribute to the common pool. The contributions of n participants to the common pool are then increased by some multiplier k and split evenly among all participants. The resulting payout P_i for each participant is the equal share of the common pool, plus the portion of his or her endowment that was kept. This payout is calculated as:

$$P_i = (x_i - d_i) + \Sigma \frac{k(d_i)}{n}$$

where i = the index denoting each independent participant in the PGG and n = the number of participants contributing to the common pool. The payout represents the overall benefit to each participant from contributing to the public good.

We used the PGG payout structure to incentivize experimental behavior. Subjects were solicited by a randomly chosen social frame representing the *solicitor* of the donations. The study subject was considered the *potential donor* and the payout each received was a representation of the assumed benefit one would derive if this were a natural setting. Each subject was provided a \$10 endowment and asked to donate to one of the five social frames (Table 10.1). The amount donated was then pooled with the contributions of three other randomly selected subjects, doubled, and then divided evenly among the four participants as in a standard PGG.

Our PGG's question format utilized a statement about a solicitor randomly assigned to one of five social frames (cues to four contextualized and one uncontex-

Table 10.1 PGG social frames

Frame	Cue
1	Close relative (CR)
2	Close friend (CF)
3	Local nonprofit member (NPM)
4	Local celebrity (LC)
5	Person (uncontextualized)

tualized social relation), and a follow-up question about the amount of the donation. Participants were asked:

> A [*social frame (1–5)*] has come to you asking for a donation of up to $10. How much will you donate?

A rational actor, termed *Homo economicus* (Persky, 1995), in a PGG is expected to contribute nothing to the common pool. By *free riding*, an individual takes advantage of the benefits provided by the public good without incurring any of the costs of funding it. However, if no individuals contribute, no public good is available to benefit, resulting in the *tragedy of the commons* (Hardin, 1977). Evidence from laboratory and field experimentation, however, indicates that across cultures individuals are more generous than this formalist economic tradition predicts (Bowles & Gintis, 2011; Gerkey, 2013; Henrich et al., 2001). Such discrepancies advise that a substantive economic approach to public goods may lead to more accurate predictions. Indeed, Gerkey (2013) accurately predicted that because fishers and herders of Kamchatka, Russia rely heavily on cooperation for successful resource procurement, they might exhibit higher mean PGG contributions when compared with groups utilizing alternative foraging strategies.

Allocation Decision Game

The allocation decision game provides a measure of prosocial relationship preferences. Four social frames were used (1 = *close relative*, 2 = *close friend*, 3 = *nonprofit member*, 4 = *celebrity*). During this game, subjects were given the option to allocate any of their $10 endowment in one dollar increments among each of the four frames. Any money not allocated could be kept by the participant. Unique to the decision game, we primed subjects, suggesting the potential benefits of donating to one frame over another. We also set a 1-min timer to induce spontaneous giving, rather than calculated greed (Rand, Greene, & Nowak, 2012).

Our ADG priming focused on the benefits associated with the cues derived from the literature.

1. Your donation to your *close relative* supports your family's interests.
2. Your donation to your *close friend's* cause increases the likelihood that they will support you when you fundraise.

3. You benefit from contributing to a *nonprofit member's* cause by improving the overall well-being in the community.
4. You benefit from contributing to a *celebrity's* cause by being publicly recognized with the celebrity.

Protocol Description

Interested subjects were escorted to a conference room furnished with a series of laptop computers and asked to be seated. A research assistant provided each volunteer with a paper copy of the game instructions and an identification number. Participants were informed to ask the assistants to clarify any questions. The subjects were then instructed to sign in through Google Forms with their requisite information, which created a method of ensuring participant's earned funds could be distributed. Payment amounts were processed and paid to student accounts at the conclusion of the study. All participant information was kept separate and confidential.

After providing consent, participants were directed to the Qualtrics (2015) survey and asked a series of practice game questions to affirm the participants understood and could follow the game's instructions. Individuals who could not demonstrate this were excluded from the study ($n_{excluded} = 1$). Successful completion of the practice questions initiated the PGG, followed by the ADG. This particular sequence of events was chosen so that subjects were introduced to all four social cues simultaneously in the ADG after being presented with the randomly chosen single frame for the PGG. Finally, participants completed a 40-question follow-up survey. This protocol follows the experimental format of the cross-cultural project of Henrich et al. (2010, 2006). Throughout the experiment, research assistants were available to answer participant's questions, and importantly, to prevent any talking or possible collusion among subjects. Groups of students were not recruited for participation so that study participants remained unacquainted. Our recruitment strategy, protocol, game script, and follow-up questionnaire were reviewed and approved by the Boise State University IRB.

Follow-Up Survey

Our 40-question follow-up survey was divided into four sections: socioeconomic status, demographic status, volunteering behavior, and social expectations. The first section inquired about income, education, type of employment organization, and any federal financial aid or assistance the respondents were receiving as income. A demographic section included questions about respondents' biological sex, relative age, household composition, residence, religion, and dependents. A volunteering section included questions about money donations, volunteer hours and frequency, and the number of organizations where the respondent volunteers. A final section explored participants' expectations and assessed the respondents' trust and distrust of people in general, community pride, community ties, and their expectations of the economic games.

Statistical Analysis

Data from game behavior and the follow-up survey was exported from Qualtrics as an Excel file and then uploaded to SPSS 20.0 (IBM SPSS, 2011) where it was cleaned and coded. Correlation matrices were created from all variables to identify possible linear relationships and to check for multicollinearity. The strength of solicitation framing in the PGG was analyzed using a one-way ANOVA and ultra-generous donations were examined using binomial logistic regression in SPSS 20.0. The strength of the solicitation framing and priming in the ADG were analyzed using a robust repeated-measures ANOVA. Potential explanatory variables for each decision frame in the ADG were analyzed using backward stepwise elimination with an elimination criterion of $p > 0.05$ in SPSS 20.0 and in RStudio (RStudioTeam, 2015). Regression models were built using the remaining variables after elimination. Shapiro–Wilk tests were conducted to test for normal distribution and where applicable (most models) a bootstrapping procedure was used to model non-normal distributions.

Sampling

For the primary study, we recruited opportunistically and face-to-face. The research team set up and staffed a table at a strategic campus location known to have a high level of foot traffic. We posted signage about the opportunity to join a study about generosity and offered a donut or healthy treat as an incentive for participating in the experiment. Subjects were told they would receive payouts calculated on their game behavior. Sixty-four subjects were recruited in this manner.

Results

Self-Report Variables

The final analysis included a sample of $N = 63$ participants. The sample was split evenly ($n_{\text{males}} = 31$, $n_{\text{females}} = 32$, $M = 24$ years) and comprised primarily of university students ($n_{\text{students}} = 58$) with $\text{Mdn}_{\text{education}} = 3$ (*some college*) reported across the entire sample. Education was strongly correlated with relative age (*Pearson's* $r = 0.55$, $p < 0.001$). Participants reported median bimonthly income of $250, median 2014 gross pretax income of $5008, and median nonessential spending at $100. When asked about religious participation, 20 of 63 respondents (31.75%) reported *yes* with a sample average of 0.49 religious events attended in the past week. This characterized our sample as mostly nonreligious.

Volunteering

To gauge the volunteerism and community behavior of our subjects, we asked them to report the frequency of their temporal and quantity of their monetary contributions to others. The information was requested for the past week, and for the past year (Table 10.2). Expectedly, past donation amounts were moderately correlated with bimonthly income ($r = 0.29$, $p < 0.05$), 2014 gross pretax income ($r = 0.55$, $p < 0.001$), and nonessential spending ($r = 0.45$, $p < 0.001$). Participants were then prompted with the following statement, "My involvement in community affairs is ______ for improving our community," and were asked to fill the survey blank with a Likert scale response (*unimportant* = 1, *somewhat unimportant* = 2, *neither important nor unimportant* = 3, *somewhat important* = 4, and *important* = 5). The sample mean for this variable was 3.70 with SD = 1.24. Volunteer frequency was moderately correlated with this community involvement importance variable ($r = 0.52$, $p < 0.001$).

Social Expectations

We asked participants to report trust and distrust using a 5-point Likert agreement scale (*strongly disagree* = 1, *disagree* = 2, *neutral* = 3, *agree* = 4, *strongly agree* = 5). The mean response to the statement, "Generally speaking, most people can be

Table 10.2 Descriptive statistics for volunteering reported in the follow-up survey

Variable	*M*	Mdn	SD	Range
Volunteer frequency	2.03	2	1.97	6
Volunteer hours (weekly)	3.97	3	3.22	13
Number of org's volunteered for (past year)	1.87	2	2.38	10
Donation amount (past year)	510.32	10	2442.33	18,000
Donation frequency	1.59	2	1.64	7
Number of org. donated to (past year)	3.58	2	2.89	9

Frequency variables were reported using a drop-down list that was coded (*never* = 0, *once a year* = 1, *once a month* = 2, *bimonthly* = 3, *once a week* = 4, *more than once a week* = 5, *daily* = 6). Weekly and past year variables were reported using a numerical write-in trusted" was 2.79, SD = 0.92. The mean response to the statement "Generally speaking, you can't be too careful with people" was 3.33 with SD = 1.03. This question was developed to measure participants' *generalized trust* (discussed in more detail below), rather than *affective trust* (Ahn & Erasey, 2008).

We inquired whether participants expected other game players to behave selfishly by contributing nothing (*free riding*), or selflessly by contributing everything (*altruism*). To these two questions, responses were recorded with a dichotomous *yes* or *no*. Overall, 40 (63.49%) anticipated *free riding* and 37 (58.73%) anticipated *altruism*. Participants were also asked to report how much they expected other game players to contribute in the PGG. The $M_{\text{contribution}} = 4.59$ was with $SD_{\text{contribution}} = 2.37$. This measure was moderately correlated with community involvement importance ($r = 0.40$, $p < 0.01$).

Descriptive Statistics and Comparison of Frames in the Public Goods Game

Observations in the PGG ($N = 63$) consisted of five subgroups each denoted by one of the randomly assigned frames (see Table 10.3), thereby reducing the number of observations for each frame to $n < 20$. Each subset included at least one individual donating the entirety of the endowment. Although solicitations framed by *close relative* and *close friend* produced greater mean donations than other frames, these differences were not statistically significant ($F(4, 58) = 2.53$, $p > 0.05$). This suggested that contextualizing the person asking for the donation in our PGG using short cues did not have significant effects on donations.

Table 10.3 Descriptive statistics for frames in each of the economic games

Frame	Mdn	*M*	SD	Range	*n*
PGG					
Close relative	7.5	6.38	3.58	0–10	16
Close friend	6	6.40	2.99	3–10	10
Nonprofit member	4	4.93	3.17	1–10	15
Celebrity	2	3.89	3.82	0–10	9
A person	5	5.77	3.92	0–10	13
ADG					
Close relative	3	3.44	2.09	0–10	63
Close friend	2	2.25	1.22	0–5	63
Nonprofit member	2	2.76	2.08	0–8	63
Celebrity	0	0.33	0.62	0–3	63

PGG means are not significantly different ($N_{\text{PGG}} = 63$, $p > 0.05$). Sample sizes for the PGG reflect the proportion of individuals that received the specific frame. In ADG, all subjects ($N_{\text{ADG}} = 63$) responded to all four frames

Logistic Regression of the PGG Results

Without precedent, 19 of 63 participants contributed the entire $10 endowment regardless of the social frame presented to them. This phenomenon resulted in a spectacularly generous distribution that showed an unexpectedly large number of $10 contributions—the entire individual endowment (Fig. 10.1). To analyze this particular distribution, PGG donations were recoded as dichotomous variables ($Donated_{\$0–9} = 0$, $Donated_{\$10} = 1$). We first used an independent samples *t*-test to check the potentially relevant control variables, including age, gender, education level, bimonthly income, annual pretax income, and employment status. There were no significant differences in means of these control variables for these two groups.

Examining other independent variables from the survey for the two groups in the PGG (i.e., those who donated none or some fraction of the endowment vs. those who donated the entire endowment), we used binary logistic regressions to test individual variables, and then combined the most significant variables in a final logistic regression. In the follow-up survey, we asked respondents to report their perceptions of other players' generosity with the question: "In Game 1, do you think at least one person contributed $9 to the group?" Those who donated their entire endowment answered "yes" to that question at a higher rate than those who kept some or all their endowment ($\beta = 1.413$, $p < 0.05$, $\exp(\beta) = 4.107$). Of the 19 players who donated their entire endowment, 15 reported that they expected at least one other person to contribute $9. Those who kept some or all their endowment were split more evenly on this question with 23 of 44 answering "no." This result indicated that a person's perception of the level of cooperation in the community may be important to that individual's willingness to be extra-generous in this game.

Respondents reported that the frequency of their own volunteering activity (recoded to *none*, *some*, and *frequent*) was significant for the change from *some* to

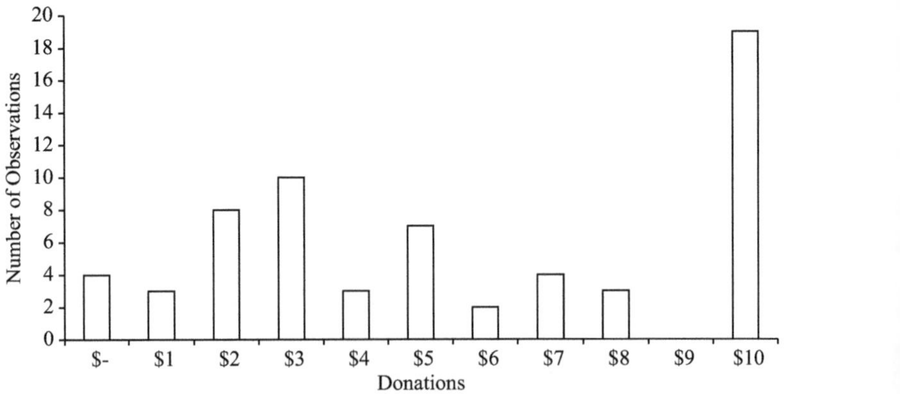

Fig. 10.1 Distribution of donation amounts in the PGG across all frames. Donations of the entire endowment ($10) are inflated

frequent volunteering ($\beta = 1.649$, $\exp(\beta) = 5.200$, $p < 0.05$). For frequent volunteers, there was a 19% increase in odds that the player donated the entire endowment. This result indicated that personal experience in donating one's time may be important in motivating the extra-generous donations in this game.

Taken together in a combined regression, the perception of altruism of other players dropped to a $p < 0.10$ level of significance. In summary, few variables predicted player behavior in the PGG, although two theoretically relevant variables (assumptions about the altruistic behavior of players, and a player's charitable experience) are suggestive. In the theoretical overview, we discuss the importance of identifying cooperators for kin selection and indirect reciprocity models.

Descriptive Statistics for the Allocation Decision Game

In the allocation decision game (ADG), players had to allocate their money to four alternative solicitors representing the four alternative social cues. Players also had the option to keep some fraction of their endowment. We first analyzed the overall distribution to the four response options, then we examine each alternative frame independently.

The differences in the mean allocations to each option in the ADG were statistically insignificant using a robust repeated-measures ANOVA (see Table 10.4). In total, *close relative* received the greatest total allocation ($217), followed by *local nonprofit member* ($174), *close friend* ($142), and self ($76), with *local celebrity* receiving the lowest total allocation ($21). A Shapiro–Wilk test of normality shows the distribution of allocations to be non-normal ($p < 0.05$) in all ADG frames. Considering the four donation options, subjects in the ADG were highly generous,

Table 10.4 ADG frame comparisons and contrasts

Group	Group	Test	SE	PSihat	CI_{LL}	CI_{UL}	α
CR	CF	3.73	0.26	0.97	0.15	1.80	True
CR	NPM	1.59	0.48	0.77	−0.76	2.30	True
CR	LC	11.88	0.27	3.18	2.33	4.03	True
CR	Self	8.12	0.34	2.79	1.70	3.88	True
CF	NPM	−0.52	0.39	−0.21	−1.45	1.04	False
CF	LC	11.37	0.19	2.21	1.59	2.82	True
CF	Self	7.16	0.25	1.82	1.02	2.63	True
NPM	LC	7.26	0.33	2.41	1.36	3.46	True
NPM	Self	5.07	0.40	2.03	0.76	3.29	True
LC	Self	−1.99	0.19	−0.38	−1.00	0.23	False

Results from robust repeated-measures ANOVA ($F(4, 58) = 3.17$, $\alpha = 0.05$)
Framed Group Cues (*CR* close relative, *CF* close friend, *NPM* local nonprofit member, *LC* local celebrity, *Self* portion of endowment not allocated)

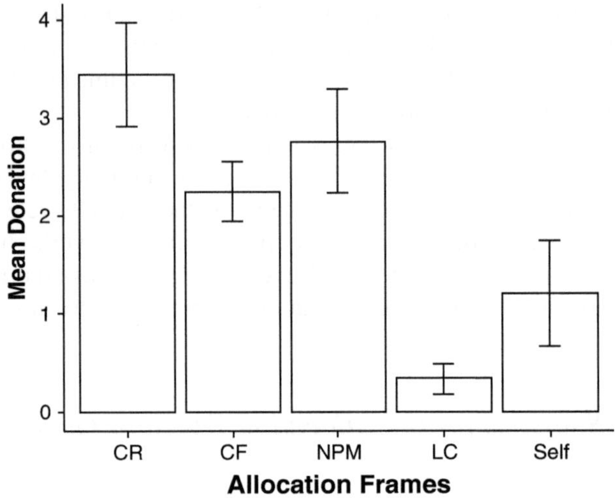

Fig. 10.2 Bar graph depicting mean donation amounts and SE for each of the social cues in the ADG

donating \$554 (87.94%) of the maximum \$630 possible. Figure 10.2 summarizes the individual donation amounts to each frame and Table 10.4 summarizes the contrasts found in the robust repeated-measures ANOVA.

Backward Stepwise Regression of Decision Frames

Our analysis used backward stepwise regression to generate a reduced best model for each frame. For consistency, we used the same eight predictors for each backward stepwise regression (i.e., expected donation amount, volunteer frequency, trust, distrust, volunteer hours weekly, log bimonthly income, log nonessential spending, and community involvement importance), generating a separate regression for each of the four decision frames in the ADG. The distribution of independent variables was not normally distributed, and inferences from these results should be subject to randomized comparisons.

We used bootstrapping method with 2000 replications to provide robust 95% confidence intervals for regression coefficients. The standard error of this bootstrapping procedure is reported for each reduced model generated from the backward stepwise regression (Tables 10.5, 10.6, 10.7 and 10.8). Backwards regressions of each donation frame with bootstrapped standard deviations were not intended to explain the overall distribution of donations, but to identify independent variables predicting donation amounts to each of the four frames at significant levels. The R^2 was interpreted as an effect size for these statistical models. Our model for donations to the nonprofit members' frame was the strongest. The R^2 results in Table 10.7

Table 10.5 Reduced model for close relative using backward stepwise regression

Model variable(s)	Coef.	SE	p
(Intercept)	4.687	1.747	0.000***
Community involvement importance	−0.571	0.485	0.014*
Expected donation	0.190	0.463	0.112

Robust bootstrapped standard errors (SE) using 2000 replicates and random replacement (Adjusted $R^2 = 0.073$; $F(2, 60) = 3.428$; $p_{\text{model}} = 0.039$)
$^{*}p < 0.05$
$^{***}p < 0.001$

Table 10.6 Reduced model for close friend using backward stepwise regression

Model variable(s)	Coef.	SE	p
(Intercept)	1.848	0.790	0.000***
Volunteer frequency	−0.214	0.376	0.020*
Community involvement importance	0.227	0.221	0.114

Robust bootstrapped standard errors (SE) using 2000 replicates and random replacement (Adjusted $R^2 = 0.060$; $F(2, 60) = 2.966$; $p_{\text{model}} = 0.059$)
$^{*}p < 0.05$
$^{***}p < 0.001$

Table 10.7 Reduced model for local nonprofit member using backward stepwise regression

Model variable(s)	Coef.	SE	p
(Intercept)	−0.061	0.762	0.940
Volunteer frequency	0.359	0.363	0.004**
Trust	0.749	0.238	0.005**

Robust bootstrapped standard errors (SE) using 2000 replicates and random replacement (Adjusted $R^2 = 0.190$; $F(2, 60) = 8.297$; $p_{\text{model}} = 0.001$)
$^{**}p < 0.01$

Table 10.8 Reduced model for local celebrity using backward stepwise regression

Model variable(s)	Coef.	SE	p
(Intercept)	0.308	0.223	0.093+
Log bimonthly income	−0.126	0.101	0.049*
Log nonessential spending	0.147	0.180	0.060+

Robust bootstrapped standard errors (SE) using 2000 replicates and random replacement (Adjusted $R^2 = 0.074$; $F(2, 60) = 3.481$; $p_{\text{model}} = 0.037$)
$^{+}p < 0.10$
$^{*}p < 0.05$

illustrate the effect size of these two variables accounted for approximately 19% of the variance in donations to this frame.

Frame 1: Close Relative. Donations allocated to the close relative frame are not associated with participant's sex, number of dependents in the household, or recent contact with kin. A strong negative relationship between the reported importance of community involvement and allocations to this frame ($r = -0.34$) suggested that individuals who perceive their involvement in community affairs as unimportant for improving community outcomes preferred to provision greater funds to close relatives. Of the eight predictors used in the initial step, community involvement importance and expected donation remained, accounting for 7.3% of the variance in donations to the close relative frame.

Frame 2: Close Friend. Donations made to the close friend frame showed a trend similar to the close relative frame, as illustrated by the marginally significant correlations observed on self-reported volunteer frequency ($r = -0.23$, $p < 0.1$). Backward stepwise regression on donations for this frame resulted in a reduced model with volunteer frequency and community involvement importance. This multiple regression explained 6% of the variance in donations to a close friend.

Frame 3: Local Nonprofit Member. Donation amounts to the local nonprofit member frame indicated strong positive correlations with reported volunteer frequency ($r = 0.33$, $p < 0.05$), generalized trust ($r = 0.32$, $p < 0.05$), and the number of organizations volunteered for in the past year ($r = 0.31$, $p < 0.05$). In the backward stepwise regression, generalized trust and volunteer frequency remained the best model for explaining allocations made to this frame ($F(2, 60) = 8.29$, $R^2 = 0.19$, $p < 0.001$). This model suggested that participants who reported more generalized trust and more frequent experiences with volunteering preferred to allocate money directly to a local nonprofit member. Donations to this frame showed strong statistical significance and the model explained 19% of the variance.

Frame 4: Local Celebrity. Allocations to the local celebrity frame were much lower than those made to other frames. We expected that a subject's income level might predict a preference for signaling. Backward stepwise regression generated a reduced model that explained 7.4% of the variance in donations to this frame with log bimonthly income and log nonessential spending as the remaining predictors.

Discussion

Trust

Generalized trust is relevant to indirect reciprocity because people who donate are counting on others to replicate that behavior. In our study, generalized trust positively influences allocations made to the local nonprofit member, a decision primed by community benefits, as predicted. Trust is described as an affective sentiment held by an individual that invites greater vulnerability to exploitation (Sargeant & Lee, 2004). Generalized social trust is considered a fundamental component of philanthropic policy-making (Payton, 1999), professional fundraising (Tempel, 1999), enduring donor–beneficiary relationships (Sargeant & Lee, 2004), and effective solicitation (Naeem & Zaman, 2016). Qualitatively different trust sentiments may be directed toward alternative members of a focal individual's social network (Ahn & Erasey, 2008). To this end, trust is a crucial facet of social capital (Putnam, 1995).

Public or generalized trust, however, is characterized by an overall lack of network directionality. Rather, it is expressed nonspecifically toward members of a community or the entire community. Some anthropologists suggest that close kin and close friend relationships have inherent trust, which may allow a greater tolerance of free riding (Xue & Silk, 2012). Others posit that different levels of trust qualitatively define these relationships, rather than by inherency (Ahn & Erasey, 2008). We cannot speak to this possibility as we did not collect any measures of affect trust. Our results only validate previous research on generalized trust for predicting community-oriented behavior.

Volunteer Experience

The volunteering experiences of our subjects are associated with increasing allocations to the local nonprofit member frame in our experiment. The frequency that an individual volunteered in the previous year is the most telling, as it predicted allocation to the nonprofit frame, and exhibited a negative relationship with donations to the *close relative* frame ($r = -0.29, p < 0.05$) and a marginal negative relationship with *close friend* frame ($r = -0.23, p < 0.1$). To better understand reported volunteer frequency, we investigated other factors that may be associated with it. We found a significant difference between the volunteer frequencies of females and males with females volunteering significantly more on average ($F(1, 61) = 3.99$, $p < 0.01$) (Fig. 10.3). However, if we control for sex effects by including sex in our backwards stepwise model of donations to the local nonprofit member frame, the regression remains significant ($F(4, 58) = 5.49$, $R^2 = 0.18$, $p < 0.01$), but sex proves to be an insignificant predictor ($t(59) = 0.37$, $p = 0.72$) in the model. This result

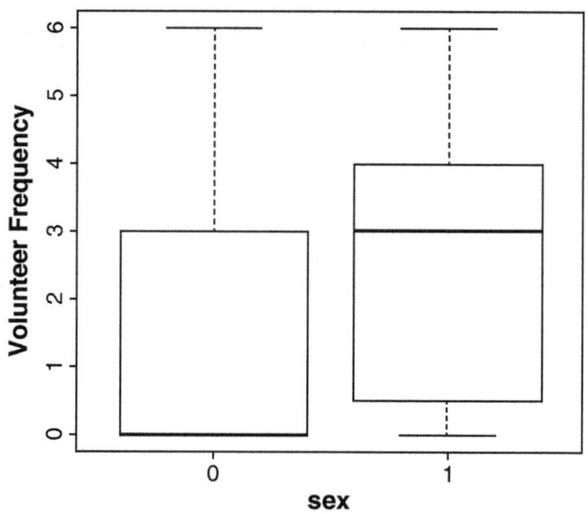

Fig. 10.3 Distribution of volunteer frequencies for males (0) and females (1) analyzed using Rstudio software (Rstudio Team, 2015). Mean frequency differs significantly between the sexes using a one-way ANOVA ($F(1, 61) = 3.99$, $p < 0.01$), suggesting significant sex effects ($M_0 = 1.42$; $M_1 = 2.63$)

indicates that while being female predicts volunteering frequency, being female does not impact donations resulting from solicitations by local nonprofit members.

Studies that find evidence that a donor's sex affects charitable giving suggest that females donate smaller amounts more frequently, while males tend to donate less frequently but in larger quantities (Rajan, Pink, & Dow, 2009). This phenomenon could be attributed to income, if there are observed income inequalities. Our survey results show that females indeed donate more frequently ($F(1, 61) = 3.99, p < 0.01$), but without any significant difference in donation amounts between the sexes ($F(1, 58) = 2.24, p > 0.10$) by one-way ANOVA. What's more, there were no significant differences between reported bimonthly income ($F(1, 60) = 4.00, p = 0.61$) or non-essential spending ($F(1, 60) = 4.00, p = 0.20$) among males and females.

Trust and Reputation in Theory

Evolutionary theorists have long regarded reciprocity to be a crucial mechanism for explaining cooperation (Bravo & Tamburino, 2008; Fehr, 2009; Nowak & Sigmund, 1998, 2005; Ostrom, 2010; Panchanathan & Boyd, 2004; Rankin & Taborsky, 2009; Saavedra, Smith, & Reed-Tsochas, 2010; Xue, 2013). Conventionally, cooperation via indirect reciprocity can be established in repeated social dilemmas when noncooperators are punished (Fehr & Gächter, 2002; Mathew & Boyd, 2011; Roberts, 2013). Alternatively, access to credible information about past outcomes, specifically the reputation of other individuals, is known to stabilize cooperation (Nowak & Sigmund, 1998; Panchanathan & Boyd, 2004). Trust is increasingly implicated as a cooperative mechanism, because a reputation for cooperating (or anything else) is only useful if an individual trusts the information the reputation provides (Ostrom, 1998).

In our study, reputation information about other players is absent. Therefore, we might expect that trust has no bearing on participant behavior—especially in a one-shot, simultaneous experimental treatment. However, trust is particularly telling when additional priming of benefits is included. This priming in our protocol may be influencing individuals who report high levels of trust, prompting them to cooperate more, or to a greater degree, with the local nonprofit member category. We can speculate that those with a history of volunteer experiences may harbor greater trust toward an individual who directly represents a charitable organization.

However, generalized trust may be more predictive of an individual that donates out of a concern for the overall well-being of others. In this way, generalized trust stands in contrast to behavior geared toward dyadic relationship solidarity. Although we can only make inferences about these relationships, our results appear to support the notion that generalized trust is markedly different from other forms of affective trust that are directed toward specific individuals (Ahn & Erasey, 2008; Xue, 2013; Xue & Silk, 2012).

Limitations

Our study has some important limitations to consider. The first is a possible systematic bias associated with our recruitment strategy. Our approach required participants to take time out of the daily campus routine to aid in our experiment. Such a behavior could be regarded as inherently generous. Thus, the high level of generosity observed in our study may be the result of this systematic bias. However, if we are interested in the behavior of donors, this bias may be fortuitous for understanding the behavior of this kind of individual. It may be that our sample comprises individuals that are more generous than the population at large.

A second limitation is in the structure of our questionnaire. The major shortcoming of our questionnaire is the small number of questions relating to psychometric variables, especially qualitatively different trust sentiments and reputation expectations. Additional questions should be developed for each of these variables so that a scale can be created and tested for validity. We would expect to see stronger evidence of separate motivations to donate to one frame or another as the psychometric measures improve.

A third limitation is the sample size of our experiment. We find several suggestive and statistically significant correlations, but additional studies are required to validate and expand these results with greater statistical power.

The final limitation of our study is that our sample is WEIRD (western, educated, industrial, rich, and democratic). This makes our results difficult to extend to non-WEIRD circumstances. Additional data collection should target populations that do not fit this description or perhaps, populations that are newly integrated into a market economy. We suggest that studies like this that address philanthropy along with other cooperative decision problems are valuable for systematically understanding variation in charitable behavior in diverse socio-ecological contexts.

Conclusion

Public goods are generated through the cooperation of multiple individuals and thus, they rely on the mobilization of part or all portions of a social network. Philanthropic solicitation is perhaps the most influential prerequisite for charitable giving and it is an interaction inherently embedded in a civic social network. Given this structural concept, the success of a solicitation relies in part on the psychology and life history of the solicited, the intrinsic characteristics of an individual, as well as the quality of the solicitation. One such quality is the social relationship that relates the potential donor to that solicitor. We find that an individual's experiences with volunteer organizations increase their likelihood to donate to a solicitor acting as a representative of a local nonprofit. In addition, individuals that harbor greater trust in their communities are more likely to donate in response to a nonprofit representative's solicitation. In contrast, those that are more distrusting, or who feel their efforts lack efficacy for influencing community affairs, appear to donate more only in response to a solicitation from a family member.

Fundraising agencies should be wary of the history of experiences embodied in the populations they consider soliciting. Individuals with volunteer experience might be targeted first for the causes with the greatest need. Similarly, if such agencies can adequately gauge the trust of their donors, high trustors likely to be responsive to charitable solicitations may be identified. This affective sentiment may be bolstered by partnering with other nonprofits, preferably those that are well-known in the community for their efficacy and reputation. Alternatively, individuals that are less trusting or who lack a history of volunteer experience may be more susceptible to a network approach to fundraising. In this way, members of a potential donor's social network may act as intermediaries between donors and beneficiaries by brokering affective trust.

Overall, this study supports the notion that life history coupled with psychological attributes are profound mediators of decision-making in social dilemmas. To fully capture donation motivations and preferences, repeated games and natural experimentation are needed. New questions uncovered through this study relate to the interaction of different forms of trust with reputation information. Evolutionary questions arise as well, concerning the transition from gift economies to institutionalized philanthropy.

Acknowledgments We are grateful to the Dan Montgomery NWEEHB Symposium Fund, The Arts and Humanities Institute's Translating Sustainability Research Cluster, and Bone and Joint Solutions, LLC (Boise, Idaho) for funding this research. We thank the members of John Ziker's Cooperation and Networks Lab—Haley Myers, Denell Letourneu, and Lisa Greer, and volunteers Hailey Moon and Ed Deckys—for their help during the experimental design and implementation. We thank Faith Brigham for her assistance with logistics and money handling, Kristin Snopkowski for her assistance with statistical analysis, and Kathryn Demps, Kendell House, and Kristin Snopkowski for providing feedback on earlier drafts of this chapter. We also thank Meng Li and an anonymous reviewer for substantive comments.

References

Ahn, T. K., & Erasey, J. (2008). A dynamic model of generalized social trust. *Journal of Theoretical Politics, 20*(2), 151–180. doi:10.1177/0951629807085816.

Alexander, R. D. (1987). *The biology of moral systems*. Hawthorne, NY: A. de Gruyter.

Allouch, N. (2013). A competitive equilibrium for a warm-glow economy. *Economic Theory, 53*, 269–282. doi:10.1007/s00199-012-0689-z.

Andreoni, J. (1989). Giving with impure altruism: Applications to charity and Ricardian equivalence. *Journal of Political Economy, 97*(6), 1447–1458. doi:10.1086/261662.

Andreoni, J. (1990). Impure altruism and donations to public goods: A theory of warm-glow giving. *The Economic Journal, 100*(401), 464–477. doi:10.2307/2234133.

Andreoni, J., & Scholz, J. K. (1998). An econometric analysis of charitable giving with interdependent preferences. *Economic Inquiry, 36*(3), 410–428. doi:10.1111/j.1465-7295.1998.tb01723.x.

Becker, G. S. (1974). A theory of social interactions. *Journal of Political Economy, 82*(6), 1063–1093. doi:10.1086/260265.

Bekkers, R. (2005). *It's not all in the ask: Effects and effectiveness of recruitment strategies used by nonprofits in the Netherlands*. Paper presented at the 34rd Annual ARNOVA-Conference, Washington, District of Columbia.

Bekkers, R., & Wiepking, P. (2011). A literature review of empirical studies of philanthropy: Eight mechanisms that drive charitable giving. *Nonprofit and Voluntary Sector Quarterly, 40*(5), 924–973. doi:10.1177/0899764010380927.

Bischoff, I., & Kauskopf, T. (2015). Warm glow of giving collectively—An experimental study. *Journal of Economic Psychology, 51*, 210–218. doi:10.1016/j.joep.2015.09.00.

Bliege Bird, R., Smith, E., & Bird, D. (2001). The hunting handicap: Costly signaling in human foraging strategies. *Behavioral Ecology and Sociobiology, 50*(1), 9–19. doi:10.1007/s002650100338.

Bowles, S., & Gintis, H. (2011). *A cooperative species: Human reciprocity and its evolution*. Princeton, NJ: Princeton University Press.

Bravo, G., & Tamburino, L. (2008). The evolution of trust in non-simultaneous exchange situations. *Rationality and Society, 20*(1), 85–113. doi:10.1177/1043463107085441.

Brown, E., & Ferris, J. M. (2007). Social capital and philanthropy: An analysis of the impact of social capital on individual giving and volunteering. *Nonprofit and Volunteer Sector Quarterly, 36*(1), 85–99. doi:10.1177/0899764006293178.

Bryant, J. H., Slaughter, H. J., Kang, H., & Tax, A. (2003). Participation in philanthropic activities: Donating money and time. *Journal of Consumer Policy, 26*(1), 43–73. doi:10.1023/A:1022626529603.

Bshary, R., & Bergmüller, R. (2008). Distinguishing four fundamental appoaches to the evolution of helping. *Journal of Evolutionary Biology, 21*(2), 405–420. doi:10.1111/j.1420-9101.2007.01482.x.

Bshary, R., & Bronstein, J. L. (2004). Game structures in mutualistic interactions: What can the evidence tell us about the kind of models we need? *Advances in the Study of Behavior, 34*, 59–102. doi:10.1016/S0065-3454(04)34002-7.

Bshary, R., & Bronstein, J. L. (2011). A general scheme to predict partner control mechanisms in pairwise cooperative interactions between unrelated individuals. *Ethology, 117*(4), 271–283. doi:10.1111/j.1439-0310.2011.01882.x.

Chapais, B. (2015). Competence and the evolutionary origins of status and power in humans. *Human Nature, 26*(2), 161–183. doi:10.1007/s12110-015-9227-6.

Dawkins, R. (1976). *The selfish gene*. New York City, NY: Oxford University Press.

Dugatkin, L. A. (1999). *Cheating monkeys and citizen bees: The nature of cooperation in humans and animals*. New York City, NY: The Free Press.

Fehr, E. (2009). On the economics and biology of trust. *Journal of the European Economic Association, 7*(2–3), 235–266. doi:10.1162/JEEA.2009.7.2-3.235.

Fehr, E., & Gächter, S. (2002). Altruistic punishment in humans. *Nature, 415*(6868), 137–140. doi:10.1038/415137a.

Fletcher, J. A., & Doebeli, M. (2009). A simple and general explanation for the evolution of altruism. *Proceedings of the Royal Society: Biological Sciences, 276*(1654), 13–19. doi:10.1098/rspb.2008.0829.

Freeman, L. C. (1977). A set of measures of centrality based on betweenness. *Sociometry, 40*(1), 35–41. doi:10.2307/3033543.

Gerkey, D. (2013). Cooperation in context: Public goods games and Post-Soviet collectives in Kamchatka, Russia. *Current Anthropology, 54*(2), 144–176. doi:10.1086/669856.

Gurven, M. (2004). To give and to give not: The behavioral ecology of human food transfers. *Behavioral and Brain Sciences, 27*(4), 543–559. doi:10.1017/S0140525X04000123.

Gurven, M., Allen-Arave, W., Hill, K., & Hurtado, M. (2000). "It's a Wonderful Life": Signaling generosity among the Ache of Paraguay. *Evolution and Human Behavior, 21*(4), 263–282. doi:10.1016/S1090-5138(00)00032-5.

Gurven, M., & Winking, J. (2008). Collective action in action: Prosocial behavior in and out of the laboratory. *American Anthropologist, 110*(2), 179–190. doi:10.1111/j.1548-1433.2008.00024.x.

Hamilton, W. D. (1964a). The genetical evolution of social behavior, I. *Journal of Theoretical Biology, 7*, 1–16. doi:10.1016/0022-5193(64)90038-4.

Hamilton, W. D. (1964b). The genetical evolution of social behavior, II. *Journal of Theoretical Biology, 7*, 17–52. doi:10.1016/0022-5193(64)90039-6.

Hardin, G. (1977). *The limits of altruism: An ecologist's view of survival*. Bloomington, IN: Indiana University Press.

Hawkes, K., O'Connell, J. F., & Blurton Jones, N. G. (2001). Hadza meat sharing. *Evolution and Human Behavior, 22*(2), 113–142. doi:10.1016/S1090-5138(00)00066-0.

Henrich, J. (2009). The evolution of costly displays, cooperation and religion. *Evolution and Human Behavior, 30*(4), 244–260. doi:10.1016/j.evolhumbehav.2009.03.005.

Henrich, J. (2012). Social science: Hunter-gatherer cooperation. *Nature, 481*(7382), 449–450. doi:10.1038/481449a.

Henrich, J., Boyd, R., Bowles, S., Camerer, C., Fehr, E., Gintis, H., & McElreath, R. (2001). In search of Homo economicus: Behavioral experiments in 15 small-scale societies. *American Economic Association, 91*(2), 73–78. doi:10.1257/aer.91.2.73.

Henrich, J., Ensminger, J., McElreath, R., Barr, A., Barrett, C., Bolyanatz, A., ... Ziker, J. (2010). Markets, religion, community size, and the evolution of fairness and punishment. *Science, 327*(5972), 1480–1484. doi:10.1126/science.1182238.

Henrich, J., Heine, S. J., & Norenzayan, A. (2010). The weirdest people in the world. *Behavioral and Brain Sciences, 33*(2-3), 61–135. doi:10.1017/S0140525x0999152x.

Henrich, J., Mcelreath, R., Barr, A., Ensminger, J., Barret, C., Bolyanatz, A., ... Ziker, J. (2006). Costly punishment across human societies. *Science, 312*(5781), 1767–1770. doi:10.1126/science.1127333.

IBM Corp. (2011). *IBM SPSS statistics for windows, Version 20.0 [software]*. Armonk, NY: IBM Corp.

Lapoint, E. C., & Joshi, P. C. (1985–1986). Economy of respect in a north Indian village. *Lambda Alpha Journal of Man, 17*(1 & 2), 41–52. Retrieved from http://ehrafworldcultures.yale.edu/document?id=aw19-008

Ledyard, J. O. (1997). Public goods: A survey of experimental research. In J. H. Kagel & A. E. Roth (Eds.), *Handbook of experimental economics* (pp. 111–251). Princeton, NJ: Princeton University Press.

Lehmann, L., & Keller, L. (2006). The evolution of cooperation and altruism—A general classification of models. *Journal of Evolutionary Biology, 19*(5), 1365–1376. doi:10.1111/j.1420-9101.2006.01119.x.

Macaulay, J. (1975). Familiarity, attraction, and charity. *Journal of Social Psychology, 95*, 27–37. doi:10.1080/00224545.1975.9923231.

Mathew, S., & Boyd, R. (2011). Punishment sustains large-scale cooperation in prestate warfare. *Proceeding of the National Academy of Sciences of the United States of America, 108*(28), 11375–11380. doi:10.1073/pnas.1105604108.

Mauss, M. (1969). *The gift: Forms and functions of exchange in archaic societies*. London: Cohen & West.

Meer, J. (2011). Brother, can you spare a dime? Peer pressure in charitable solicitation. *Journal of Public Economics, 95*(7), 926–941. doi:10.1016/j.jpubeco.2010.11.026.

Meskill, J. M. (1979). *A Chinese pioneer family* (1st ed.). Princeton, NJ: Princeton University Press.

Moll, J., Krueger, F., Zahn, R., Pardini, M., de Oliveria-Souza, R., & Grafman, J. (2006). Human fronto-mesolimbic networks guide decisions about chartiable donation. *Proceedings of the National Academy of Sciences of the United States of America, 103*(42), 15623–15628. doi:10.1073/pnas.0604475103.

Naeem, S., & Zaman, A. (2016). Charity and gift exchange: Cultural effects. *Voluntas, 27*(2), 900–919. doi:10.1007/s11266-015-9655-2.

Nowak, M. A., & Roch, S. (2007). Upstream reciprocity and the evolution of gratitude. *Proceedings of the Royal Society B: Biological Sciences, 274*(1610), 605–609. doi:10.1098/rspb.2006.0125.
Nowak, M. A., & Sigmund, K. (1998). Evolution of indirect reciprocity by image scoring. *Nature, 393*(6685), 573–577. doi:10.1038/31225.
Nowak, M. A., & Sigmund, K. (2005). Evolution of indirect reciprocity. *Nature, 437*(7063), 1291–1298. doi:10.1038/nature04131.
Ostrom, E. (1998). The comparative study of public economies. *American Economist, 42*(1), 3–15. doi:10.1177/056943459804200101.
Ostrom, E. (2010). Analyzing collective action. *Agricultural Economics, 41*, 155–166. doi:10.1111/j.1574-0862.2010.00497.x.
Panchanathan, K., & Boyd, R. (2004). Indirect reciprocity can stabilize cooperation without the second-order free rider problem. *Nature, 432*(7016), 499–502. doi:10.1038/nature02978.
Payton, R. L. (1999). Philanthropy and trust. *New Directions for Philanthropic Fundraising, 1999*(26), 5–10. doi:10.1002/pf.2601.
Persky, J. (1995). Retrospectives: The ethology of Homo economicus. *The Journal of Economic Perspectives, 9*(2), 221–231. Retrieved from http://www.jstor.org/stable/2138175.
Pfeiffer, T., Rutte, C., Killingback, T., Taborsky, M., & Bonhoeffer, S. (2005). Evolution of cooperation by generalized reciprocity. *Proceedings of the Royal Society B: Biological Sciences, 272*(1568), 1115–1120. doi:10.1098/rspb.2004.2988.
Putnam, R. D. (1995). Bowling alone: America's declining social capital. *Journal of Democracy, 6*(1), 65–78. doi:10.1353/jod.1995.0002.
Qualtrics. (2015). *Qualtrics survey platform [Software]*. Provo, UT. http://qualtrics.com
Radley, A., & Kennedy, M. (1995). Charitable giving by individuals: A study of attitudes and practice. *Human relations, 48*(6), 685–709. doi:10.1177/001872679504800605.
Rajan, S. S., Pink, G. H., & Dow, W. H. (2009). Sociodemographic and personality characteristics of Canadian donors contributing to international charity. *Nonprofit and Voluntary Sector Quarterly, 38*(3), 413–430. doi:10.1177/0899764008316056.
Rand, D. G., Greene, J. D., & Nowak, M. A. (2012). Spontaneous giving and calculated greed. *Nature, 489*(7416), 427–430. doi:10.1038/nature11467.
Rankin, D. J., & Taborsky, M. (2009). Assortment and the evolution of generalized reciprocity. *Evolution, 63*(7), 1913–1922. doi:10.1111/j.1558-5646.2009.00656.x.
Roberts, G. (2013). When punishment pays. *PLoS One, 8*(3), e57378. doi:10.1371/journal.pone.0057378.
RStudio Team. (2015). *RStudio: Integrated development for R [Software]*. Boston, MA: RStudio. Retrieved from http://www.rstudio.com.
Saavedra, S., Smith, D., & Reed-Tsochas, F. (2010). Cooperation under indirect reciprocity and imitative trust. *PLoS One, 5*(10), 1–6. doi:10.1371/journal.pone.0013475.
Sahlins, M. (1972). *Stone age economics*. Chicago, IL: Aldine-Atherton.
Sargeant, A., & Lee, S. (2004). Trust and relationship commitment in the United Kingdom voluntary sector: Determinants of donor behavior. *Psychology and Marketing, 21*(8), 613–635. doi:10.1002/mar.20021.
Sargeant, A., & Woodliffe, L. (2007). Gift giving: An interdisciplinary review. *International Journal of Nonprofit and Voluntary Sector Marketing, 12*(4), 275–307. doi:10.1002/nvsm.308.
Simpson, B., & Willer, D. (2005). The structural embeddedness of collective goods: Connection and coalitions in exchange networks. *Sociological Theory, 23*(4), 386–407. doi:10.1111/j.0735-2751.2005.00260.x.
Simpson, B., & Willer, R. (2008). Altruism and indirect reciprocity: The interaction of person and situation in prosocial behavior. *Social Psychology Quarterly, 71*(1), 37–52. doi:10.1177/019027250807100106.
Sulek, M. (2010). On the modern meaning of philanthropy. *Nonprofit and Voluntary Sector Quarterly, 39*(2), 193–212. doi:10.1177/0899764009333052.
Tempel, E. R. (1999). Trust and fundraising as a profession. *New Directions for Philanthropic Fundraising, 1999*(26), 51–58. doi:10.1002/pf.2604.

Tonin, M., & Vlassopoulos, M. (2014). An experimental investigation of intrinsic motivations for giving. *Theory & Decision, 76*, 47–67. doi:10.1007/s11238-013-9360-9.

Trivers, R. (1971). The evolution of reciprocal altruism. *Quarterly Review of Biology, 46*(1), 35–57. doi:10.1086/406755.

Wang, L., & Graddy, E. (2008). Social capital, volunteering, and charitable giving. *Voluntas, 19*(1), 23–42. doi:10.1007/s11266-008-9055-y.

Wiessner, P. (2002). Hunting, healing, and hxaro exchange: A long-term perspective on! Kung (Ju/'hoansi) large-game hunting. *Evolution and Human Behavior, 23*(6), 407–436. doi:10.1016/S1090-5138(02)00096-X.

Wood, B. M., & Marlowe, F. W. (2013). Household and kin provisioning by Hadza men. *Human Nature, 24*(3), 280–317. doi:10.1007/s12110-013-9173-0.

Xue, M. (2013). Altruism and reciprocity among friends and kin in a Tibetan village. *Evolution and Human Behavior, 34*, 323–329. doi:10.1016/j.evolhumbehav.2013.05.002.

Xue, M., & Silk, J. B. (2012). The role of tracking and tolerance in relationship among friends. *Evolution & Human Behavior, 33*(1), 17–25. doi:10.1016/j.evolhumbehav.2011.04.004.

Yörük, B. K. (2012). Do charitable solicitations matter? A comparative analysis of fundraising methods. *Fiscal Studies, 33*(4), 467–487. doi:10.1111/j.1475-5890.2012.00169.x.

Zahavi, A. (1975). Mate selection-a selection for a handicap. *Journal of Theoretical Biology, 53*(1), 205–214. doi:10.1016/0022-5193(75)90111-3.

Zahavi, A., & Zahavi, A. (1997). *The handicap principle: A missing piece of Darwin's puzzle*. Oxford: Oxford University Press.

Ziker, J. P. (2002). *Peoples of the tundra: Northern Siberians in the post-communist transition*. Long Grove, IL: Waveland Press.

Ziker, J. P., Rasmussen, J., & Nolin, D. A. (2016). Indigenous Siberians solve collective action problems through sharing and traditional knowledge. *Sustainability Science, 11*(1), 45–55. doi:10.1007/s11625-015-0293-9.

Ziker, J., & Schnegg, M. (2005). Food sharing at meals: Kinship, reciprocity, and clustering in the Taimyr Autonomous Okrug, northern Russia. *Human Nature, 16*(2), 178–211. doi:10.1007/s12110-005-1003-6.

Index

M. Li, D.P. Tracer (eds.), *Interdisciplinary Perspectives on Fairness, Equity, and Justice*, DOI 10.1007/978-3-319-58993-0

MIX
Papier aus verantwortungsvollen Quellen
Paper from responsible sources
FSC® C105338

If you have any concerns about our products,
you can contact us on
ProductSafety@springernature.com

In case Publisher is established outside the EU,
the EU authorized representative is:
Springer Nature Customer Service Center GmbH
Europaplatz 3, 69115 Heidelberg, Germany

Printed by Libri Plureos GmbH
in Hamburg, Germany